WEYERHAEUSER ENVIRONMENTAL CLASSICS

Paul S. Sutter, Editor

WEYERHAEUSER ENVIRONMENTAL CLASSICS
Paul S. Sutter, Editor

Weyerhaeuser Environmental Classics are reprinted editions of key works that explore human relationships with natural environments in all their variety and complexity. Drawn from many disciplines, they examine how natural systems affect human communities, how people affect the environments of which they are a part, and how different cultural conceptions of nature powerfully shape our sense of the world around us. These are books about the environment that continue to offer profound insights about the human place in nature.

Weyerhaeuser Environmental Classics is a subseries within Weyerhaeuser Environmental Books, under the general editorship of Paul S. Sutter. A complete listing of the series appears at the end of this book.

ENVIRONMENTAL JUSTICE IN POSTWAR AMERICA

A Documentary Reader

EDITED BY
CHRISTOPHER W. WELLS

UNIVERSITY OF WASHINGTON PRESS
Seattle

Environmental Justice in Postwar America is published with the assistance of a grant from the Weyerhaeuser Environmental Books Endowment, established by the Weyerhaeuser Company Foundation, members of the Weyerhaeuser family, and Janet and Jack Creighton.

22   21   20   5   4   3

University of Washington Press
www.washington.edu/uwpress

LIBRARY OF CONGRESS CATALOGING-IN-PUBLICATION DATA ON FILE

ISBN (hardcover): 978-0-295-74368-4
ISBN (paperback): 978-0-295-74369-1
ISBN (ebook): 978-0-295-74370-7

For Marianne

CONTENTS

FOREWORD

The Age of Environmental Inequality

PAUL S. SUTTER

Environmental injustice is an age-old problem, yet the environmental justice *movement* as an organized political effort is a surprisingly recent development, dating only from the early 1980s. This disjuncture between the deep history of environmental injustice and the late emergence of a social movement to oppose it is something of a historical riddle: Why did self-conscious environmental justice activism take so long to coalesce, and what was it about postwar America that finally led to its arrival? These are the questions that animate Christopher W. Wells's exciting new primary source collection, *Environmental Justice in Postwar America: A Documentary Reader*.

Some of the answers to this riddle are predictable. To the extent that the environmental inequalities of postwar America resulted from differential exposure to pollutants, the development of a new generation of highly toxic chemicals magnified the perils of exposure. In that sense, environmental justice concerns were part and parcel of a new technological era of toxicity. But the rise of environmental justice activism was about more than new threats. Americans experienced a fundamental reorganization of space after World War II—a remaking of industrial, residential, and recreational geography—that is also essential to understanding why the postwar years became an age of environmental inequality. In part 1 of *Environmental Justice in Postwar America*, Wells offers a series of documents that methodically depict this reorganization of American space as a necessary precondition for the birth of environmental justice activism. Many Americans, most of them white and well off, moved out of harm's way in the decades after World War II, often to exclusive suburbs whose environmental amenities—large leafy house lots, nearby parks and playgrounds, clean air and water—were a major part of the attraction. As they did so, they fashioned for themselves a vision of nature as wild and untouched, taking little account of the increasingly dire conditions that poor and working class people, many of them people of color, faced in the crumbling urban areas to which they had been consigned. African Americans felt this reorganization of space with particular poignancy, for as they moved out of the rural South and into the nation's cities during the Great Migration, they continued to face the persistent forces of segregation in law and practice. African Americans often lived in substandard housing, worked in the lowest paying and most dangerous jobs, and had limited access to parks and other natural spaces for their recreation. A growing consciousness of environmental injustice, then, was specific to this postwar spatial history.

Another way of understanding the late arrival of environmental justice activism is to focus on the two momentous social movements that were its prerequisites: the civil rights movement and the environmental movement. Before these movements came along, environmental justice activism was difficult to imagine. The civil rights movement gave environmental justice much of its organizational force, even as the claims of the environmental movement reshaped the traditional civil rights agenda. But if the environmental justice movement was the offspring of these two parents, it developed as the product of a troubled marriage. Arising in the blind spots of the maturing environmental movement, it emerged largely as a critique of the nation's narrow environmental commitments. Environmental justice activists argued that the persistence of environmental inequities in American society was a product of a mainstream environmental movement that had not taken seriously the environmental concerns of poor people and people of color. More surprisingly, they also argued that many of the apparent successes of the environmental movement had made environmental injustice markedly worse in postwar America. How could this be? To give one example, regulations that required polluters to control their emissions rather than broadcasting them into the environment often resulted in concentrated forms of hazardous waste that had to be put somewhere, and not surprisingly this waste often ended up in and around poor communities and communities of color. The problem, then, was not just that a new regime of environmental regulation did not reach these communities; it was that this regime actually targeted them in ways that magnified these unequal burdens. The documents that Wells has carefully chosen for part 2 of this volume beautifully illustrate the fascinating relationships between the civil rights and environmental movements in the years between the first Earth Day in 1970 and the rise of a self-conscious environmental justice movement in the 1980s and beyond. More than that, they illustrate a powerful irony that Andrew Hurley noted several decades ago in his pioneering environmental history of Gary, Indiana: "The age of ecology was also the age of environmental inequality."

In the documents that Wells features in part 3 of this reader, we witness the consolidation and growing influence of the environmental justice movement in the late twentieth and early twenty-first centuries. We see environmental justice activism proliferate and then come together in a national movement, with sophisticated organizations, inspiring leaders, and polished manifestos. We see environmental justice activism expanding beyond its early focus on differential toxic exposure and finding a place in federal environmental policy making as well as in mainstream environmental organizations. We see events, from the Flint water crisis to the Dakota Access Pipeline protests, foregrounding environmental justice issues. We also see how the globalization of the environmental movement raised profoundly important environment and development questions. We see, in short, how the maturation of an environmental justice movement transformed the mainstream environmental agenda in the early twenty-first century. Wells skillfully uses the documents in the final section of *Environmental Justice in Postwar America* to make an intriguing argument: that the shift to "sustainability" concerns over the last quarter century has been one of the most important legacies of environmental justice activism.

The first reader of its kind, *Environmental Justice in Postwar America* is a powerful real-time accounting of a movement that remade modern American environmental politics. By collecting the classic documents from the movement's short history, Christopher Wells has crafted a primary-source portrait of the emergence of environmental justice claims and the social activism that made them politically potent. More than that, though, Wells gives us the materials to understand the movement in its rich historical context. The environmental justice movement was not the preordained result of civil rights and environmental ideologies meeting and mingling. Rather, environmental justice activists conceived and built their movement in a distinctive age of environmental inequality.

ACKNOWLEDGMENTS

This book got its start in the classroom, where I found myself struggling alongside my students to make sense of the complicated and often tense historical relationship between mainstream environmentalists and advocates for environmental justice. Why hadn't environmentalists championed environmental protections in the nation's most obviously polluted neighborhoods during the "environmental decade" of the 1970s? Why did the early environmental movement, which drew in so many obvious ways on the powerful example of the civil rights movement, have so few direct bridges between the two movements? Why did it take a separate movement, led by people of color, to get such a pressing and morally unambiguous set of issues onto the national agenda? Even to frame the questions in such a way sat uncomfortably with my environmental studies students, who tended to care about questions of social justice as much as they were compelled by environmental ones, and who tended to see social justice and environmental degradation as more obviously unified than easily separable. The number of former students that I can list here is constrained, but I hope that Josie Ahrens, Laura Bartolomei-Hill, Eva Beal, Brianna Besch, Aaron Brown, Timothy Den Herder-Thomas, Asa Diebolt, Sophie Downey, Jeff Jay, Matt Kazinka, Madeline Kovacs, Maria Langholz, Ruby Levine, Alice Madden, Grace Newton, Diego Ruiz, Akilah Sanders-Reed, Essie Schlotterbeck, and Hannah White—among others—can all see themselves (and our conversations) reflected here.

Although the theme of environmental inequalities has animated the work of environmental historians in increasingly significant ways, the lion's share of the scholarship on environmental justice comes from other places, with scholar-activists from disciplines like sociology, geography, urban studies, and legal studies leading the charge. As I began to read widely in the environmental justice literature, which overflows with sophisticated theoretical and technical analyses, my reflex as a historian was to turn to primary sources to sharpen and clarify my understanding of the literature and to help answer the questions that kept recurring in my classes. One of the movement's slogans—"We speak for ourselves!"—provided constant inspiration and helped me realize that the primary documents I had been collecting might be useful for others as well. Bill Cronon and Marianne Keddington-Lang helped me recognize that I had been working on a book without realizing it, and when they stepped aside from the Weyerhaeuser Environmental Books series, Paul Sutter, Regan Huff, and Catherine Cocks were there with advice and encouragement to keep me going. They all have my profound thanks.

The serendipity of the card catalog, the magic of the archives, and the footnote trails of other scholars account for most of the documents in this collection, but some of the very best documents here are the direct result of generous friends and colleagues sharing advice and recommendations. My sincere appreciation goes to everyone who helped in ways large and small, with special thanks to Eric Carter, Nathan Connolly, Michael Egan, Rob Gioielli, Aram Goudsouzian, Josh Howe, Steve Kantrowitz, Connie Karlin, Matt Klingle, Erik Kojola, Christie Manning, Brian McCammack, Ginny Moran, Akilah Sanders-Reed, Kendra Smith-Howard, David Stradling, George Vrtis, and Carl Zimring, as well as the University of Washington Press's anonymous reviewers. When it came time to write, Jim Feldman and Margot Higgins both read drafts of the introduction and offered insightful suggestions and critiques. I also owe a special thank you to Giulia Girgenti, who spent a summer working with me to track down a range of obscure sources and talk through various issues while I was making a first pass at organizing the material into a usable collection.

Just as this book depended on the help and insight of many friends and colleagues, it also depended on a huge range of individuals, archives, libraries, and institutions who allowed me to reprint their work for free or at a greatly reduced cost. Without the help and generosity of the Virginia Key Beach Park Trust, the Tougaloo College Archives, Timothy Benally and the Navajo Uranium Miner Oral History and Photography Project, the United Farm Workers of America, the Edmund Muskie Archives and Special Collections Library at Bates College, Don Coombs, Penelope Ploughman, the University at Buffalo Libraries, Jenny Labalme, the United Church of Christ, Sam Kittner, Richard Moore, Mark Gutierrez, the *Los Angeles Times*, Public Citizen, *High Country News*, the Center for Public Integrity, Amy Perkins, Democracy Now!, Kathy Jetñil-Kijiner, *CityLab*, the *Minnesota Women's Press*, and the World Rainforest Movement, the quality and range of documents in this collection would have been greatly diminished. A special thank-you as well to the innumerable environmental justice advocates who produced these documents but more importantly have done the hard work of building the movement.

My biggest debts, as always, are to my family. My children, Jack, Annie, and Meg, are still just on verge of being old enough to understand the importance of the topics in this book, but they give me profound hope for a better future. My wife, Marianne Milligan, understands the issues all too well, and has helped me grapple with them through the whole long process of putting this book together. I dedicate it to her.

ENVIRONMENTAL JUSTICE IN POSTWAR AMERICA

INTRODUCTION

The environmental justice movement sprang to life on September 15, 1982, when fifty-five nonviolent protesters lay down in the middle of a highway in rural Warren County, North Carolina. Their goal was to block a squadron of dump trucks from entering the state's first toxic waste landfill, a new 142-acre facility that opponents had tried and failed over several years of court battles to prevent from opening. The protests had begun earlier in the day, when an interracial group of 130 protesters staged a two-mile march from Coley Springs Baptist Church, a local African American congregation, to the new landfill. There they waited for the first of what would eventually amount to 7,223 dump trucks, each carrying dirt laced with high concentrations of polychlorinated biphenyls (PCBs), toxic man-made organic chemicals that are linked to a range of serious human health problems, including cancer, and do not break down readily in the environment or in human bodies.[1] When the protesters began lying down in the highway, police responded by arresting and removing them to clear a way for the trucks, triggering a story on the *CBS Evening News with Dan Rather*. "They didn't expect us to organize, but we're gonna fight," proclaimed one protester. "It's one thing to be poor, it's another to be poor and poisoned."[2] Over the next several weeks, with trucks continuing to stream toward the landfill, the number of protesters grew—and the number of arrests swelled to 523.

The fact that African Americans dominated the protests added an additional layer of drama to the events and stood in stark contrast to most environmental protests of the time. Indeed, photographs of the protests evoke less a typical postwar environmental protest than the pitched civil rights campaigns of the 1950s and 1960s—demonstrators marching arm in arm under hand-lettered signs; protesters chanting, clapping, and singing as a battalion of armed officers lines up behind them; helmeted police officers carrying limp protestors toward yellow school buses adapted as makeshift paddy wagons. The pattern of arrests reinforced the sense that this was as much a civil rights protest as an environmental one. No national environmental leaders were among those arrested, for example, though several prominent civil rights leaders were, including the Reverend Joseph E. Lowery (president of the Southern Christian Leadership Conference, the organization founded by Martin Luther King Jr. in the wake of the Montgomery bus boycott victory); Walter E. Fauntroy (Washington, DC's congressional delegate, who had helped coordinate the 1963 March on Washington); and the Reverend Benjamin Chavis (deputy director of the United Church of Christ's Commission for Racial Justice and the author of *An American Political Prisoner Appeals for Human Rights*, which he authored while wrongfully imprisoned in a North Carolina jail).[3]

The optics of the protests—an interracial coalition in which civil rights leaders marched arm in arm with environmentalists—prompted a *Washington Post* editorial to describe the events in Warren County as a "marriage of civil rights activism with environmental concerns," noting that it was "good to see a broadening of the traditionally white, upper-middle-class environmental movement."[4] Yet the underlying meaning and significance of the Warren County protests turned out to be much more complicated than the metaphor of marriage suggests. In truth, the flowering of the environmental justice (or "EJ") movement challenged many of the most basic premises, assumptions, and strategies of 1970s-era environmentalism. Indeed, as the EJ movement gained steam, its leaders quickly concluded that the policies enacted during the so-called "environmental decade" of the 1970s—during which environmentalists achieved so many legislative and administrative triumphs—had fallen woefully short. The "age of ecology" may have dramatically improved the quality of the environment for most Americans, EJ advocates argued, but had done so in ways that left minority populations systematically exposed to the heaviest and most toxic environmental burdens. At best, the regulations and practices that the mainstream environmental movement championed had failed to resolve these unequal burdens; at worst, they had actually amplified them.

WARREN COUNTY AND THE EJ CHALLENGE
TO MAINSTREAM ENVIRONMENTALISM

The protests that erupted in Warren County in 1982, together with the events that called them into being, illustrate both the common ground that environmental justice shared with mainstream environmentalism and the fundamental challenges that EJ posed to business-as-usual environmentalism. The Warren County protests, for example, grew from what initially looked like common environmental problems of the era. The chain of events began in 1978 when Robert "Buck" Ward, owner of the Raleigh-based Ward Transformer Company, and his long-time friend, Robert Burns, conspired to save Ward money and help Burns pay off part of a substantial loan from Ward by finding a surreptitious (but patently illegal) way to get rid of a large accumulation of insulating fluid that Ward's company had drained from old electrical transformers. The fluid was laced with PCBs, which the electrical industry had used extensively for decades because of their excellent insulating properties. By the mid-1970s, however, as the extreme toxicity of PCBs was becoming better understood, they had become subject to a federal environmental law known as the Toxic Substance Control Act of 1976 (TSCA, pronounced "tosca"). As one of environmentalists' many legislative victories of the era, TSCA established rules for their safe use and disposal and banned further PCB production after July 1979.[5]

To help Ward avoid the costs associated with TSCA's more stringent regulations, Burns gathered a crew at the Ward Transformer Company facility and equipped a truck with a 750-gallon tank concealed inside a large wooden box. In June, test dumping runs to secluded parts of the Fort Bragg military base revealed that none of the spots with sandy soil that Burns had picked out as promising disposal sites absorbed the oily liquid as well as he had hoped. Undeterred, and after some discussion with Ward, he rigged the tank with a valve and spigot that allowed the truck to spray the fluid along the roadside in a greasy four- to six-inch-wide swath. Then, over a two-week stretch in late July and early August, Burns's sons, Randall and Timothy, made a series of late-night dumping runs during which they sprayed some 31,000 gallons of the toxic liquid alongside over two hundred miles of North Carolina highways spread across fourteen counties.[6]

The conspirators were quickly discovered, and the perpetrators eventually landed in jail, but the state still had to deal with the clear threat to public health created by the toxic roadside mess. Initially, officials erected roadside warning signs and sent notices to area farmers, advising them to destroy crops near the poisoned roadsides and recommending that they prevent their livestock from grazing there.[7] In an earlier era, things might have stopped there, but TSCA required the state to clean everything up. As a result, state officials made a series of seemingly technical decisions to mitigate the threat, developing plans to scrape up the contaminated soil and deposit it in a state-of-the-art "dry tomb" PCB landfill. In contrast to the Resource Conservation Recovery Act of 1976, however, which included mechanisms that required public participation in the siting process of hazardous waste disposal facilities, TSCA regulations did not require states to consider public feedback or incorporate public participation in the siting process for facilities handling substances like PCBs, which were categorized as "toxic" rather than "hazardous." There was thus no formal mechanism for the residents of Warren County to participate in—or even be made aware of—the decision-making process that ultimately led to the designation of their home as the location for the state's first toxic waste landfill.

As a result, shortly before Christmas in 1978, Deborah and Ken Ferruccio were surprised to hear a media report that a farm four miles down the road from their home in rural Warren County—located in a poor part of the state near the Virginia border—had been chosen as the site for the state's first toxic waste dump. In addition to being surprised, the Ferruccios, a well-educated white couple who had moved to Warren County from Ohio the year before in part to live a life they hoped would be closer to nature, were also incensed. They pulled together a small group of neighbors, including Carol and Larry Limer, and jumped into action, each taking a few pages torn from the local Warrenton phone directory to use as a calling list. Word spread quickly and opposition mounted. By the day after Christmas, they had formally organized a protest group, Warren County Citizens Concerned about PCBs, and named Ken as its spokesperson.[8]

Three years of vigorous opposition followed, during which the original group of white organizers evolved into an interracial coalition that better reflected the fact that Warren County had the highest percentage of African American residents in the state, at 64 percent, and that Shocco Township, where the toxic waste landfill was located, had a 75 percent African American majority. Despite three lawsuits and a series of public hearings, however, the courts declined to block the state from completing the project. Opponents argued that the state had targeted the impoverished African American county to host the facility because its minority-dominated population was too economically and politically weak to resist. But the courts disagreed. "There is not one shred of evidence," a state judge wrote in August 1982, rejecting a final request for an injunction to block the landfill, "that race has at any time been a motivating factor for any decision taken by any official—state, federal, or local—in this long saga."[9] A month later, the roadside cleanup began, dump trucks rolled, and protesters made the national news.

As these events unfolded, four significant lines of disagreement opened between the Warren County protesters and the various officials charged with enforcing federal environmental regulations. These disagreements foreshadowed the significant cleavages that split EJ advocates and members of the environmental movement over the next decade or two, and highlight many of the themes that permeate the documents in this book. This makes them worth understanding in some detail.

First and most fundamentally, protesters vehemently disputed how officials in the Environmental Protection Agency (EPA) defined the "environmental problem" that needed to be solved. For EPA officials and other proponents of TSCA, the obvious environmental problem was the toxic mess that Ward and the Burnses had created. The solution, as they saw it, was to scrape up the contaminated soil and put it in a certified, carefully engineered landfill where it could be monitored and contained. For the Warren County activists, on the other hand, the pertinent environmental problem was not the contaminated roadsides—it was the new toxic waste facility opening in their neighborhood. Viewed from this perspective, the environmental threat emanated not from the illegal actions of Ward and the Burnses, but from the legal process itself. It was not, after all, the midnight dumpers who had brought thousands of PCB-filled dump trucks to their doorsteps. Instead, that responsibility lay with the state officials, EPA experts, and judges who had decided that the best way to manage the environmental cleanup was to dump all of the PCBs in Warren County, despite vigorous local objections.

Second, mainstream environmentalists and the Warren County protesters disagreed over the integrity of a siting process that failed to include any local voices. From the perspective of the officials in charge, the process followed a clear set of rules. When first confronted with the magnitude of the PCB contamination along the state's highways, for example, officials had considered various possible solutions, including trucking the contaminated soil to an existing toxic waste landfill in Alabama, sending it to an EPA-licensed incinerator, or using one of a few different processes to detoxify or neutralize the PCBs where they were. The first two options had prohibitive costs, and the third failed after the EPA denied the state's request for a waiver to allow an experimental roadside treatment. Because the state did not already have a certified toxic waste facility, however, it could not remove the contaminated soil until after it built and licensed a new toxic waste landfill. This in turn prompted a study of ninety sites around the state to find a suitable location that would meet the EPA's various technical licensing criteria. Only after this lengthy review did the state settle on Warren County as the location, and only after surviving several court challenges did the state proceed with remediation. From the perspective of local protesters, on the other hand, this lengthy process had a fatal flaw: it lacked local representation. The people who determined Warren County's fate were all white, lived elsewhere, and were entrusted with the state's decision-making power; by contrast, those who would have to live with the facility were predominantly poor and African American, and had been excluded from the decision-making process.

Third, the two sides disagreed over how much trust to place in experts, how much faith to have in technological systems, and how to assess reasonable levels of risk. Environmental regulators argued that they possessed sufficient expertise to evaluate the merits of the proposed landfill and concluded that its "dry tomb" design was sufficiently well engineered that it should not present any problems—even though it was a new, untested design. State officials went so far as to describe it as the "cadillac of landfills."[10] Protesters, on the other hand, focused on the fact that in certifying the site, the EPA had waived a key technical criterion—

that the facility be located at least fifty feet from groundwater—which protesters believed should have prevented Warren County from being chosen. They also pointed out that decision-makers had ignored expert testimony that the site's subsoil was unsuitable for forming a slowly permeable liner. Without such a liner, the soil would not prevent the PCBs from migrating if water got into the landfill. Locals believed that it was inappropriate for nonlocal officials to issue waivers for key technical criteria since doing so imposed all of the risks of an untested engineering solution on the residents of Warren County.

Finally, protesters questioned the motives of decision-makers. Crying foul, protesters claimed that the whole process appeared to be rigged to save the state money and hassle, not to minimize environmental risks. If that had not been the case, they asked, why had the state not chosen to send the contaminated soil to the existing toxic waste facility in Alabama, which did not require any waivers to operate? To opponents, the state seemed to have chosen to build a new toxic waste landfill because it was the cheapest available option, and then to site it in a poor, isolated, minority-dominated area that would be too politically weak to resist its construction. Although the courts disagreed with the protesters' assessment, protesters were convinced that the elaborate siting process did not reflect the sort of dispassionate, apolitical process that environmentalists had intended, in which technical and scientific criteria were applied to minimize the risks of toxic contamination. In addition, the apparent politicization of the EPA's agenda under Anne M. Gorsuch, who resigned as EPA administrator in 1983 during a congressional investigation into mismanagement of monies designated for cleaning up toxic waste, added an additional layer of distrust.[11] To critics, the entire process was little more than a fig leaf designed to cover the political reasoning and racism that protesters were convinced had guided state decision-makers.

In the years after the first protests in Warren County, a national movement marching under the EJ banner built on these and other insights. Working together, activists, scholars, and citizens identified, documented, and fought against the unequal environmental burdens that communities of color and low-income communities routinely shouldered. In doing so, they challenged the fundamental approaches, priorities, and composition of mainstream environmental advocacy groups, and campaigned to change the ways courts and government agencies interpreted and implemented environmental laws, policies, and regulations. Though the movement suffered some failures, it also enjoyed many successes, including a gradual expansion of the mainstream environmental coalition, both at home and abroad, and convincing environmentalists to think more critically about the ways environmental and social justice issues intersect.

UNEQUAL BURDENS AND THE ENVIRONMENTAL JUSTICE MOVEMENT IN THE POSTWAR UNITED STATES

Although the environmental justice movement did not form until the 1980s, the underlying issues that shaped its rise have a much longer history. Some of these, such as state-sanctioned racial discrimination, have roots that trace all the way back to the nation's origins. Others, such as the pollution and racial segregation endemic to American cities, evolved in the period of rapid industrial growth and urban expansion stretching from the 1870s to the 1920s. The documents in this book, however, date primarily from the period after World War II, during which social movements emerged to confront both the legacies of segregation and the thorny new environmental problems that came with remaking the country as an affluent, suburbanizing, industrial nation. These two movements—the civil rights movement and the environmental movement—had many points of overlap and shared much common ground. Nevertheless, they proceeded largely independently of one another through most of the postwar era. The two came into productive conversation around the first Earth Day in 1970, but then largely separated again for the remainder of the decade. When they finally came back into direct dialogue in the early 1980s, it was in the fraught context of EJ's direct challenge to the priorities of mainstream environmentalism.

In the decades after World War II, segregation exerted a profound influence over the environments occupied by people of color. In the decade or two after each world war, for example, people of color were among those who flocked in huge numbers to American cities, where structural forces almost invariably funneled them into ghettos— segregated areas dominated by one or more minority groups and characterized by inferior and usually overcrowded housing. This pattern applied not only to African Americans who congregated in neighborhoods like Harlem in New York, Black Bottom and Paradise Valley in Detroit, and Chicago's South Side, but also to other racial groups, as illustrated by the presence of big-city Chinatowns and Spanish-speaking barrios. Racial segregation also extended into the workplace. In the postwar United States, racial minorities disproportionately held the most physically demanding, unpleasant, and low-paying jobs: working in blast furnaces and coke rooms, doing janitorial and sanitation work, and performing the most dangerous and difficult jobs in construction and agriculture. Segregation also restricted access to environmental amenities and opportunities for outdoor recreation in places as varied as parks, beaches, golf courses, and campgrounds.

During the postwar period, the American economy entered a period of prolonged change and growth that created unprecedented levels of affluence but came at the cost of a host of new environmental problems. One of the trickiest new questions was how to safely dispose of a dizzying range of new types of toxic wastes. Most of these new toxics had direct ties to the innovations that helped transform the nation's postwar economy, including industrial manufacturing processes, new synthetic organic compounds ranging from plastics to pesticides, and both the threats and opportunities of the dawning atomic age. In addition to being dangerous to human health, many of these toxic substances were surprisingly long lived, breaking down only very slowly, if at all, in the environment. In part because of their durability and longevity, many of them—such as radioactive fallout from nuclear tests and the class of chemicals known as persistent organic pollutants (POPs), which were the basis for products ranging from PCBs to potent new agricultural pesticides—moved through ecosystems in surprising ways. Both radioactive fallout and POPs circulated through natural systems over great distances from their point of release. In addition, through a process known as biomagnification, they moved up through food chains in ways that caused them to accumulate in human bodies in much higher concentrations than in the rest of the environment.

In the same postwar decades, the quality of the urban environment in American cities deteriorated significantly. Many of the biggest problems confronted by cities were the direct product of rapid suburbanization and white flight. Just as minorities were pouring into cities all over the country, white residents were flooding out into the green fields of burgeoning new suburbs—and many offices, manufacturing concerns, and retail operations went with them. The result was not just rapid demographic change but a growing sense of crisis as cities struggled with an eroding tax base, aging infrastructure, deteriorating housing stock, and serious traffic and air quality problems. Many of the solutions embraced by cities, such as slum clearance, urban renewal developments, and the construction of big infrastructure projects like the new interstate highways, amounted to radical urban surgery. Such projects were justified on the grounds that they would raise the overall quality of urban life, but were particularly disruptive to the immediate neighborhoods in which they were located. In addition, like other locally undesirable urban land uses that could also be justified as public goods—such as garbage transfer stations, incinerators, landfills, and pollution-emitting factories—the most severe pain of dramatically reconfiguring cities disproportionately affected minority neighborhoods.

Although many Americans celebrated what they perceived as the undeniable social and economic benefits of suburbanization, the new interstate highway system, and the almost magical range of new consumer products pouring out of American factories, many also worried about the costs of these advances. A growing number focused in particular on the deteriorating environmental quality of American cities. How should the nation respond to changes that seemed to be pointing cities toward a state of crisis? Especially after the publication of Rachel Carson's path-breaking book, *Silent Spring* (1962), which brought the environmental dangers of the widely used pesticide DDT to a broad audience, Americans struggled publicly with the intractable problems of safe use and disposal raised by the expanding presence of new toxic materials. If the government did not intend to ban outright the toxic materials that helped spur economic growth and material affluence, what steps did it need to take to protect human health? How should it handle dangerous substances that could not be disposed of through traditional channels, had surprisingly long life spans, and required the constant vigilance of scientific experts to monitor and contain? In short, what was the nation to do with large and expanding quantities of deadly poisons, many of which would never really go away or cease to pose a threat to human health?

The answers to both the urban environmental crisis and the threat of toxics rested in part on the combined strengths and limitations of scientific knowledge and technical expertise at the time, and in part on the ways a political system steeped in the legacies of segregation unequally distributed the era's new environmental burdens along lines of race and class. The truth was that a wide range of urban activities with broad social utility—including pollution-emitting factories, waste-handling facilities, and big infrastructure projects like the interstates—had negative effects on their immediate environment. And a disproportionate number of these locally undesirable features concentrated most heavily in places dominated by people of color. The unfortunate reality was that this pattern did not emerge by accident, but rather as the intentional product of a dense thicket of laws, policies, and practices that had evolved during the long period in which legal segregation existed across the United States.

As the civil rights movement mounted a furious challenge to segregation in the 1950s and 1960s, it recognized and sought to alleviate all of these unequal burdens—but rarely defined them as environmental. Instead, civil rights leaders tended to focus on overturning the many practices—formal and informal—that perpetuated segregation and condoned racial discrimination. As a result, they campaigned for legislation designed to achieve goals like fair housing and equal employment opportunity. At the same time, they challenged the constitutionality of laws that allowed states to provide segregated public facilities. Most famously, civil rights challenges to the "separate but equal" doctrine resulted in court-ordered desegregation of schools and transportation systems, including buses and trains, but these victories also included winning access to facilities that had been set aside as environmental amenities for public use, like parks, beaches, and campgrounds.

For a brief moment in the late 1960s and early 1970s, discussion about race and the environment took a new turn as both civil rights activists and environmentalists wrestled with new ways to frame the relationship between various pressing environmental problems and the overlapping realities of race and poverty. In this environmental moment, (largely minority) civil rights leaders took seriously the fundamental concerns that animated the new environmentalism and began to describe many civil rights issues in ways that incorporated an environmental critique. At the same time, (largely white) environmentalists began to consider what it would mean to try to tackle environmental inequalities. Although some of these conversations anticipated future developments, mainstream environmentalists ultimately failed during the 1970s to give racial minorities a meaningful place in their coalition or to embrace the subjects of most concern to people of color.

As a result, it took EJ's rise as a separate, minority-led movement to put environmental inequalities squarely on the nation's political agenda. In the process, EJ advocates directly challenged many of the basic orthodoxies and approaches that animated mainstream environmentalism. Perhaps most importantly, they challenged basic assumptions among environmentalists about how to define the environment—and by extension, how to identify environmental problems. As Dana Alston famously put it in a speech at the First National People of Color Environmental Leadership Summit, held in Washington, DC, in October 1991, people of color understood the environment not only or even primarily as beautiful, natural places unsullied by human activities, but as the everyday places "where we live, where we work and where we play."[12] These places bore the unmistakable imprint of human activity, were often heavily constructed rather than primarily natural, and suffered much too frequently from extreme contamination. These places, too, were environments worthy of attention. Environmental problems should thus be understood to include a broader range of issues than those addressed by establishment environmental organizations, including adequate housing, occupational exposure to harmful pollution, and the pronounced tendency of locally undesirable land uses to congregate disproportionately in minority neighborhoods.

During the presidential administrations of Ronald Reagan and George H. W. Bush, environmentalists and EPA officials often responded defensively in the face of criticism, pointing out that environmental policies during the 1970s had been tremendously successful in protecting endangered species and habitats, cleaning up serious air and water pollution, banning harmful chemicals, and curbing the environmentally destructive behavior of big corporate actors. Environmental protection "is about *all* of us: it benefits *all* of us," declared Bush's EPA administrator, William Reilly, in 1992. "In fact, it improves our health, defends our natural systems, and involves us in the humanly defining enterprise of stewardship."[13] Leaders within the EJ movement rejected this position, however, presenting evidence that even under the best of circumstances, the strong legacies of racial segregation meant that the even-handed enforcement of "race-blind" environmental laws too often translated into leaving minority populations to bear an unequal share of the heaviest environmental burdens. Worse, they pointed out that environmental laws were often enforced unevenly—to the point of reflecting what critics denounced as "environmental racism," or deliberate efforts to force people of color to play host to the worst kinds of environmental burdens. The result was to create "sacrifice zones," whereby officials turned a blind eye to extreme environmental contamination in minority-dominated areas so that society at large could continue to reap the rewards of a robust consumer economy and a strong military.

After a decade of EJ activism, which advocates spent identifying, documenting, and protesting a wide range of environmental injustices, the movement achieved one of its signal advances early in Bill Clinton's first term as president, when he signed Executive Order 12898. This order gave the movement institutional footing within the federal government, directing every federal agency to "make achieving environmental justice part of its mission by identifying and addressing, as appropriate, disproportionately high and adverse human health or environmental effects of its programs, policies, and activities on minority populations and low-income populations in the United States."[14] Although the executive order was no silver bullet and suffered from a lack of funding for implementation, it did elevate the movement's national profile and energize grassroots organizations. Clinton's presidency also marked the rise of numerous influential EJ research centers, including Beverly Wright's Deep South Center for Environmental Justice at Xavier University (which moved to Dillard University in 2005), Robert Bullard's Environmental Justice Resource Center at Clark-Atlanta University, and a group of influential EJ scholars in the University of Michigan's School of Natural Resources, including Bunyan Bryant, Dorceta Taylor, and Paul Mohai.

In the twenty-first century, as EJ continued to grow and evolve, it developed a new relationship with environmentalism as that movement became more attuned to issues of social and economic justice, often couched within the framework of sustainability. From an institutional perspective, EJ's national fortunes waxed and waned from one presidential administration to the next. During George W. Bush's presidency, for example, the EPA watered down its definition of environmental justice in a way that softened its focus on racial disparities, leaving state environmental agencies, foundations, and nonprofits to fund and advance the work without federal help. In addition, the movement suffered a series of setbacks in the courtroom, where judges proved reluctant to apply antidiscrimination laws to environmental disparities. During Barack Obama's administration, on the other hand, fighting for environmental justice again became a priority within the EPA, which supported ongoing EJ work around the country and produced two sets of agency guidelines known as *Plan EJ 2014* and *Plan EJ 2020*.[15] Across both the Bush and Obama presidencies, many of the environmental issues that received significant coverage in the press, such as Hurricane Katrina under Bush and the Flint water crisis and the Dakota Access Pipeline showdown at Standing Rock under Obama, were fundamentally environmental justice issues.

Perhaps the most interesting development during the early twenty-first century, however, has been the ways the EJ movement has prompted more critical and creative thinking about the broader interconnections between environmental issues and social justice concerns, both in the United States and abroad. EJ battles tend to occur at the local level, with grassroots organizations fighting specific environmental threats to a particular community. The focus has tended to be either on locally undesirable land uses, such as refineries, toxic waste facilities, incinerators, high-emitting factories, and garbage transfer stations, or on combating acute health problems, such as lead poisoning, asthma, or cancer, which disproportionately affect local minority populations. Yet as a movement, EJ activism has never been just local: building broader coalitions and finding common cause among affected populations were primary motivations for the First National People of Color Environmental Leadership Summit in 1991, where participants drafted a set of principles calling for "a national and international movement of all peoples of color." The next year, some of the summit's leaders then carried those principles—translated into Spanish and Portuguese—to the United Nations Conference on Environment and Development in Rio de Janeiro, Brazil, where they joined NGO participants pushing for a definition of sustainability that treated issues of social equity on a par with environmental and economic concerns.

As mainstream environmental organizations became less exclusively white and EJ concerns gained traction among environmental decision-makers, the "three-legged stool" of sustainability, with its emphasis on environment, economy, and equity, began to compete with environmentalism as a framework for thinking about environmental issues. In this atmosphere, EJ sprouted offshoots focused on new types of environmental inequalities. Activists began to adapt the insights and social justice orientation of traditional EJ work to a whole new range of environmental issues, launching campaigns for things like food justice, transit justice, green-collar jobs, and climate justice, which might be understood as much in terms of the environment and justice as environmental justice. With this expansion, the "marriage" of environmentalism and civil rights appears, perhaps, to have finally occurred.

READING THE DOCUMENTS

The documents in this collection will not always be easy to read. This is true in two ways. First, as is the case with all primary documents, you need to consider them in the context in which they originated to understand them fully. You must ask yourself: Who wrote this? For what audience and purpose? When? With what effect? Second, and perhaps more difficult, many of these documents contain both big ideas and specific language about race, class, and the environment that are, in a word, fraught. Some of the authors represented here use *language* that in today's context ranges from the politically incorrect to the outright hateful. I have chosen not to edit out even the most hateful and racist language, in part because those who used it did so to advance specific agendas that must be identified, and in part because editing it out would mask the role that white supremacy played in crafting the public policies that created and maintained segregation.

In addition to using problematic language, many of the authors wield *ideas* about racial superiority and inferiority, and about the use and abuse of power, that might disturb or even offend you. You might be tempted to dismiss them out of hand based on the conclusion that only bad people would hold such ideas, and that bad people do not deserve your attention. Yet if your goal is understanding, then you will need to think both critically and historically, even—or perhaps especially—when you are reading about ideas, practices, and attitudes that you find deeply objectionable. You do not need to suspend moral judgments as you read or to change your personal beliefs about right and wrong, but real understanding is unlikely to come from a position that begins and ends with a moral judgment. Why did people believe what they did? How did they express their views, and how did those views shape their actions? And when, if ever, did people change their minds . . . and why?

As you read, you might find it helpful to start with some of these questions:

- How did the practices of racial segregation affect the distribution of environmental burdens in the postwar years? When considering the unequal distribution of things like pollution-emitting factories, toxic waste facilities, or interstate highways, how important is the presence (or absence) of evidence that siting decisions were guided by malicious, racially motivated intent? Are there categories other than race—such as class or colonial relationships—that might also help explain why marginalized groups consistently shoulder an unequal share of environmental burdens? To what extent are these other categories separable from race?
- Early civil rights leaders were well aware of issues like dirty jobs, bad housing, and heavily polluted minority neighborhoods but did not define these issues as environmental. Why not? Do you think they would have been more or less effective if they had? Why?
- Environmentalists grappled with how to think about various racial disparities through an environmental lens in the years around the first Earth Day in 1970, but environmental leaders never adopted questions related to race and racial discrimination

as a central part of the agenda of mainstream environmentalism. How did those who saw issues related to race and class in environmental terms describe them as such? And how did those who rejected them as legitimate issues for environmentalists make that argument?

- Why have EJ activists so frequently been critical of mainstream environmentalism? What did they want environmentalists to do differently? Why did leaders of mainstream environmental organizations believe the things EJ leaders wanted would be challenging to implement? Over time, how successfully have mainstream environmental organizations incorporated EJ issues and a social justice perspective into their work?
- Why were EJ activists so critical of the EPA? Where has the EPA succeeded in advancing the work of EJ? Where has it failed?
- EJ activists have embraced Dana Alston's definition of the environment as "where we live, where we work and where we play"—sometimes adding "where we study" and "where we pray" to the definition. Through most of the EJ movement's history, though, EJ leaders have focused on combating locally undesirable land uses in marginalized communities like high-emitting factories and toxic waste facilities, even as they have worked to build national and international coalitions. How have new issues like access to healthy food, "green collar" jobs, and a stable climate system changed EJ? How have EJ ideas about sustainability changed the ways environmentalists understand environmental problems?
- Many of the documents in this collection are visual rather than textual. What are the strengths and weaknesses of visual sources as a type of historical evidence? What questions should we be asking ourselves as we interpret visual sources?

Finally, it is important to recognize that the documents in this collection are not comprehensive. They do not include, for example, many of the complicated debates that have roiled the field, such as the strengths and weaknesses of adopting different geographical units as the subject of analysis, the complications involved in trying to determine the health effects of various types of toxic exposure, or the legal intricacies of different strategies to combat environmental inequalities in the courts. Each of these important topics could easily form another, very different, volume. Instead, this collection pays special attention to the lasting legacy of segregation as a force that continues to shape the kinds of environments that different groups of people inhabit and experience, and highlights the underlying tensions and points of disagreement between environmental justice activists and the mainstream environmental movement. Its overarching goal is to help readers develop a wide-ranging historical understanding of the rise, growth, and evolution of the postwar environmental justice movement in the United States.

NOTES

1   "Carolinians Angry over PCB Landfill," *New York Times*, August 11, 1982.
2   Jenny Labalme, *A Road to Walk: A Struggle for Environmental Justice* (Durham, NC: Regulator Press, 1987), 5.
3   Labalme, *A Road to Walk*, 2–5.
4   "Dumping on the Poor," *Washington Post*, October 12, 1982.
5   L. Fleming Fallon, "Toxic Substances Control Act (1976)," in *Environmental Encyclopedia*, ed. Marci Bortman, Peter Brimblecombe, and Mary Ann Cunningham (Detroit: Gale, 2003), 1409–11.
6   US v. Robert Ward, Jr, No. 676 F.2d 94 (US Court of Appeals, 4th Cir. April 14, 1982); "No Dumping: A PCB Spill Fires Up a Town," *Time*, November 1, 1982, 29.
7   "No Dumping," 29.
8   Cheryl Katz, "Birth of the Movement: 'People Have to Stand up for What Is Right,' A Q&A with Two Environmental Justice Pioneers," *Environmental Health News*, June 20, 2012, www.environmentalhealthnews.org/ehs/news /2012/pollution-poverty-people-of-color-day-9-qa-with-environmental -justice-pioneers.
9   Labalme, *A Road to Walk*, 4.
10 Labalme, *A Road to Walk*, 4.
11 Eileen McGurty, *Transforming Environmentalism: Warren County, PCBs, and the Origins of Environmental Justice* (New Brunswick, NJ: Rutgers University Press, 2009), 21–49.
12 See Dana Alston, "Moving beyond the Barriers," in *The First National People of Color Environmental Leadership Summit, Proceedings*, ed. Charles Lee (New York: United Church of Christ, 1992), 103–6, in this volume.
13 William K. Reilly, "Environmental Equity: EPA's Position," in this volume.
14 William J. Clinton, Executive Order 12898, in this volume.

15　"Plan EJ 2014," in this volume. For an overview of federal level approaches to environmental justice, see Brentin Mock, "Can the Environmental Justice Movement Survive a Trump Administration?" CityLab, December 14, 2016, www.citylab.com/politics/2016/12/environmental-justice-enters-its-age-of -anxiety/510416.

PART I

THE NATURE OF SEGREGATION

A fundamental tenet of the environmental justice movement, as Dana Alston first gave it voice in 1991, is the notion that the environment should be understood to encompass not only places dominated by Nature with a capital N, but also the everyday places "where we live, where we work and where we play." Historically, this definition has mattered for people of color because deeply rooted practices of racial segregation have shaped the environments they occupy in fundamental ways. Throughout the period after World War II, in every region of the country and across the spectrum from rural to urban, formal and informal practices of segregation have systematically shunted people of color into the least desirable places and barred them from the most desirable ones. In postwar America, separate environments have seldom been created equal.

"WHERE WE LIVE"

This section focuses on the domestic spaces and neighborhoods where people of color lived starting in the era of segregation and moving into the civil rights era. The first four documents come from a stunning collection of images held by the Library of Congress, known as the Farm Security Administration and Office of War Information photographs (FSA/OWI). This New Deal project, which employed documentary photographers to chronicle American life, produced some 175,000 photographs in the years immediately before and during World War II, between 1935 and 1944. The first, from November 1938, is a photograph of the home of a family of African American farmers in Louisiana. The second, taken in 1941, shows an African American slum district in Norfolk, Virginia, in which the backed-up sewer is only the most obvious indication of neglect. The third, from 1935, shows the kitchen of a slum rental apartment's kitchen, with chipped plaster and peeling paint, located near the US Capitol Dome in Washington, DC. The fourth, taken in California's Imperial Valley in 1937, shows a migratory Mexican field-worker's home on the edge of a field. When you encounter photographs in this book, it is reasonable to wonder how representative they are. What are the strengths and limits of this kind of evidence? How should we interpret what we see? It is also reasonable to wonder how evidence from the years immediately preceding World War II compares to conditions after the war. What might have changed, and how would we know?

The next five documents reflect some of the racially discriminatory legal and financial practices that affected the type and location of housing available to people of color. The first document, a data sheet from a Home Owners Loan Corporation (HOLC) appraisal of a Los Angeles neighborhood in 1939, illustrates the practice of redlining. The practice derived its name from the color-coded rating system devised by the HOLC, which had been created in 1933 as part of the New Deal's efforts to save the struggling housing industry. By assigning different colors to different neighborhoods, HOLC maps allowed banks (and the Federal Housing Administration) to assess the risks of issuing loans based on a home's location. Green and blue neighborhoods were "best" and "still desirable," respectively. Yellow areas were "definitely declining." Red areas, on the other hand, signaled neighborhoods characterized by older housing, physical deterioration, and poverty, and were deemed too risky for investment. According to the HOLC's underwriting criteria, neighborhoods could earn a red designation simply for having African American residents.

Two obvious effects of this system were to bar most African Americans from taking advantage of postwar federal homeownership programs that fostered upward mobility and to drain postwar African American neighborhoods of capital and investment. But the HOLC's emphasis on maintaining racially "homogenous" populations and on the "prevention of infiltration" by "inharmonious racial groups" also created enormous financial incentives for white homeowners to protect their home values by maintaining rigid segregation. The next two documents depict the perverse extremes that such a policy could inspire: in this case, a half-mile-long concrete wall, erected by a developer in 1941 to separate a new (white) development from an adjacent (black) neighborhood in Detroit. Without the wall, the FHA did not approve the project. With it, it did.

The next document illustrates a very different but also effective technique that maintained segregated housing. It collects various examples of "restrictive covenants," or clauses written into property deeds that legally restricted members of named minority groups from buying, renting, or occupying certain properties, even when owners were otherwise willing. Used widely across the country between the First World War and 1948, when the Supreme Court declared them unenforceable, restrictive covenants like these were a key legal mechanism for maintaining racially segregated housing and confining people of color to segregated ghettos.

In the years after World War II, in the context of an acute housing shortage in which vast quantities of new housing were needed, the question of whether or not discriminatory practices like redlining and racially restrictive covenants should be allowed to continue sparked public debate. Some, like Charles Abrams, a leading housing reformer and public intellectual, cast the question in stark moral terms. Would federal policy aim to "[recast] our communities in a democratic mold," he asked in 1947, or would it cave in to "pressures to perpetuate segregation"?[1]

Pressure to maintain segregation came in different forms, as the next several documents show. One of the most obvious forms of pressure came in overt expressions of hatred and violence. The first document, a famous photograph taken by Arthur Siegel in February 1942, is part of a series documenting a riot at the new Sojourner Truth housing project in Detroit, which broke out when white neighbors tried to prevent its first African American tenants from moving in. The next document, an excerpt from a 1954 *Saturday Evening Post* feature article on William Levitt, the president of the country's largest suburban developer, Levitt and Sons, explains his family's choice not to "sell their houses to Negroes." This is followed by a *Saturday Evening Post* exposé, published in 1962, that explains the lucrative practice known as "block busting," by which speculators capitalized on the volatile cocktail of racial tensions, housing shortages, financial incentives, and prevailing real estate practices to "drive the whites from a block whether or not they want to go, then move in Negroes." The author uses crude language that displays obvious individual bigotry, but he also makes clear that his personal feelings about race are a small part of a much bigger pattern. More important than his individual attitudes is the fact that his actions—and those of other blockbusters—enjoy the full sanction of local politicians, police, realty organizations, and the press.

The final four documents in this section illustrate the importance of housing-related issues as a key item on the civil rights movement's agenda. The first is a photo of the Civil Rights March on Washington, DC, on August 28, 1963, which is best known as the venue for Martin Luther King Jr.'s iconic "I Have a Dream" speech. It shows leaders Roy Wilkins (NAACP), A. Philip Randolph (AFL-CIO), and Walter Reuther (UAW) holding hands in the foreground, with marchers carrying signs behind them that proclaim various priorities. The second photo shows three picketers outside the Seattle offices of the National

Association of Real Estate Boards protesting the discriminatory practices of realtors. The third document, an excerpt from the Fair Housing Act of 1968, marks one of the civil rights movement's signal legal victories, the Civil Rights Act of 1968, which President Lyndon Johnson signed into law in the midst of nationwide riots in the wake of Martin Luther King Jr.'s assassination. The fourth document, excerpted from a US Commission on Civil Rights pamphlet, "Understanding Fair Housing" (1973), explains the significance of efforts to secure equal housing, while cautioning that even sweeping legal victories were unlikely to eliminate segregation.

NOTE

1   Charles Abrams, "Race Bias in Housing: The Great Hypocrisy," *Nation*, July 19, 1947, 67–69.

RUSSELL LEE

SHACK OF NEGRO FAMILY FARMERS LIVING NEAR JARREAU, LOUISIANA, 1938

Russell Lee, *Shack of Negro Family Farmers Living near Jarreau, Louisiana,* Nov. 1938, Farm Security Administration—Office of War Information Photograph Collection, Library of Congress Prints and Photographs Division, LC-USF33- 011891-M4 [P&P], www.loc.gov/pictures/resource/fsa.8a24792.

JOHN VACHON

BACKED UP SEWER IN NEGRO SLUM DISTRICT, NORFOLK, VIRGINIA, 1941

John Vachon, *Backed Up Sewer in Negro Slum District, Norfolk, Virginia*, March 1941, Farm Security Administration—Office of War Information Photograph Collection, Library of Congress Prints & Photographs Division, LC-USF34-062567-D, www.loc.gov/pictures/item/fsa2000043236/PP.

CARL MYDANS

KITCHEN OF NEGRO DWELLING IN SLUM AREA NEAR HOUSE OFFICE BUILDING, WASHINGTON, D.C., 1935

Carl Mydans, *Kitchen of Negro Dwelling in Slum Area near House Office Building, Washington, D.C.*, Sept. 1935, Farm Security Administration—Office of War Information Photograph Collection, Library of Congress Prints and Photographs Division, LC-USF33- 000115-M1, www.loc.gov/pictures/item/fsa1997000120/PP.

DOROTHEA LANGE

MIGRATORY MEXICAN FIELD WORKER'S HOME ON THE EDGE OF A FROZEN PEA FIELD, IMPERIAL VALLEY, CALIFORNIA, 1937

Dorothea Lange, *Migratory Mexican Field Worker's Home on the Edge of a Frozen Pea Field, Imperial Valley, California,* March 1937, Farm Security Administration— Office of War Information Photograph Collection, Library of Congress Prints and Photographs Division, LC-USF34- 016425-C, www.loc.gov/item /fsa2000001016/PP.

LOS ANGELES DATA SHEET D52, 1939

AREA DESCRIPTION
Security Map of _____ LOS ANGELES COUNTY _____

1. **POPULATION:** a. Increasing _____ - _____ Decreasing _____ - _____ Static __Yes__

   b. Class and Occupation __WPA workers, laborers, low scale clericals, factory workers, etc__ Income $700 to $1500

   c. Foreign Families __40 %__ Nationalities __Mexicans, Japanese and low class Italians__ d. Negro __50 %__

   e. Shifting or Infiltration __Encroachment of industry a threat.__

2. **BUILDINGS:**

	PREDOMINATING	85%	OTHER TYPE	%
a. Type and Size	5 rooms			
b. Construction	Frame			
c. Average Age	35 years			
d. Repair	Very poor			
e. Occupancy	97%			
f. Owner-occupied	20%			
g. 1935 Price Bracket	$2000-2750	% change	$	% change
h. 1937 Price Bracket	$2500-3500	20 %	$	%
i. 1939 ___ Price Bracket	$2500-3500	- %	$	%
j. Sales Demand	Fair			
k. Predicted Price Trend (next 6-12 months)	Slowly down			
l. 1935 Rent Bracket	$25.00-30.00	% change	$	% change
m. 1937 Rent Bracket	$27.50-35.00	13 %	$	%
n. 1939 ___ Rent Bracket	$27.50-35.00	- %	$	%
o. Rental Demand	Fair			
p. Predicted Rent Trend (next 6-12 months)	Static			

3. NEW CONSTRUCTION (past yr.) No. 3 ___ Type & Price 5 rms.$4000 ___ How Selling __Slowly__

4. OVERHANG OF HOME PROPERTIES: a. HOLC __9__ b. Institutions __Few__

5. SALE OF HOME PROPERTIES (3 yr.) a. HOLC __74__ b. Institutions __Few__

6. MORTGAGE FUNDS __None__ 7. TOTAL TAX RATE PER $1000 (193__) 1937-8 $ 52.80

8. DESCRIPTION AND CHARACTERISTICS OF AREA:

   Terrain: Level. No flood or construction hazards. Land improved 90%. Zoning is mixed, but improvements are largely single family dwellings. Conveniences are all readily available. This is the "melting pot" area of Los Angeles, and has long been thoroughly blighted. The Negro concentration is largely in the eastern two thirds of the area. Original construction was evidently of fair quality but lack of proper maintenance is notable. Population is uniformly of poor quality and many improvements are in a state of dilapidation. This area is a fit location for a slum clearance project.
   The area is accorded a "low red" grade.

9. LOCATION __Central Ave.Dist.__ SECURITY GRADE __4th -__ AREA NO. __D-52__ DATE __3-3-39__
   400

Home Owners Loan Corporation data sheet D52, March 1939, Los Angeles, from *Mapping Inequality*, dsl.richmond.edu/panorama/redlining/#loc=11/34.0051/-118 .3701&opacity=0.86&city=los-angeles-ca&sort=16&area=D52.

JOHN VACHON

NEGRO CHILDREN STANDING IN FRONT OF HALF MILE CONCRETE WALL, DETROIT, MICHIGAN, 1941

John Vachon, *Negro Children Standing in Front of Half Mile Concrete Wall, Detroit, Michigan. This Wall Was Built in August 1941, to Separate the Negro Section from a White Housing Development Going Up on the Other Side*, Aug. 1941, Farm Security Administration—Office of War Information Photograph Collection, Library of Congress Prints and Photographs Division, LC-USF34-063679-D and -063680 [P&P], www.loc.gov/pictures/resource/fsa.8c20121 and /fsa.8c20122.

EXAMPLES OF RACIALLY RESTRICTIVE
REAL ESTATE COVENANTS

No part of the land hereby conveyed shall ever be used or occupied or sold, demised, transferred, conveyed unto, or in trust for, leased, rented, or given to Negroes, or any person of the Semitic race or origin, which racial designation shall be deemed to include Armenians, Jews, Hebrews, Persians, Egyptians.[1]

This property shall not be used or occupied by any person or persons except those of the Caucasian race.[2]

Hereafter no part of said property or any portion thereof shall be . . . occupied by any person not of the Caucasian race, it being intended hereby to restrict the use of said property . . . against the occupancy as owners or tenants of any portion of said property for resident or other purpose by people of the Negro or Mongolian race.[3]

No person of any race other than (race to be inserted) shall use or occupy any building or any lot, except that this covenant shall not prevent occupancy by domestic servants of a different race domiciled with an owner or tenant.[4]

That said premises shall not at any time hereafter be sold, leased or transferred to any colored person or persons or to any person or persons of the Ethiopian or Semetic Race or to any descendant of either of said races and said premises shall not be used or occupied by any such person or persons at any time as a residence or otherwise and these presents are made upon the express condition that upon the sale, lease or transfer of title to any colored person or persons or to any person or persons of the Ethiopian or Semetic Race, or to any descendant of either of said races, then the estate hereunder shall become immediately forfeited and all rights, title and interest therein shall thereupon revert to the grantors, their heirs, executors, administrators or assigns.[5]

He will make no sale, contract of sale, conveyance, lease or agreement and give no license or permission in violation of such restriction or provisions, which are as follows:

1. The restriction that no part of said premises shall in any manner be used or occupied directly or indirectly by any negro or negroes, provided that this restriction shall not prevent the occupation, during the period of their employment as janitors' or Chauffeurs' quarters in the basement or in a barn or garage in the rear, or of servants' quarters by negro janitors, employed as such for service in and about the chauffeurs or house servants, respectively, actually employed as such for service in and about the premises by the rightful owner or occupant of said premises.

2. The restriction that no part of said premises shall be sold, given, conveyed or leased to any negro or negroes, and no permission or license to use or occupy any part thereof shall be given to any negro except house servants or janitors or chauffeurs employed thereon as aforesaid.

3. The covenants, restrictions, and agreements herein contained shall be considered as appurtenant to and running with the land, and shall be binding upon and for the benefit of each party hereto and may be enforced by any of the parties hereto by any permissible legal or equitable proceedings, including proceedings to enjoin violation and for specific performance; provided, however, that in any action brought to set aside any deed made in violation of any of the provisions of this agreement, it shall be a good defense thereto that prior to the institution of each suit, the title to the premises then in question had become vested in, and was then owned by a corporation or a white person, for value; and provided further, that the lien of no mortgage or trust deed in the nature of a mortgage shall be impaired or invalidated by reason of the breach of any of the

provisions of this agreement, whether any such breach shall have occurred prior or subsequent to the recording of any such mortgage or trust deed; and provided further, that nothing contained in the foregoing provisos shall in any manner impair the right of any person or persons interested to enforce at all times and against all persons the restrictions in this agreement contained prohibiting the use or occupation of all or any part of said premises by a negro or negroes.[6]

NOTES

1   As quoted in Sara Lamport, "New Dred Scott Case," *Nation*, January 31, 1948, 124.

2   As quoted in John Doebele, "Hope in Court," *Commonweal*, September 12, 1947, 523–27.

3   As quoted in US Commission on Civil Rights, "Understanding Fair Housing" (Washington, DC: US Government Printing Office, 1973), 4.

4   Model covenant, as quoted in Charles Abrams, "Race Bias in Housing: The Great Hypocrisy," *Nation*, July 19, 1947, 69.

5   From Wendy Plotkin, "Racial and Religious Covenants in the U.S. and Canada," www.wbhsi.net/~wendyplotkin/DeedsWeb.

6   From "Racial Restrictive Covenant of Washington Park Subdivision in the City of Chicago," supporting document in Hansberry v. Lee, 311 U.S. 32 (1940), as reproduced on www.wbhsi.net/~wendyplotkin/DeedsWeb/cc.html.

ARTHUR S. SIEGEL

DETROIT, MICHIGAN. RIOT AT THE SOJOURNER TRUTH HOMES, A NEW U.S. FEDERAL HOUSING PROJECT, CAUSED BY WHITE NEIGHBORS' ATTEMPT TO PREVENT NEGRO TENANTS FROM MOVING IN, 1942

Arthur S. Siegel, *Detroit, Michigan. Riot at the Sojourner Truth Homes, a New U.S. Federal Housing Project, Caused by White Neighbors' Attempt to Prevent Negro Tenants from Moving In. Sign with American Flag "We Want White Tenants in Our White Community," Directly Opposite the Housing Project,* February 1942, Farm Security Administration—Office of War Information Photograph Collection, Library of Congress Prints and Photographs Division, LC-USW3-016549-C [P&P] LOT 661, www.loc.gov/item/owi2001018484/PP.

CRAIG THOMPSON

"GROWING PAINS OF A BRAND-NEW CITY," 1954

It was in July of 1951 that William J. Levitt—president and principal executive of Levitt and Sons—publicly affirmed his intention to construct 16,000 dwellings in lower Bucks County adjacent to U. S. Steel's new Fairless works near Morrisville, Pennsylvania. Presently, several sample houses went up and Levitt advertised that, beginning December eighth, he would take orders for thousands like them as yet unbuilt....

By mid-1954 at prices ranging from $8990 to $16,500, some 9000 houses had been built, sold and occupied. Barring unpredictable delays, the 16,000th will be finished by the end of 1955, and what, four years before, had been 5500 acres of farmland, scrub woods and swamp will be a city of 70,000 people.

Concerning these people, surveys have established certain generalities. Levittowners are young—most, family heads are under thirty and most of their children not yet five. They are able—no family earns less than $4000 a year, the minimum required by the Federal Housing Administration for a mortgage guarantee. They are responsible—no applicant gets a house without a good credit rating. Finally, though 90 per cent of Levittowners came from nearby Philadelphia and Trenton, most of them had never met before. Levittown, then, begins as a community of strangers who pay their bills and possess the hopeful vitality of youth....

Within Levittown, many residents say, the atmosphere is more tolerant and neighborly than any other place they ever lived. However,

Levittowners collectively have not yet come to grips with one problem that could give rise to a really tense situation. This is the problem of Negro exclusion.

The Levitts do not sell their houses to Negroes. This, as William Levitt explains it, is not a matter of prejudice, but one of business.

"The Negroes in America," he says, "are trying to do in four hundred years what the Jews in the world have not wholly accomplished in six thousand. As a Jew, I have no room in my mind or heart for racial prejudice. But, by various means, I have come to know that if we sell one house to a Negro family, then ninety to ninety-five per cent of our white customers will not buy into the community. That is their attitude, not ours. We did not create it, and cannot cure it. As a company, our position is simply this: we can solve a housing problem, or we can try to solve a racial problem. But we cannot combine the two."

Over the years, Levitt has been the butt of much sharp criticism on this subject, which he has learned to take philosophically, although it rankles him at times to know that his most vigorous critics are those who refuse to accept what he regards as the realities of his position. But there is another reality involved that many people have not understood. Once the title to a Levitt house passes from the builder to the buyer, that buyer is free to sell it to anyone. Because of this fact, Friends Association Chairman Blanshard confidently predicts that a day will come when a Negro family will move into Levittown. And Levitt replies, "If that should happen, there is nothing I can, or would, do about it."

NORRIS VITCHEK

"CONFESSIONS OF A BLOCK-BUSTER," 1962

I specialize in locating blocks which I consider ripe for racial change. Then I "bust" them by buying properties from the white owners and selling them to Negroes—with the intent of breaking down the rest of the block for colored occupancy. Sometimes the groundwork—the initial block-busting—has already been done by some other speculator by the time I arrive on the scene. In that case all I have to do is to work on the remaining whites and reap my share of the harvest.

I make my money—quite a lot of it, incidentally—in three ways: (1) By beating down the prices I pay the white owners by stimulating their fear of what is to come; (2) by selling to the eager Negroes at inflated prices; and (3) by financing these purchases at what amounts to a very high rate of interest. I'll have more to say about these techniques later.

Block-busting is a relatively new business—only ten to fifteen years old actually—but already it is a crowded field. Block-busters also operate in Washington, D.C, Baltimore, Philadelphia, New York City, Boston, Cleveland, Detroit, St. Louis and other cities and in some of their suburbs. Chicago alone has more than 100 of us. Because few Negroes can command the necessary financing to enter this occupation, most of us are white, as I am. Over the past ten years we have helped "change" an average of two to three blocks a week in Chicago. Even now, with the overall housing market rather quiet, we bust a new block in Chicago every four to eight days.

With the nation's Negro population exploding and continuing to concentrate in urban areas, the demand simply never lets up. More than half the citizenry of Washington, D. C, is Negro. Philadelphia is one fourth Negro. In Chicago the Negro population, now one fourth of our citizenry, has nearly doubled in the past ten years and probably will double again in the next thirty, rising to 1,700,000 persons, or half the city's present population. Even its suburbs, now mostly white, are expected to contain nearly 700,000 Negroes by 1990.

AVERAGE CITIZENS, AVERAGE PREJUDICES

If you are an average white citizen, with average prejudices, you may regard all this as the ruin of metropolitan neighborhoods. I think of it merely as more business for what already is a growth industry. My attitude stems from the fact that few white neighborhoods welcome Negroes who can afford to buy there; yet the need for homes for Negroes keeps growing. I assist in the solution of this problem. My function, which might be called a service industry, is to drive the whites from a block whether or not they want to go, then move in Negroes.

You might think it would be difficult to bust a block, especially your block. It isn't really. In most blocks someone almost always is being transferred, wanting a larger or smaller home, or moving away for his health. If I offer enough money, I can buy any building I want—if not directly, then through a front. It doesn't matter whether Negroes now live nearby. The shock effect of the block-busting, plus my ready financing, can cave in enough of the block to make my efforts successful.

But I prefer blocks near others where Negroes already live—especially old, middle-class blocks with a mixture of frame homes and walk-up apartments. Whites already there have been conditioned to insecurity by the inexorable march of the color line in their direction. This makes these blocks setups for the quick turnover, large volume and the large profits I like. . . .

"We'll organize," some residents said. "We'll keep the niggers out." But other speculators and I already were buying buildings in adjacent blocks and holding them until we thought the area was ready to be turned for maximum profit.

You can't appreciate the psychological effect of such a color-line march unless you have seen it. First, Negro students begin enrolling in neighborhood schools. Then, churches and businesses in the area quit fixing up facilities as they normally might. Parks which have been all white suddenly become all Negro. A homeowner applies to his bank for a home-improvement loan and is turned down. "Too close to the color line," he is told.

Small businesses begin to close. New whites, if they move into the area at all, are apt to be of lower economic class than before, and they are tenants, not owners. Because lending institutions always blacklist an area for regular mortgages when change appears imminent, whites can't buy there if they want to. . . .

FIRST "BREAK" CAN BRING TROUBLE

. . . Now admittedly, although somebody would perform this economic function if I did not, these dealings are not always pleasant. In the first place, the Negro able to buy property usually doesn't want trouble. Yet, being the first to "break" an all-white block, or even second or third, can and often does bring trouble.

For example, there was the case of a Negro salesman who had just been promoted to a supervisory position in his firm. He came to a speculator seeking an income property into which he could move with his family. The speculator told him about a three-flat building he had just bought from whites. "The place we're renting is bad," the Negro said, "but we don't want any trouble. Has the block been busted?" The speculator owned another building there, but the block hadn't been busted, in the sense that Negroes already were living there. However, knowing the three-flat building would be a good investment for the Negro and that he should be able to carry it financially, the speculator told him, "It's OK."

In the first few days after the Negro moved in, a bottle was thrown through his front window, his wife was insulted by several whites who lived in the block, and his two children were harassed on their way home from school.

Few Negroes or whites on Chicago's West Side have forgotten the riots involving thousands, three summers ago, after a speculator's sale of a building to Negroes on West Jackson Boulevard. Luckily only the building got hurt. And, fortunately, any incidents connected with the move-ins I handle are so minor in comparison to what Negroes already have experienced that they soon are forgotten.

Actually, block-busting probably is tougher on the whites than the Negroes. Nobody who has lived in a neighborhood for years, seen his children grow up there, remodeled his home exactly to his liking and become accustomed to nearby school, church and shopping facilities likes to be uprooted. This is particularly true if it happens so suddenly that he has no new neighborhood in mind, if he has to accept less living space and a higher-interest mortgage than he previously had and if he must sell his property at a loss. Several elderly persons have died because of the anguish and upheaval involved.

As a result of my business dealings, I have been cursed, called "nigger lover," "vulture," and "panic peddler," had doors slammed in my face and even been chased by an irate woman with a broom. "You're Communist and un-American!" one owner shouted at me. "You've sold out your own race!" others have yelled. . . .

But no matter how emotional or awkward some situations may be, there is one compensation for it all—money. Some brokers or investors make a good return only on some deals. I make it on every deal in the three ways I mentioned earlier.

You may believe your home is worth $15,000, for example. If I bust your block, I will expect to buy it for $12,000 cash. The odds are that eventually you will sell for that price, if not to me, then to another speculator. If you and your white neighbors did not run, you probably would gain, rather than lose. More than four fifths of the white neighborhoods into which Negroes move hold their own or enjoy an increase in value, according to a five-year Fund for the Republic study of 10,000 transactions in Northern interracial neighborhoods. But the myth that "Negroes lower property values" persists—so whites run, and we block-busters clean up. Within a few days comes profit No. 2: I advertise and sell it to a Negro not for $15,000, but for $18,000. Financing the deal myself, I will accept $500 to $1500 down, with the remainder on contract. The easy-payment plan, I believe it is called—that is, $150 to $200 a month until the contract is fulfilled. When is that? This is profit No. 3, the big one. The contract is fulfilled when I have been paid principal and interest totaling $36,000.

These terms, I am told, force Negroes to overcrowd and overuse their buildings by renting out part of them, or to skimp on maintenance, starting the neighborhood on the way to blight. (In most Negro neighborhoods in Chicago the population density is five times that of white areas.) The contract burden, I also am told, forces Negro mothers to work, despite the presence of youngsters at home, compels fathers to take two jobs, and can lead to numerous other problems because of the financial strain and anxiety.

Even so, the number of Negro buyers who default on their payments is small. When it does happen in my own business, it is no loss to me, since I retain title to property until contracts are completed. I keep all the payments made until that time, evict the owners and either rent the building or resell it on about the same terms.

The Urban League of Chicago says we speculators make nearly $1,000,000 a month in our city in "abnormal" profit from Negroes who buy former white property on contract. This could be. I know that I make four times the profit I could for the same amount of effort in all-white real estate. If anybody who is well established in this business in Chicago doesn't earn $100,000 a year, he is loafing.

"A dirty business," you say? One that whites should fight?

White people in dozens of neighborhoods have tried fighting. They have pressured neighborhood banks and savings-and-loan associations to quit blacklisting their areas, resulting in token concessions. They have held block meetings to warn homeowners not to deal with those of us who advertise "Quick Cash Sales" in newspapers or the classified phone directory, have passed out leaflets listing speculators' names and have ripped up "Sold by" signs which were of larger size or were posted longer than city ordinance allows. They even won a fraud-and-misrepresentation case against two block-busting brokers in Chicago, thanks to several blunders which no established operator would have made. Despite all such resistance, once a block has been busted, only rarely has its complete breakdown been halted. Too many forces are working for us speculators.

ORDAINING THE "CAVE-IN" METHOD

The Chicago Real Estate Board, an organization of the city's most prominent realtors, all but ordained the "cave-in" method in a policy laid down in 1917: "It is desired in the interest of all that each block shall be filled solidly (with Negroes) and that further expansion shall be confined to contiguous blocks. . . . "

The board, which is all white, no longer makes a copy of this statement available in its office, but the policy never has been rescinded or repudiated. None of the board's 1700 members violates it. No member, if he deals with Negroes at all, is likely to arrange for a sale to them in a white neighborhood that is not next to a "Negro block." Once a neighborhood begins changing, none will show homes there to whites.

Lending institutions' "no-Negro" or "no-integrated area" loan policies further perpetuate the trend, restricting Negroes to blocks we bust and forcing them to rely mainly on our contract sales for financing.

The City Council and Mayor Richard J. Daley, who, like his two immediate predecessors, comes from the all-white Bridgeport area of the city, also help. They regularly table every request for open-occupancy ordinances, which by opening up any neighborhood to Negroes who could afford to buy there would take the pressure off the few collapsing ones which are open.

The police put down violence promptly in any blocks which are busted in a "permissible" area. Yet, if a Negro is leapfrogged into a home beyond this zone, the protests somehow always get out of hand. In one case a policeman guarding a Negro's new home was seen showing several youths how to make a Molotov-cocktail incendiary bomb. . . .

RELENTLESS MARCH OF THE COLOR LINE

. . . Newspapers, too, help prepare the way. Their only stories in this field usually concern the "panic" aspects. If they print stories about Negroes, it's only in connection with crime or welfare problems or population increases, not with Negro church activity or business and educational success or other aspects of normal life in good Negro neighborhoods.

The Board of Education contributes by writing off a school once it begins to change racially, consigning it to overcrowding, double shifts and supervision by the least experienced and lowest-paid teachers— and by giving it the lowest proportion of counselors.

Then there are my financial sources, which are among the most reputable in the city. My credit is good in almost any bank or savings-and-loan association in town. It also is good with insurance companies, including several Negro firms. Merely by placing an ad in a daily newspaper, I can raise cash by selling my contract paper at a discount to some of the most reputable doctors, dentists, lawyers and other business and professional men in town.

With forces such as these on my side, why should I feel guilty? Am I really the basic cause of whites' fleeing? Do I depress their property values and inflate prices for Negroes? When a Negro has been turned away from a bank, do I "trap" him into accepting a contract sale?

And what alternative can you provide for my function? Would you try to influence your bank or savings-and-loan association to begin lending to Negroes? Would you help remove the pressure on "busted" areas by welcoming a Negro family into your block? Do you even care that my business operates as it does? Whatever my faults and whatever the social stigma I endure, I don't believe I am hypocritical about all this. Can you honestly say the same?

CIVIL RIGHTS MARCH ON WASHINGTON, D.C., 1963

Civil Rights March on Washington, D.C., August 28, 1963, RG 306: Records of the U.S. Information Agency, 1900–2003, National Archives and Records Administration, NWDNS-306-SSM-4C(36)6.

FAIR HOUSING PROTEST, SEATTLE, WASHINGTON, 1964

Seattle Municipal Archives, *Fair Housing Protest, Seattle, Washington, 1964*
[Confronting Racial Discrimination in Housing Sales], 1964, Item 63897, Records
of the Office of the Mayor (Record Series 5210-01), Seattle Municipal Archives.

FAIR HOUSING ACT OF 1968

DISCRIMINATION IN SALE OR RENTAL OF HOUSING
AND OTHER PROHIBITED PRACTICES

SEC. 804.   As made applicable by section 803 of this title and except as exempted by sections 803(b) and 807 of this title, it shall be unlawful—

(a) To refuse to sell or rent after the making of a bona fide offer, or to refuse to negotiate for the sale or rental of, or otherwise make unavailable or deny, a dwelling to any person because of race, color, religion, sex, familial status, or national origin.

(b) To discriminate against any person in the terms, conditions, or privileges of sale or rental of a dwelling, or in the provision of services or facilities in connection therewith, because of race, color, religion, sex, familial status, or national origin.

(c) To make, print, or publish, or cause to be made, printed, or published any notice, statement, or advertisement, with respect to the sale or rental of a dwelling that indicates any preference, limitation, or discrimination based on race, color, religion, sex, handicap, familial status, or national origin, or an intention to make any such preference, limitation, or discrimination.

(d) To represent to any person because of race, color, religion, sex, handicap, familial status, or national origin that any dwelling is not available for inspection, sale, or rental when such dwelling is in fact so available.

Civil Rights Act of 1968, Title VIII, U.S.C., vol. 42, 1968 [Fair Housing Act].

(e) For profit, to induce or attempt to induce any person to sell or rent any dwelling by representations regarding the entry or prospective entry into the neighborhood of a person or persons of a particular race, color, religion, sex, handicap, familial status, or national origin.

DISCRIMINATION IN THE FINANCING OF HOUSING

SEC. 805.   After December 31, 1968, it shall be unlawful for any bank, building and loan association, insurance company or other corporation, association, firm or enterprise whose business consists in whole or in part in the making of commercial real estate loans, to deny a loan or other financial assistance to a person applying therefor for the purpose of purchasing, constructing, improving, repairing, or maintaining a dwelling, or to discriminate against him in the fixing of the amount, interest rate, duration, or other terms or conditions of such loan or other financial assistance, because of the race, color, religion, or national origin of such person or of any person associated with him in connection with such loan or other financial assistance or the purposes of such loan or other financial assistance, or of the present or prospective owners, lessees, tenants, or occupants of the dwelling or dwellings in relation to which such loan or other financial assistance is to be made or given: *Provided*, That nothing contained in this section shall impair the scope or effectiveness of the exception contained in section 803(b).

DISCRIMINATION IN THE PROVISION
OF BROKERAGE SERVICES

SEC. 806.   After December 31, 1968, it shall be unlawful to deny any person access to or membership or participation in any multiple-listing service, real estate brokers' organization or other service, organization, or facility relating to the business of selling or renting dwellings, or to discriminate against him in the terms or conditions of such access, membership, or participation, on account of race, color, religion, or national origin.

US COMMISSION ON CIVIL RIGHTS

"UNDERSTANDING FAIR HOUSING," 1973

It is the policy of the United States to provide, within constitutional limitations, for fair housing throughout the United States.

With this preamble, Congress, in 1968, incorporated fair housing legislation into the Nation's body of civil rights law. Housing was the last of the major civil rights areas to receive legislative attention from Congress. Yet equal housing is of overriding importance. It is a major determinant of the quality of life afforded to minorities. Its achievement is necessary for progress in other areas of equal opportunity. Above all, it is vital to the Nation's well-being.

Few rights are as basic as acquiring a home of one's choice. The home and neighborhood are the environment in which families live and rear their children. For minorities, the home usually means housing vacated by whites who, because of their race as well as ability to pay, are able to acquire a more desirable dwelling elsewhere. The neighborhood is often a deteriorating ghetto or barrio isolated from the rest of the community.

Housing is a key to improvement in a family's economic condition. Homeownership is one of the important ways in which Americans have traditionally acquired financial capital. Tax advantages, the accumulation of equity, and the increased value of real estate property enable homeowners to build economic assets. These assets can be used to educate one's children, to take advantage of business opportunities, to meet financial emergencies, and to provide for retirement. Nearly two of every three majority group families are homeowners, but less than two

Excerpted from US Commission on Civil Rights, "Understanding Fair Housing" (Washington, DC: US Government Printing Office, 1973), 1–2.

of every five nonwhite families own their homes. Consequently, the majority of nonwhite families are deprived of this advantage.

Housing is essential to securing civil rights in other areas. Segregated residential patterns in metropolitan areas undermine efforts to assure equal opportunity in employment and education. While centers of employment have moved from the central cities to suburbs and outlying parts of metropolitan areas, minority group families remain confined to the central cities, and because they are confined, they are separated from employment opportunities. Despite a variety of laws against job discrimination, lack of access to housing in close proximity to available jobs is an effective barrier to equal employment.

In addition, lack of equal housing opportunity decreases prospects for equal educational opportunity. The controversy over school busing is closely tied to the residential patterns of our cities and metropolitan areas. If schools in large urban centers are to be desegregated, transportation must be provided to convey children from segregated neighborhoods to integrated schools.

Finally, if racial divisions are to be bridged, equal housing is an essential element. Our cities and metropolitan areas consist of separate societies increasingly hostile and distrustful of one another. Because minority and majority group families live apart, they are strangers to each other. By living as neighbors they would have an opportunity to learn to understand each other and to redeem the promise of America: that of "one Nation indivisible."

In addition to the Federal Fair Housing Law, Title VIII of the Civil Rights Act of 1968, other laws exist which ban discrimination in housing. President Kennedy's Executive order on equal opportunity in housing, issued in November 1962, prohibits discrimination in housing with funds obtained through federally assisted programs. Title VI of the Civil Rights Act of 1964 forbids discrimination in a variety of federally assisted programs, including low-rent public housing and urban renewal. And the 1968 decision of the Supreme Court of the United States in *Jones v. Mayer* bars discrimination in all housing, public and private. In addition, more than half the States and thousands of municipalities in the country have enacted fair housing laws.

But these acts have not reversed the pattern of residential segregation. Between 1960 and 1970 residential segregation actually increased.

Some minority group families are moving to the suburbs, but in far smaller numbers than white families. Many suburban black families merely exchange an inner-city ghetto for a suburban black enclave. That the housing laws have not had an impact on reversing the patterns of segregated housing underscores the complexity of the denial of equal housing opportunity to minority groups.

The Nation's problems of fair housing have not been widely discussed and their complexity is not understood. Slogans like "forced housing" and "open housing" are used as substitutes for rational analysis. Judgments of the causes of housing segregation are often based on unsupported assumptions rather than on documented evidence. There is not even common understanding of the statutory term, "fair housing" which Congress left undefined. In short, the American people have not been well served by the public discussion of equal housing opportunity.

The problems of discrimination in housing and residential segregation involve a variety of issues. Many of these are legal in nature, involving the scope of protection against housing discrimination afforded by our laws and Constitution. Others involve fundamental questions of the relationship between Government and the people and how to strike the proper balance between protection of the rights of home seekers and those of property owners. Still others involve practical questions such as the effect of racial integration on property values and the relative importance of economics and discrimination as factors that determine where people live.

These issues also involve fundamental questions of the kind of world we want our children to inherit. The way we resolve problems of equal housing opportunity will go far in answering these questions, in determining whether we leave to future generations a racially divided or a racially united country.

The U.S. Commission on Civil Rights is convinced that the problems of discrimination in housing and residential segregation can be resolved wisely and compassionately. It is essential that the American people be fully informed of the true nature of the issues involved. The Commission speaks out in the hope that it can shed light on these issues and, by so doing, contribute to public understanding of what has been so grossly misunderstood.

"WHERE WE WORK"

The documents in this section focus on segregated workplaces, where racial minorities held a disproportionate share of the most physically demanding, unpleasant, and low-paying jobs. Working in blast furnaces and coke rooms, doing janitorial and sanitation work, cleaning homes and doing laundry, and performing the most dangerous and difficult work in construction and agriculture, people of color were overrepresented in jobs with challenging work environments and high levels of occupational exposure. The first document, a photograph of African American cotton pickers in Mississippi, was taken in 1940 but could easily be mistaken for an earlier era. The second document, also a photograph from 1940, shows two African American steelworkers in Maryland, and illustrates one of the unpleasant but higher-paying jobs that from 1940 to 1970, during the Second Great Migration, helped draw over 5 million African Americans from the South to the industrial cities of the Northeast and Midwest.

Although the percentage of African Americans living in poverty fell substantially during this period, problems persisted. As the third document suggests, African American workers were often the last hired and first fired. In addition, as the fourth document explains, even within industries that employed relatively large numbers of African Americans, such as the auto industry, opportunities for people of color—skilled and unskilled alike—were confined almost exclusively to the least desirable positions. In the American Southwest, for example, as Cold War tensions prompted an arms race between the United States and the Soviet Union, mining companies like the Vanadium Corporation of America and Kerr-McGee operated uranium mines to supply the country's growing nuclear arsenal. As the fifth document illustrates, although large numbers of Navajo workers found employment in the mines, the positions available to them came with significant workplace hazards that had long-term health implications. The next document, an interview with the author Mildred Pitts Walter, highlights some of the typical jobs available to women of color in the postwar era.

The final three documents illustrate some of the ways that battling against segregated workplaces, like fighting segregated housing, animated the civil rights agenda, even though they do not frame the dirt and danger of the workplace as environmental issues. The first document, an excerpt from the watershed Equal Employment Opportunity provisions of the Civil Rights Act of 1964, banned discrimination on the basis of "race, color, religion, sex, or national origin" in hiring, compensating, promoting, or firing employees. In the second document, President Lyndon Johnson's commencement address to Howard University's graduating class of 1965, he draws on what he calls the "special thing" that is "American justice" to advocate for a more comprehensive approach to helping African Americans "emerge from poverty and prejudice." The third document is a campaign flyer distributed to sanitation workers in Memphis as part of Martin Luther King Jr.'s final campaign, during which he was assassinated. The campaign began as a fight against the low pay and dirty, dangerous working conditions that prevailed among the city's almost exclusively African American garbage haulers, who were responsible for keeping the city's environment clean. Although it did not describe these as environmental issues, it did stress the goals of justice and dignity.

RUBY T. LOMAX

[COTTON PICKING SCENES ON ROGER WILLIAMS PLANTATION IN THE DELTA, NEW DREW, MISSISSIPPI], 1940

Ruby T. Lomax, *[Cotton Picking Scenes on Roger Williams Plantation in the Delta, New Drew, Mississippi]*, October 24, 1940, Lomax Collection, Library of Congress Prints and Photographs Division, LC-DIG-ppmsca-38793, www.loc.gov/item/2015645813.

JOHN VACHON

STEEL MILL WORKERS, BETHLEHEM COMPANY, SPARROWS POINT, MARYLAND, 1940

John Vachon, *Steel Mill Workers, Bethlehem Company, Sparrows Point, Maryland,* 1940, Farm Security Administration—Office of War Information Photograph Collection, Library of Congress Prints & Photographs Division, LC-USF34-061333-D, www.loc.gov/item/fsa2000041960/PP.

HELP WANTED WHITE ONLY

Help Wanted White Only, "America's Black Holocaust Museum | The Five Pillars of Jim Crow," abhmuseum.org/the-five-pillars-of-jim-crow.

LLOYD H. BAILER

"THE NEGRO AUTOMOBILE WORKER," 1943

Negroes were largely confined to the most undesirable jobs in the industry. Most of them were unskilled. A small minority performed semiskilled and even skilled operations, but the latter were almost invariably
hot, noisy, dirty, dusty, hazardous, or required exceptional physical
exertion....

Nearly three-fourths of them were found in unskilled capacities as
against one-fourth of the whites. Approximately one-half of the white
employees but only one-eighth of the Negroes were white-collar or
skilled workers. Were Ford employment eliminated from these figures,
the Negro's concentration in the lower occupational classifications
would have appeared much greater, for his occupational distribution
in that concern (where nearly half of the Negro automobile workers
were found) has been much broader than in the rest of the industry.

These statistics do not tell the whole story, however, for jobs within
the same classification as to skill vary greatly in their desirability. Outside of the coreroom nearly all foundry jobs are unpleasant, yet a substantial portion of them are semiskilled and skilled. The same holds
true for the heat-treat and sanding and paint operations. Yet most of
the semiskilled and skilled Negro workers were found in such departments, where they were confined to the most hazardous or otherwise
undesirable occupations—such jobs, for example, as shear-operator,
heater, sprayman, chipper, rough-snag-grinder, and sand-blaster.
Likewise, Negro unskilled workers filled the more undesirable jobs
in that broad occupational category. In brief, Negroes were not only

Excerpted from Lloyd H. Bailer, "The Negro Automobile Worker," *Journal of
Political Economy* 51, no. 5 (1943): 415–28. Used with permission.

concentrated in occupations requiring less skill but were also attached to the worst jobs within each occupational classification. The sole exception to this general characterization was the Ford Rouge plant— though here, as described below, the difference was largely one of degree.

The pre-war position of Negroes in Chrysler plants may be taken as typical of those plants where Negroes were used in substantial numbers. In March, 1940, 51 per cent of the approximately two thousand Negro employees of Chrysler were classed as unskilled (production helpers, janitors, common laborers, etc.); 30 per cent as foundry workers; 5 per cent as paint-department employees (chiefly sanders and sprayers); and 14 per cent were classified in "miscellaneous occupations." All of these employees were found in the Chrysler Michigan plants, no Negro workers being employed in the company's Indiana and California establishments. In fact, most of the relatively few Negro automobile workers found in all assembly and parts plants located outside the Michigan-Ohio-Indiana region were janitors, porters, material handlers, and other unskilled employees.

The number of Negroes in supervisory positions (exclusive of the Ford Rouge plant) was negligible. Only six Negro foremen were found in nineteen motor-vehicle and twenty-one body and parts companies surveyed in the spring of 1940. The number of straw bosses was somewhat larger. In every case Negro foremen and straw bosses supervised all-Negro crews. . . .

It was nevertheless true that Negro wage-earners were disproportionately concentrated in the less desirable occupations and divisions. Thus they constituted nearly half of the production workers and over one-third of all workers in the foundry, but less than 1 per cent of the tool and die makers. In the most disagreeable jobs the proportion of Negro workers was over 50 per cent, as exemplified by the following percentages on Negro proportion of total employment: shakeout, 56.97; molding, 62.62; reels, 55.97; melting, 51.86; and chipping, 51.06.

Thus, at Ford's, as in the rest of the industry, Negroes were employed in greatest numbers in those jobs and in those sections where the general nature of the work was least desirable. . . .

NAVAJO MINERS WORK AT THE KERR-MCGEE URANIUM MINE AT COVE, ARIZ., 1953

Navajo Miners Work at the Kerr-McGee Uranium Mine at Cove, Ariz., May 7, 1953.
Associated Press file photo.

"BIOGRAPHICAL SKETCH,"
SEPTEMBER 28, 2017

I was born in Louisiana in 1922 to Paul and Mary Pitts, the seventh of three girls and one boy. My father was an itinerant worker for Long Bell Lumber who moved from place to place where the trees were plentiful. He went to work in Mississippi while my mother remained with us in Louisiana, where she felt was better for us.

I grew up in a segregated environment where the all black schools and all black churches helped us to resist accepting that we were inferior by stressing that we hold our heads high with dignity and humility, for humility could not be humiliated. That we stay in school and strive for excellence in our actions. From the time I was seven years old I worked in service. In high school, I worked every morning cleaning a white beauty shop before school and on weekends in the homes of white people.

I graduated from high school and went to Southern University, an all-black school in Scotlandville, Louisiana. There black intellectuals help to still resist what segregation tried to instill in us. We were capable of learning and knowing who we are.

In my senior year, I went to visit my sister, who lived in the state of Washington near the Vancouver shipyards. I went for just one semester to earn enough money to graduate. That was my first time out of the south. I had had experience working in the personnel office, and

Mildred Pitts Walter, "Biographical Sketch," modified and edited by Mildred Pitts Walter on September 28, 2017, from "Mildred Pitts Walter Oral History Interview Conducted by David P. Cline in San Mateo, California," Civil Rights History Project collection (afc2010039_crhp0059), American Folklife Center, Library of Congress, 2013.

thinking things might be different, I applied for a job in personnel in the shipyard. I was laughed at. Instead of personnel, I worked the grave-yard shift cleaning, preparing ships for trial runs. I was lucky, because some of the people cleaning ships used carbon tetrachloride, which gave them lung problems. There was discrimination in the shipyards and in the small town where my sister lived. All the black people lived in the same area with their own church. The children went to an inte-grated school but did not form relationships in the community with white students.

I graduated from Southern in 1944. The only jobs available for us in Louisiana were teaching or manual labor. I could have gone to work at Camp Polk in the laundry or something like that. I applied for a teach-ing job and was offered a position teaching high school English and manning the library for fifty dollars a month. I felt that out of Louisiana I could form a career and earn more money. With my mother's blessing, I went to Los Angeles.

At that time, there was only one African American teacher in the Los Angeles schools. I applied and was told I had to have a California credential. So I went to Cal State L.A., and got a credential, but first I was employed by the school board as a clerk in the classified section office, where tests were given for people who did noncertificated work: clerks, janitors, construction work, etc.

I married Earl Walter, who was chairman of the local chapter of the Congress of Racial Equality (CORE). After I earned an elementary school teaching credential from California State College in Los Ange-les, I was hired in 1954 in a school that had predominately black students and teachers.

In the meantime, I continued to work with Earl in CORE, testing the California Unruh Act that outlawed discrimination in public hous-ing, hotels and motels. We would go to public places and seek service. When denied, a white couple would follow and be served. We would sue and change that practice. Prior to the fifties and sixties, there was discrimination in hiring in many public places. Blacks were limited to maintenance jobs or no jobs in many places. So we picketed and negotiated with businesses to hire qualified people and train them for managerial positions.

We also picketed at new housing tracts that refused to sell to African Americans and other people of color. I did my actions on weekends and never let it affect my teaching job. I was fortunate to have a principal who respected my right to do what I was doing. When I was arrested in a housing tract that discriminated, I pleaded with the newspaper reporter not to include my name. I wanted to tell the principal of the school where I worked myself. They honored my request.

Earl was active in CORE until he died in 1965, leaving two sons, Lloyd, seventeen, and Craig, eleven. I became a single parent who saw our sons become men. Their father would have been proud to have them bear his name. I continued my activities in different ways, consulting in areas of diversity and writing books for children. Having voted for the first time for Franklin D. Roosevelt, I can say I have seen a lot. There have been changes for the better, and things that have affected my people negatively have remained the same.

I am pleased to say I lived to see an African American president. I hope to see the nation lose its guilt and fear by finally discussing slavery and Jim Crow and become reconciled, living together in peace and harmony.

CIVIL RIGHTS ACT OF 1964, TITLE VII: EQUAL EMPLOYMENT OPPORTUNITY

DISCRIMINATION BECAUSE OF RACE, COLOR, RELIGION, SEX, OR NATIONAL ORIGIN

SEC. 703. (a) It shall be an unlawful employment practice for an employer—

(1) to fail or refuse to hire or to discharge any individual, or otherwise to discriminate against any individual with respect to his compensation, terms, conditions, or privileges of employment, because of such individual's race, color, religion, sex, or national origin; or

(2) to limit, segregate, or classify his employees in any way which would deprive or tend to deprive any individual of employment opportunities or otherwise adversely affect his status as an employee, because of such individual's race, color, religion, sex, or national origin.

(b) It shall be an unlawful employment practice for an employment agency to fail or refuse to refer for employment, or otherwise to discriminate against, any individual because of his race, color, religion, sex, or national origin, or to classify or refer for employment any individual on the basis of his race, color, religion, sex, or national origin.

(c) It shall be an unlawful employment practice for a labor organization—

(1) to exclude or to expel from its membership, or otherwise to discriminate against, any individual because of his race, color, religion, sex, or national origin;

Excerpted from *Civil Rights Act of 1964* [Equal Employment Opportunity] (Pub. L. 88–352, Title VII, July 2, 1964).

(2) to limit, segregate, or classify its membership, or to classify or fail or refuse to refer for employment any individual, in any way which would deprive or tend to deprive any individual of employment opportunities, or would limit such employment opportunities or otherwise adversely affect his status as an employee or as an applicant for employment, because of such individual's race, color, religion, sex, or national origin; or

(3) to cause or attempt to cause an employer to discriminate against an individual in violation of this section.

(d) It shall be an unlawful employment practice for any employer, labor organization, or joint labor-management committee controlling apprenticeship or other training or retraining, including on-the-job training programs to discriminate against any individual because of his race, color, religion, sex, or national origin in admission to, or employment in, any program established to provide apprenticeship or other training. . . .

LYNDON B. JOHNSON

COMMENCEMENT ADDRESS
AT HOWARD UNIVERSITY:
"TO FULFILL THESE RIGHTS," 1965

Dr. Nabrit, my fellow Americans:
I am delighted at the chance to speak at this important and this historic
institution. Howard has long been an outstanding center for the education of Negro Americans. Its students are of every race and color and
they come from many countries of the world. It is truly a working example of democratic excellence. . . .

In far too many ways American Negroes have been another nation:
deprived of freedom, crippled by hatred, the doors of opportunity
closed to hope.

In our time change has come to this Nation, too. The American
Negro, acting with impressive restraint, has peacefully protested and
marched, entered the courtrooms and the seats of government, demanding a justice that has long been denied. The voice of the Negro was
the call to action. But it is a tribute to America that, once aroused, the
courts and the Congress, the President and most of the people, have
been the allies of progress.

LEGAL PROTECTION FOR HUMAN RIGHTS

Thus we have seen the high court of the country declare that discrimination based on race was repugnant to the Constitution, and therefore

Excerpted from Lyndon B. Johnson, "Commencement Address at Howard University: 'To Fulfill These Rights,'" June 4, 1965, reproduced in Gerhard Peters
and John T. Woolley, *The American Presidency Project*, www.presidency.ucsb.edu
/ws/?pid=27021.

void. . . . The voting rights bill will be the latest, and among the most important, in a long series of victories. But this victory—as Winston Churchill said of another triumph for freedom—"is not the end. It is not even the beginning of the end. But it is, perhaps, the end of the beginning."

That beginning is freedom; and the barriers to that freedom are tumbling down. Freedom is the right to share, share fully and equally, in American society—to vote, to hold a job, to enter a public place, to go to school. It is the right to be treated in every part of our national life as a person equal in dignity and promise to all others.

FREEDOM IS NOT ENOUGH

But freedom is not enough. You do not wipe away the scars of centuries by saying: Now you are free to go where you want, and do as you desire, and choose the leaders you please.

You do not take a person who, for years, has been hobbled by chains and liberate him, bring him up to the starting line of a race and then say, "you are free to compete with all the others," and still justly believe that you have been completely fair. . . .

To this end equal opportunity is essential, but not enough, not enough. Men and women of all races are born with the same range of abilities. But ability is not just the product of birth. Ability is stretched or stunted by the family that you live with, and the neighborhood you live in—by the school you go to and the poverty or the richness of your surroundings. It is the product of a hundred unseen forces playing upon the little infant, the child, and finally the man.

PROGRESS FOR SOME

This graduating class at Howard University is witness to the indomitable determination of the Negro American to win his way in American life.

The number of Negroes in schools of higher learning has almost doubled in 15 years. The number of nonwhite professional workers has more than doubled in 10 years. The median income of Negro college women tonight exceeds that of white college women. And there are also

the enormous accomplishments of distinguished individual Negroes—
many of them graduates of this institution, and one of them the first
lady ambassador in the history of the United States.

These are proud and impressive achievements. But they tell only the
story of a growing middle class minority, steadily narrowing the gap
between them and their white counterparts.

A WIDENING GULF

But for the great majority of Negro Americans—the poor, the unemployed, the uprooted, and the dispossessed—there is a much grimmer
story. They still, as we meet here tonight, are another nation. Despite
the court orders and the laws, despite the legislative victories and the
speeches, for them the walls are rising and the gulf is widening.

Here are some of the facts of this American failure.

Thirty-five years ago the rate of unemployment for Negroes and
whites was about the same. Tonight the Negro rate is twice as high.

In 1948 the 8 percent unemployment rate for Negro teenage boys
was actually less than that of whites. By last year that rate had grown
to 23 percent, as against 13 percent for whites unemployed.

Between 1949 and 1959, the income of Negro men relative to white
men declined in every section of this country. From 1952 to 1963 the
median income of Negro families compared to white actually dropped
from 57 percent to 53 percent.

In the years 1955 through 1957, 22 percent of experienced Negro
workers were out of work at some time during the year. In 1961 through
1963 that proportion had soared to 29 percent.

Since 1947 the number of white families living in poverty has
decreased 27 percent while the number of poorer nonwhite families
decreased only 3 percent.

The infant mortality of nonwhites in 1940 was 70 percent greater
than whites. Twenty-two years later it was 90 percent greater.

Moreover, the isolation of Negro from white communities is increasing, rather than decreasing as Negroes crowd into the central cities and
become a city within a city.

Of course Negro Americans as well as white Americans have shared
in our rising national abundance. But the harsh fact of the matter is

that in the battle for true equality too many—far too many—are losing ground every day. . . .

SPECIAL NATURE OF NEGRO POVERTY

For Negro poverty is not white poverty. Many of its causes and many of its cures are the same. But there are differences—deep, corrosive, obstinate differences—radiating painful roots into the community, and into the family, and the nature of the individual.

These differences are not racial differences. They are solely and simply the consequence of ancient brutality, past injustice, and present prejudice. They are anguishing to observe. For the Negro they are a constant reminder of oppression. For the white they are a constant reminder of guilt. But they must be faced and they must be dealt with and they must be overcome, if we are ever to reach the time when the only difference between Negroes and whites is the color of their skin.

Nor can we find a complete answer in the experience of other American minorities. They made a valiant and a largely successful effort to emerge from poverty and prejudice.

The Negro, like these others, will have to rely mostly upon his own efforts. But he just can not do it alone. For they did not have the heritage of centuries to overcome, and they did not have a cultural tradition which had been twisted and battered by endless years of hatred and hopelessness, nor were they excluded—these others—because of race or color—a feeling whose dark intensity is matched by no other prejudice in our society.

Nor can these differences be understood as isolated infirmities. They are a seamless web. They cause each other. They result from each other. They reinforce each other.

Much of the Negro community is buried under a blanket of history and circumstance. It is not a lasting solution to lift just one corner of that blanket. We must stand on all sides and we must raise the entire cover if we are to liberate our fellow citizens. . . .

TO FULFILL THESE RIGHTS

There is no single easy answer to all of these problems.

Jobs are part of the answer. They bring the income which permits a man to provide for his family.

Decent homes in decent surroundings and a chance to learn—an equal chance to learn—are part of the answer.

Welfare and social programs better designed to hold families together are part of the answer.

Care for the sick is part of the answer.

An understanding heart by all Americans is another big part of the answer.

And to all of these fronts—and a dozen more—I will dedicate the expanding efforts of the Johnson administration. . . .

WHAT IS JUSTICE

For what is justice?

It is to fulfill the fair expectations of man.

Thus, American justice is a very special thing. For, from the first, this has been a land of towering expectations. It was to be a nation where each man could be ruled by the common consent of all— enshrined in law, given life by institutions, guided by men themselves subject to its rule. And all—all of every station and origin—would be touched equally in obligation and in liberty.

Beyond the law lay the land. It was a rich land, glowing with more abundant promise than man had ever seen. Here, unlike any place yet known, all were to share the harvest.

And beyond this was the dignity of man. Each could become whatever his qualities of mind and spirit would permit—to strive, to seek, and, if he could, to find his happiness.

This is American justice. We have pursued it faithfully to the edge of our imperfections, and we have failed to find it for the American Negro. . . .

"EXHIBIT 1 IN CITY OF MEMPHIS VS. MARTIN LUTHER KING, JR.," 1968

Dr. Martin Luther King, Jr.

and

Community On the Move for Equality

INVITE YOU

To March for Justice and Jobs

FRIDAY, MARCH 22, 1968

9:00 A.M.
From Clayborn Temple A.M.E. Church
280 Hernando

We ask you to stay away from work or school and walk with more than 10,000 people who want Memphis once and for all to learn that it must be a city for all people. A man is a man. God requires that a man be treated like a man.

Memphis must do so in work, play, education, housing, by the police and in all other ways, the rights of each man must be upheld. This will be a march of dignity. The only force we will use is soul-force which is peaceful, loving, courageous, yet militant.

MARCH INSTRUCTIONS:

1. Come to the church from Vance Street only.
2. THE ROUTE: Hernando to Beale
    To Main
    To Poplar
    To Second
    To Beale
    To Hernando
    To Clayborn Temple where we will disperse

3. Be ready to follow the instructions of the March Marshalls who will wear yellow arm bands.
4. We will march in the street.
5. Each organization can prepare a banner, no bigger than 6'x3' attached to at least two poles, which can carry the sign up above the heads of the marchers.

6. Walk gently, do not crowd those in front, when those stop you stop.

"Exhibit 1 in City of Memphis vs. Martin Luther King, Jr.," NARA, RG 21 Records of District Courts of the United States, 1685–2009, Series Civil Cases, 1/1965–12/1975, File City of Memphis vs. Martin Luther King, Jr., et al, Civil C-68-80, catalog.archives.gov/id/279325.

"WHERE WE PLAY"

Just as segregation shaped the home and workplace environments, it also restricted people of color's access to outdoor environmental amenities and their opportunities to enjoy places as varied as parks, beaches, golf courses, and campgrounds. The first document in this section, the introduction to the 1950 edition of the *Negro Motorist Green Book*, highlights the ways segregation made long-distance and overnight travel difficult for people of color. Published annually between 1936 and 1966, the *Green Book* compiled the names and addresses of individuals and establishments that were known to "cater to the Negro trade." Its aim was to help travelers avoid the frustrations and potential dangers of seeking meals and accommodations in unknown places. The second and third documents, photos of segregated campgrounds at Shenandoah National Park in Virginia and the segregated Virginia Key Beach in Miami, highlight the reach of formally segregated facilities beyond the better-known examples of schools, public transportation facilities, and restaurants.

The next three documents illustrate the civil rights movement's challenge to segregated outdoor recreational facilities. The first document presents the Supreme Court's unanimous decision in November 1955 to uphold a federal appeals court ruling striking down the "separate but equal" standard for public recreational facilities like parks, playgrounds, beaches, and golf courses. Even after this legal decision, many such places remained segregated in practice, and some cities even moved to privatize public recreational facilities rather than integrate them. The second document is a photo taken during a series of "wade-in" protests at Fort Lauderdale's segregated public beach between July 4 and August 8, 1961, which captured national headlines and ultimately led, after additional court action, to integration of the beaches. The third document, a letter from local NAACP branches in Jackson, Mississippi, to various city and state officials in May 1963, announced its intention to pursue an end to ongoing practices of racial segregation in all of the city's public facilities, including its parks and playgrounds, by all legal means at its disposal.

VICTOR H. GREEN, ED.

INTRODUCTION, *THE NEGRO MOTORIST GREEN BOOK: 1950*

With the introduction of this travel guide in 1936, it has been our idea to give the Negro traveler information that will keep him from running into difficulties, embarrassments and to make his trips more enjoyable.

The Jewish press has long published information about places that are restricted and there are numerous publications that give the gentile whites all kinds of information. But during these long years of discrimination, before 1936 other guides have been published for the Negro, some are still published, but the majority have gone out of business for various reasons.

In 1936 the Green Book was only a local publication for Metropolitan New York, the response for copies was so great it was turned into a national issue in 1937 to cover the United States. This guide while lacking in many respects was accepted by thousands of travelers. Through the courtesy of the United States Travel Bureau of which Mr. Chas. A. R. McDowell was the collaborator on Negro Affairs, more valuable information was secured. With the two working together, this guide contained the best ideas for the Negro traveler. Year after year it grew until [in] 1941 "PM" one of New York's great white newspapers found out about it. Wrote an article about the guide and praised it highly. At the present time the guide contains 80 pages and lists numerous business places, including whites which cater to the Negro trade.

Schomburg Center for Research in Black Culture, Jean Blackwell Hutson Research and Reference Division, New York Public Library, Victor H. Green, ed., *The Negro Motorist Green Book: 1950*, New York Public Library Digital Collections, digitalcollections.nypl.org/items/283a7180-87c6-0132-13e6-58d385a7b928.

There are thousands of first class business places that we don't know about and can't list, which would be glad to serve the traveler, but it is hard to secure listings of these places since we can't secure enough agents to send us the information. Each year before we go to press the new information is included in the new edition.

When you are traveling please mention the Green Book, in order that they might know how you found their place of business, as they can see that you are strangers. If they haven't heard about this guide, ask them to get in touch with us so that we might list their place. If this guide has proved useful to you on your trips, let us know. If not, tell us also as we appreciate your criticisms and ideas in the improvement of this guide from which you benefit.

There will be a day sometime in the near future when this guide will not have to be published. That is when we as a race will have equal opportunities and privileges in the United States. It will be a great day for us to suspend this publication for then we can go wherever we please, and without embarrassment. But until that time comes we shall continue to publish this information for your convenience each year.

LEWIS MOUNTAIN ENTRANCE SIGN, SHENANDOAH NATIONAL PARK

Lewis Mountain Entrance Sign, Shenandoah National Park, "Lewis Mountain and Other Segregated Facilities, 1939–1950," National Park Service, home.nps.gov /common/uploads/photogallery/ner/park/shen/1E6321B9-155D-451F-6793AC4 FC782160A/1E6321B9-155D-451F-6793AC4FC782160A.jpg.

COLORED ONLY SIGN

Colored Only Sign, Virginia Key Beach Park Trust, University of Miami Libraries, Collaborative Archive from the African Diaspora, caad.library.miami.edu/?p= digitallibrary/digitalcontent&id=20.

MAYOR AND CITY COUNCIL OF BALTIMORE CITY V. DAWSON, 1955

PER CURIAM.

These appeals were taken from orders of the District Court dismissing actions brought by Negro citizens to obtain declaratory judgments and injunctive relief against the enforcement of racial segregation in the enjoyment of public beaches and bathhouses maintained by the public authorities of the State of Maryland and the City of Baltimore at or near that city. Notwithstanding prior decisions of the Supreme Court of the United States striking down the practice of segregation of the races in certain fields, the District Judge, as shown by his opinion, 123 F. Supp. 193, did not feel free to disregard the decision of the Court of Appeals of Maryland in Durkee v. Murphy, 181 Md. 259, 29 A.2d 253, and the decision of this court in Boyer v. Garrett, 4 Cir., 183 F.2d 582. Both of these cases are directly in point since they related to the field of public recreation and held, on the authority of Plessy v. Ferguson, 163 U.S. 537, 16 S.Ct. 1138, 41 L.Ed. 256, that segregation of the races in athletic activities in public parks or playgrounds did not violate the 14th Amendment if substantially equal facilities and services were furnished both races.

Our view is that the authority of these cases was swept away by the subsequent decisions of the Supreme Court. . . .

The combined effect of these decisions of the Supreme Court is to destroy the basis of the decision of the Court of Appeals of Maryland in Durkee v. Murphy, and the decision of this court in Boyer v. Garrett.

Excerpted from *Mayor and City Council of Baltimore City v. Dawson*, 350 U.S. 877, 76 S. Ct. 133 (1955).

The Court of Appeals of Maryland based its decision in Durkee v. Murphy on the theory that the segregation of the races in the public parks of Baltimore was within the power of the Board of Park Commissioners of the City to make rules for the preservation of order within the parks; and it was said that the separation of the races was normal treatment in Maryland and that the regulation before the court was justified as an effort on the part of the authorities to avoid any conflict which might arise from racial antipathies.

It is now obvious, however, that segregation cannot be justified as a means to preserve the public peace merely because the tangible facilities furnished to one race are equal to those furnished to the other. The Supreme Court expressed the opinion in Brown v. Board of Education of Topeka, 347 U.S. 492 to 494, 74 S.Ct. 690 to 691, that it must consider public education in the light of its full development and its present place in American life, and therefore could not turn the clock back to 1896 when Plessy v. Ferguson was written, or base its decision on the tangible factors only of a given situation, but must also take into account the psychological factors recognized at this time, including the feeling of inferiority generated in the hearts and minds of Negro children, when separated solely because of their race from those of similar age and qualification. With this in mind, it is obvious that racial segregation in recreational activities can no longer be sustained as a proper exercise of the police power of the State; for if that power cannot be invoked to sustain racial segregation in the schools, where attendance is compulsory and racial friction may be apprehended from the enforced commingling of the races, it cannot be sustained with respect to public beach and bathhouse facilities, the use of which is entirely optional. . . .

CIVIL RIGHTS DEMONSTRATION
AT FORT LAUDERDALE'S SEGREGATED
PUBLIC BEACH, 1961

Civil Rights Demonstration at Fort Lauderdale's Segregated Public Beach, July 24, 1961, Image No. PR05161, State Archives of Florida, Florida Memory, www.florida memory.com/items/show/4524.

JACKSON NAACP BRANCHES TO CITY AND STATE OFFICIALS, MAY 12, 1963

Dear Sir:

The NAACP is determined to put an end to all forms of racial segregation in Jackson. This means that we want to end the discriminatory practices in the businesses that now do not give fair employment opportunities to colored citizens. We also insist that segregation now practiced in the restroom and restaurant and other facilities of these establishments be ended. As the patrons who help to make it possible for these businesses to continue to operate at a profit, we know that we have the economic strength to back up our requests with effective action. A selective buying campaign is already underway. Unless we get results through peaceful negotiations undertaken in good faith, we have no alternative but to step up and broaden our selective buying campaign to produce the results that will make Jackson a place of fair play for all persons without regard to race.

We are determined to end all state and local government sponsored segregation in the parks, playgrounds, schools, libraries and other public facilities. To accomplish this we shall use all lawful means of protest—picketing, marches, mass meetings, litigation, and whatever other legal means we deem necessary.

At this time we wish to let the city, the state, the nation and the world know that we want to meet with city officials and community

---

Jackson NAACP branches to city and state officials, May 12, 1963, Ernst Borinski Collection (T/005; Box 15, Folder 39) of Tougaloo College Civil Rights Collection, Mississippi Department of Archives and History.

leaders to make good faith attempts to settle grievances and assure immediate full citizenship rights for all Americans. We earnestly hope that those who have the best interests of the city at heart will accept our offer to reach a speedy and orderly settlement. We call upon President John F. Kennedy and any other national loaders who share our love of freedom to use their good offices in helping to get those discussions started.

Sincerely yours,
Jackson NAACP branches
1072 West Lynch Street

(Signed by:)

Mr. Medgar W. Evers
Field Secretary

Mrs. Doris Allison
President, Jackson Branch

Mr. John R. Salter
Advisor, Youth Council

PART 2

A MORE INCLUSIVE ENVIRONMENTALISM? FROM EARTH DAY TO ENVIRONMENTAL JUSTICE

Although some activists spent the "environmental decade" of the 1970s pushing for a broad, inclusive approach to environmentalism, by the end of the decade the environmental movement still lacked a meaningful role for people of color. Instead, it took the rise of a separate environmental justice movement in the 1980s to call national attention to environmental inequalities and to challenge mainstream environmentalism's priorities. Activists called attention to the ways segregated neighborhoods and segregated jobs disproportionately exposed people of color to environmental hazards. They documented the ways "race-blind" environmental cleanup laws failed to protect society's most marginalized members in landscapes that remained heavily segregated by race. And they called attention to the ways mainstream environmental organizations—which overwhelmingly had white, affluent memberships—failed to represent the voices of people of color or to engage with the serious environmental problems confronted by minority populations. Slowly, in piecemeal fashion, the EJ critique gained force, and new approaches to addressing environmental inequalities began to acquire institutional force.

A NEW CIVIL RIGHTS CRITIQUE

In the years before and after the first Earth Day in 1970, during a period of swelling environmental consciousness nationwide, civil rights activists from a range of minority groups began to frame long-standing concerns in more explicitly environmental terms. In November 1969, for example, when the Native American group Indians of All Tribes launched a fourteen-month occupation of Alcatraz Island in San Francisco Bay, they declared it "Indian land" and announced their intention to turn the former prison into a Native American studies center, an American Indian museum, and an ecology center. In the "Alcatraz Proclamation" (December 1969), they offered a biting environmental critique, highlighting the twin legacies on most reservations of dispossession and heavy environmental burdens.

The second document, from the Navajo Uranium Miner Oral History and Photography Project's interview with Timothy Benally, highlights the toxic legacy of the Cold War arms race borne by Navajo miners. The third document, from the United Farm Workers of America's newsletter, *El Malcriado*, which was published in 1969 during the pivotal Delano grape boycott, protests heavy pesticide exposure among Mexican American workers.

The final document, Wilbur Thomas Jr.'s "Black Survival in Our Polluted Cities," appeared in *Proud*, an African American magazine based in Saint Louis. Thomas, a scientist who coordinated the Environmental Field Program at Barry Commoner's Center for the Biology of Natural Systems at Washington University in Saint Louis, did early and innovative work on the intersection of social justice issues with environmental problems. Best known for spearheading field surveys of childhood lead exposure in inner city housing, Thomas's team also anticipated the future work of the environmental justice movement by investigating such issues as air and water pollution, infant mortality, and rat problems in African American neighborhoods. He also wrote regularly about these issues in *Proud* in a column called "Black Ecology."

"THE ALCATRAZ PROCLAMATION," 1969

Proclamation to the Great White Father and All His People

We, the native Americans, re-claim the land known as Alcatraz Island in the name of all American Indians by right of discovery.

We wish to be fair and honorable in our dealings with the Caucasian inhabitants of this land, and hereby offer the following treaty:

We will purchase said Alcatraz Island for twenty-four dollars ($24) in glass beads and red cloth, a precedent set by the white man's purchase of a similar island about 300 years ago. We know that $24 in trade goods for these 16 acres is more than was paid when Manhattan Island was sold, but we know that land values have risen over the years. Our offer of $1.24 per acre is greater than the 47¢ per acre that the white men are now paying the California Indians for their land. We will give to the inhabitants of this island a portion of that land for their own, to be held in trust by the American Indian Affairs [*sic*] and by the bureau of Caucasian Affairs to hold in perpetuity—for as long as the sun shall rise and the rivers go down to the sea. We will further guide the inhabitants in the proper way of living. We will offer them our religion, our education, our life-ways, in order to help them achieve our level of civilization and thus raise them and all their white brothers up from their savage and unhappy state. We offer this treaty in good faith and wish to be fair and honorable in our dealings with all white men.

We feel that this so-called Alcatraz Island is more than suitable for an Indian Reservation, as determined by the white man's own standards. By this we mean that this place resembles most Indian reservations in that:

Indians of All Tribes, "The Alcatraz Proclamation," December 1969, www.history isaweapon.com/defcon1/alcatrazproclamationandletter.html.

1. It is isolated from modern facilities, and without adequate means of transportation.
2. It has no fresh running water.
3. It has inadequate sanitation facilities.
4. There are no oil or mineral rights.
5. There is no industry and so unemployment is very great.
6. There are no health care facilities.
7. The soil is rocky and non-productive; and the land does not support game.
8. There are no educational facilities.
9. The population has always exceeded the land base.
10. The population has always been held as prisoners and kept dependent upon others.

Further, it would be fitting and symbolic that ships from all over the world, entering the Golden Gate, would first see Indian land, and thus be reminded of the true history of this nation. This tiny island would be a symbol of the great lands once ruled by free and noble Indians.

TIMOTHY BENALLY

"'SO A LOT OF THE NAVAJO LADIES BECAME WIDOWS'"

The Navajo Nation was still in its childhood stages of economic development in the early 1940's, mainly recovering from the devastating stock reduction period of 1930. To meet the economic gap that was created by this stock reduction, Navajo men sought work away from the reservation on railroads in the western states. Families who had no livestock sought farm work in Phoenix and California.

Employment sources were the Bureau of Indian Affairs (BIA), traders on the reservation and a few of the border town businesses. Employment was based on the amount of education the person had, especially with the BIA which had about 90% Anglos.

The Bureau of Indian Affairs, through the Treaty of 1868, had responsibility to care for Navajo economic, education and health services. The Navajos' needs became greater as the population increased. During the 1930's, BIA built elementary day schools throughout the Navajo reservation and a few high schools.

When World War II broke out many Navajo men aborted their education and went into the military. High schools were closed for lack of students. The Cold War followed the end of WW II. The Navajo Nation was still dependent on BIA for its economic needs. The Tribe now had

---

Timothy Benally, "'So a Lot of the Navajo Ladies Became Widows,'" in Timothy Benally and Phil Harrison, *Memories Come to Us in the Rain and the Wind: Oral Histories and Photographs of Navajo Uranium Miners and Their Families* (Boston, MA: Navajo Uranium Miner Oral History and Photography Project, 1997), 2–3. Reprinted with permission of Timothy Benally and the Navajo Uranium Miner Oral History and Photography Project.

a council and hired some of its people. States and counties were getting involved in Navajo affairs.

The U.S. had gone into the nuclear age, and the Navajo were still struggling economically. The U.S. Government's demand for uranium started mining booms in the Four Corners area. On the Navajo reservation, uranium was discovered in Cove, Arizona and then in other parts of the reservation. Work became available right near home and the young men dug the uranium. This was a time when transportation was still by horse-drawn wagons, horse-back riding and walking to get to a place. In our community, with a population of about 3,000, only four families had motor vehicles.

When the mines started on the reservation, most families were very thankful that they had employment. This is what they express when they come to the office of the Navajo Uranium Workers. They said, "we were glad that our husband had a job and that he didn't have to go away to other places to do railroad work. The job was right here and he could go from home to the mine and it was great. But what the people that operated these mines didn't tell us was, that danger was associated with uranium mining, and this is what is hurting us today. If they had told us that danger was there, we might have done something else to find employment. But they didn't tell us and we just enjoyed our people working."

The miners and the widows themselves found out about this danger on their own, from actually experiencing the sickness themselves. The reports they made were very sad. They said that they tried every kind of medicine; they tried western medicine and went to the hospitals, but the doctors didn't know what was wrong with their husbands. Until it got to the real bad stage of lung cancer, then they told them he was dying from what's called lung cancer. And most of these were at an advanced stage, there was no more that could be done for them. So a lot of the Navajo ladies became widows.

"GROWERS SPURN NEGOTIATIONS ON POISONS," 1969

DELANO, January 16—A special meeting of 250 boycott organizers and community leaders from all over California has been scheduled for Saturday, January 25, to consider escalation of the boycott and concern over the use of economic poisons in the vineyards.

The meeting was called after grape growers refused to reply to a recent letter sent out by Cesar Chavez to the Southern Central Farmers Commission, the California Grape and Tree F[ruit] League, and the Desert Grape League.

Chavez's letter, calling once again for negotiations with the growers to avoid escalation of the boycott during the coming season, said,

"There is one critical issue of such overriding importance that it demands immediate attention, even if other labor relations problems have to wait. I mean the harmful effects of spraying grapes with pesticides, or economic poisons, as they are called. We have recently become more aware of this problem through an increasing number of cases coming into our clinic."

"We will not tolerate the systematic poisoning of our people. Even if we cannot get together on other problems, we will be damned—and we should be—if we will permit human beings to sustain permanent damage to their health from economic poisons."

Chavez said Union representatives would be willing to meet with the growers on the sole issue of pesticides, even if the growers are "not prepared to begin full-scale collective bargaining at present."

"Growers Spurn Negotiations on Poisons," *El Malcriado: The Voice of the Farm Worker,* January 15, 1969, 3. Used with permission of the United Farm Workers of America.

Growers, however, did not reply to the letter.

Chavez told EL MALCRIADO there was no intention on the part of the Union to abandon its drive for collective bargaining agreements with California's table grape growers, but that Union officials were unanimous in their belief that the question of economic poisons used in the vineyards was the most dangerous problem faced by farm workers.

"The increasing number of children reporting to our clinic after having eaten table grapes in the fields where their parents were working frightens all of us," Chavez said.

"The dangers of chemical pesticides to those who cultivate and consume grapes must be faced."

Chavez said he had hoped talks on the subject of the poisons might lead to further negotiations on other questions of importance but that the refusal of the growers to answer the letter meant the Union had no choice but to prepare for a third season of active boycott organization.

He said he had called the January 25 meeting to consider the escalation of the boycott and the concern of the Union about the dangerous chemicals used on table grapes.

UFWOC General Counsel Jerome Cohen recently was denied access to public records on the use of the poisons by the Kern County Agricultural Commissioner. UFWOC researchers have also been denied access to public State records on the use of pesticides in Fresno, Tulare and Riverside counties.

Research on the use of the poisons has shown that many of the chemicals used for insect and disease control in the vineyards were similar to those developed by Nazi Germany for extermination of humans.

"There is talk at both federal and state levels of farm labor legislation. If we cannot agree on wages, hours and working conditions—or at the very minimum even talk about the most important issue of all, which is the protection of human life from the dangers of economic poisons—then how can we ever agree on legislation? What alternatives do you have? You won't be able to break our Union or stop our boycott. So if you won't negotiate with us, the only route open to you will be repressive legislation which the American people will not accept," the letter concluded.

WILBUR L. THOMAS JR.

"BLACK SURVIVAL IN OUR POLLUTED CITIES," 1970

Is the current emphasis on "saving the environment" just another attempt to ignore the critical needs of the Black community as perceived by the community; or is the environment, particularly the urban environment, rapidly becoming uninhabitable?

Are the urban Black[s] disproportionally exposed to greater environmental hazards than non-Blacks?

Will the war on pollution end up like the war on poverty?

What strategy is available to urban residents concerned with protecting their community from the mounting environmental insults?

In my opinion, the answers to these intriguing questions represent the basic relevancy of environmental pollution as it relates to the Black community.

Last year at the session concerned with the same problem, environmental pollution and the Black community, it was brought out that man is threatened by a variety of crises that may well end his presence on the planet. These crises include nuclear destruction, runaway population growth and the world food shortage, the potential exhaustion of

---

Excerpted from Wilbur L. Thomas Jr., "Black Survival in Our Polluted Cities," *Proud*, April 1970, 10–13.

the world's oxygen supply, the general pollution of our environment to the point where life is being made intolerable, if not impossible. Now, a year later, the public concern about these newly received threats to man's survival is spreading throughout the land in geometric proportions with an arousing awareness in the public that human survival no longer remains as a guaranteed eventuality. Interestingly enough, the segment of the population best equipped to survive is the most outspoken advocate of preserving environmental integrity. Yet, that segment of the population least equipped to survive to date, has been conspicuously silent on the subject, namely Black folks. They are least equipped to survive because the existing basic political, economical, and social systems that have worked for most non-Blacks have [been], and continue to be in most part, unresponsive to the needs of the Black community, and, in fact, are primarily responsible for the prevalence of widespread urban decay. However for both the silent and the vocal segments, time is running out if the current rate of intrusions on the environment continues. . . .

The 'nitty gritty' issue relevant to Blacks is simply the fact that a disproportional number of Blacks are exposed to more environmental health hazards than non-Blacks in addition to the regular burden. Exposure to additional hazards such as lead poisoning, infant mortality, air pollution and land pollution, and rat control are all indigenous problems to most Black communities.

For example, lead poisoning is characterized by the affliction of children six years and younger as the result of eating substances containing lead, usually in the form of peeling paint and broken plaster readily available in substandard, archaic, and slum housing, often located conveniently next to the children's beds. The behavior of little children putting any and everything in their mouths, commonly referred to as pica, is very characteristic of all children regardless of socioeconomic standing as any distraught mother would readily acknowledge after a day of regular playing.

Unfortunately the real issue is that this kind of health problem exists almost exclusively within the Black community where people live in "lead chambers" because of their economic inability to move in the more desirable residences and because of wanton neglect by absentee landlords in providing adequate maintenance and consistent supportive services. Because of the stark nakedness of most families' immediate environment, their children suffer more with this problem. Yet meaningful prevention can be executed by replacement of faulty, inadequate housing with sound and sturdy houses coupled with the approval of appropriate legislation to penalize those persons responsible for permitting such circumstances.

Both the short-and-long-term consequences of adverse health effects are being documented by ecologists, physicians, and other suitably trained individuals throughout the community which will be useful for pointing out the hidden health effects.

However, the real issue of Black survival is again the fact that most Black folk by virtue of their location are subsidizing the polluters in that the money required to eliminate harmful omission is not being spent, and hence, ends up within the corporate framework as profit. Yet it is, in one way or another, the same money that will have to be spent by the recipient to counteract the harmful effects of the needless fallout. . . .

Land pollution is another example of an environmental burden restricted to Black communities more than any other. Land pollution is characterized by highways, escape roads for suburbanites, absence of plants and other useful vegetation, and the prevalence of noise all of which concentrate on Blacks more than on others.

This kind of affliction is a direct example of what happens when people lose control or do not possess control of neighborhoods, etc., and the other powers in the community develop programs for their convenience under the guise of alleged benefit for those in the affected areas.

These examples show how Blacks encounter another set of environmental hazards in addition to the universal burden on all, and hence receive a double dose of ecological backfires.

In essence the threat of death is not new to Black people. Environmental pollution represents only another one amidst many, whereas for non-Blacks, it represents for the first time threats toward their survival. This accounts for their greater involvement in the current ecologic movement.

However, this current imbalance and concern should not be interpreted to mean that Black Americans should allow the present battle to be waged on their behalf by others with good intentions. The traditional dangers are of course that the outcome might not provide the Black community with the safeguards and substantive changes required to restore neighborhoods to former quality. For example, lead poisoning and rat infestation are almost one hundred percent preventable.

If slum housing, characterized by peeling paint, dilapidated superstructure, inadequate and antiquated external and internal facilities, was completely replaced with sound and sturdy adequately designed homes, the incidence of these public health hazards would disappear. . . .

Most black folks are confronted with a unique pattern of environmental pollution characterized by two kinds of exposure. The first of which is like air and water pollution and the indiscriminatory use of pesticides, which ignores geographical, political, and economic boundaries and poses serious threats for the health of all.

The second type is the existence within the Black community more than any other, of certain health hazards such as lead poisoning, infant mortality, and air pollution.

Thus the answer to my opening question is "yes," the environment is being seriously stressed, increasingly beyond the point of no return, and accordingly Black people must include in their everyday fight to survive appropriate steps to survive in a polluted world. We must become aware of the types of problems existing in our community such as lead poisoning, air pollution, the lingering effect of DDT, and other similar pesticides.

Black unity must develop and push for any and everything that could help improve living conditions such as support of enforceable ordinances that could eliminate health hazards such as air pollution, lead poisoning, inadequate housing, and indiscriminate use of pesticides. Concerned citizens must also insist that environmental health information become readily available at the neighborhood level, to keep residents abreast of community hazards and preventative measures.

Black people must join with other non-health forces within the community who are concerned with the other vital issues of the provision of improved and adequate housing, as well as the provision of neighborhood health facilities—both of which are currently woefully absent from practically all Black and poor neighborhoods. According to noted ecologists, there is very little doubt as to what is more needed financially in order to more effectively mobilize the key resources of the country to combat this environmental crisis. The total cost in money alone, would far outstrip the mere $10 billion suggested to fight the problem of water pollution, by the Nixon administration. The war on pollution will fail as brutally as the war on poverty if funded in spurts or in less than adequate amounts. One must face up to the fact that the critical humane needs of Blacks have never received substantial financing and appropriate priority. Instead those in power have delivered eloquent speeches along the lines of motherhood and apple pie rhetoric.

Ecologically, this type of traditional approach will not be adequate to finance the war on people survival. Survival for all will be difficult; for Black people it will be doubly difficult.

RACE, ENVIRONMENTALISM, AND ENVIRONMENTAL GOVERNANCE

While some activists were busy developing new ways to think about civil rights issues in more environmental terms, environmental activists debated the relationship between their traditional concerns and social justice issues. The first document, a speech by Senator Edmund Muskie (D-ME), reflects the views of a politician who contributed in notable ways to both environmental and civil rights legislation. Nicknamed "Mr. Clean" for his work on antipollution legislation, Muskie was also a strong supporter of the Civil Rights Act of 1964. In much of his work, he expressed the view that environmental issues and social justice issues should be understood as interconnected. His speech on the first Earth Day in 1970, excerpted here, stresses this theme. "I hope," he enjoined the crowd at a rally in Philadelphia, "that your view of the environment will not be a narrow one."

The next document, an excerpt from an Environmental Protection Agency (EPA) report published in 1971 during its first year of operation—a time when summer interns could apparently write entire portions of reports—makes the case for viewing urban poverty and racial inequality through an environmental lens. The next document, John H. White's photograph "Chicago Ghetto on the South Side," from May 1974, was taken as part of the EPA's Documerica Project. Echoing the New Deal's FSA/OWI photography project, Documerica employed more than one hundred photographers between 1971 and 1977 to document environmental conditions in the United States before and after EPA programs went into effect. Both documents illustrate the degree to which the EPA, in its early years, was open to considering urban problems generally—and the problems of impoverished slums specifically—as environmental issues.

The final document, a 1972 membership survey conducted by the Sierra Club, one of the nation's largest and most influential environmental organizations, shows that its leaders, too, were considering similar questions. In addition to collecting demographic information about its members, the survey asked how much attention the club should pay to "special groups" such as the "urban poor and minorities." The answers revealed both the club's overwhelmingly white, affluent membership and a clear generational split in attitudes toward urban environmental issues. Nevertheless, the majority opinion steered the club away from greater engagement. With big environmental organizations like the Sierra Club steering away from social justice issues, activists advocating for a more inclusive environmentalism that would tackle issues like housing, jobs, and urban environmental problems found themselves increasingly marginalized.

EDMUND S. MUSKIE

SPEECH AT THE PHILADELPHIA EARTH WEEK RALLY, FAIRMOUNT PARK, PHILADELPHIA, APRIL 22, 1970

One hundred and eighty-three years ago, a small group of men gathered in this city in an effort to bring order out of chaos. They met in the shadow of failure. America had won her independence but was now in danger of breaking up into small and quarrelsome states. Their objective was to build "a more perfect union."

We have met in this city to help build a whole society—for we have seen the birthright of a free nation damaged by exploitation, spoiled by neglect, choked by its own success, and torn by hatred and suspicion.

The Founding Fathers did build "a more perfect union." They created a nation where there was none, and they built a framework for a democratic society which has been remarkable for its successes. We are now concerned with its failures.

We have learned that their creation was not infallible, and that our society is not indestructible.

We have learned that our natural resources are limited and that, unless those limitations are respected, life itself may be in danger.

We have also learned that, unless we respect each other, the very foundations of freedom may be in danger.

And yet we act as though a luxurious future and a fertile land will continue to forgive us all the bad habits which have led us to abuse our physical and our social environment.

If we are to build a whole society—and if we are to insure the

Excerpted from Edmund S. Muskie, speech at the Philadelphia Earth Week rally, Fairmount Park, Philadelphia, April 22, 1970, Edmund S. Muskie Archives and Special Collections Library, Bates College.

achievement of a life worth living—we must realize that our shrinking margins of natural resources are near the bottom of the barrel.

There are no replacements, no spare stocks with which we can replenish our supplies. . . .

Our nation—and our world—hang together by tenuous bonds which are strained as they have never been strained before—and as they must never be strained again.

We cannot survive an undeclared war on our future.

We must lay down our weapons of self-destruction and pick up the tools of social and environmental reconstruction.

These are the dimensions of the crisis we face:

No major American river is clean anymore, and some are fire hazards.

No American lake is free of pollution, and some are dying.

No American city can boast of clean air, and New Yorkers inhale the equivalent of a pack and a half of cigarettes every day—without smoking.

No American community is free of debris and solid waste, and we are turning to the open spaces and the ocean depths to cast off the products of our effluent society.

We are horrified by the cumulative impact of our waste, but we are told to expect the use of more than 280 billion non-returnable bottles in the decade of the seventies.

Man has burst upon the environment like an invader—destroying rather than using, discarding rather than saving, and giving the environment little chance to adapt.

We have depleted our resources and cluttered our environment—and only recently have we been shocked by the enormity of our errors.

As long as Americans could escape the confines of the soot and clutter, pollution was isolated by the size and openness of America.

A river here a forest there, a few industrialized cities—these examples of environmental destruction seemed a small price to pay for prosperity. . . .

We have to choose, to say no, and to give up some luxuries. And these kinds of decisions will be the acid test of our commitment to a healthy environment.

It means choosing cleaner cars rather than faster cars, more parks instead of more highways, and more houses and more schools instead of more weapons and more wars.

The whole society that we seek is one in which all men live in brotherhood with each other and with their environment. It is a society where each member of it knows that he has an opportunity to fulfill his greatest potential.

It is a society that will not tolerate slums for some and decent houses for others, rats for some and playgrounds for others, clean air for some and filth for others.

It is the only kind of society that has a chance. It is the only kind of society that has a future.

To achieve a whole society—a healthy total environment—we need change, planning, more effective and just laws and more money better spent.

Achieving that whole society will cost heavily—in foregone luxuries, in restricted choices, in higher prices for certain goods and services, in taxes, and in hard decisions about our national priorities. It will require a new sense of balance in our national commitments.

It does not make sense to say we cannot afford to protect our environment—just yet.

It does not make sense to say that we cannot afford to win the fight against hunger and poverty—just yet.

It does not make sense to say we cannot afford to provide decent housing and needed medical care—just yet.

We can afford to do these things, if we admit that there are luxuries we can forego, false security we can do without, and prices we are willing to pay.

I believe that those of you who have gathered here to save the earth are willing to pay the price to save our environment.

I hope, however, that your view of the environment will not be a narrow one.

The environmental conscience which has been awakened in our nation holds great promise for reclaiming our air, our water and our land. But man's environment includes more than these natural resources. It includes the shape of the communities in which he lives:

his home, his schools, his places of work, and those who share this planet and this land.

If the environmental conscience which has brought us together this day is to have any lasting meaning for America, it must be the instrument to turn the nation around. If we use our awareness that the total environment determines the quality of life, we can make those decisions which can save our nation from becoming a class-ridden and strife-torn wasteland.

The study of ecology—man's relationship with his environment—should teach us that our relationships with each other are just as intricate and just as delicate as those with our natural environment. We cannot afford to correct our history of abusing nature and neglect the continuing abuse of our fellow-man.

We should have learned by now that a whole nation must be a nation at peace with itself.

We should have learned by now that we can have that peace only by assuring that all Americans have equal access to a healthy total environment.

That can mean nothing less than equal access to good schools, to meaningful job opportunities, to adequate health services, and to decent and attractive housing.

For the past ten years we have been groping toward the realization that the total environment is at stake.

We have seen the destructiveness of poverty, and declared a war on it.

We have seen the ravages of hunger, and declared a war on it.

We have seen the costs of crime, and declared a war on it.

And now we have awakened to the pollution of our environment, and we have declared another war.

We have fought too many losing battles in these wars to continue this piece-meal approach to creating a whole society.

The only strategy that makes sense is a total strategy to protect the total environment.

The only way to achieve that total strategy is through an Environmental Revolution—a commitment to a whole society.

The Environmental Revolution must be one of laws, not men; one of values, not ideology; and one of achievement, not unfulfilled promises.

We are not powerless to accomplish this change, but we are powerless as a people if we wait for someone else to do it for us. . . .

Martin Luther King once said that "Through our scientific and technological genius we have made of this world a neighborhood. Now through our moral and spiritual genius we must make of it a brotherhood."

For Martin Luther King, every day was an Earth Day—a day to work toward his commitment to a whole society. It is that commitment we must keep.

EPA TASK FORCE ON THE ENVIRONMENTAL
PROBLEMS OF THE INNER CITY

OUR URBAN ENVIRONMENT AND OUR MOST ENDANGERED PEOPLE, 1971

The Environmental Protection Agency was established in December 1970, when it had become evident that the need to act on environmental problems requires special attention by the Federal Government. The Agency brought together environmental programs of several Executive departments. Though the programs are diverse in their focus, they are related in their aim of improving the environment.

Today, there are few who are unaware of the ecological devastation of pollution, but our awareness must go further to an understanding of the effect that this has on the human community. The programs of the Environmental Protection Agency are designed to meet the needs of communities throughout the nation. Among the most pressing needs are those found in our urban communities. Many cities are served by projects already in existence, but solutions to the problems of the cities require comprehensive long-range policy aimed at the roots of the most urgent social problems.

The problems of today's urban poor represent a complexity of conditions, none of which can be considered in isolation. We have too often been project-oriented in designing solutions to problems such as poverty, racial inequality, crime, disease and drugs, and rarely ever considered them as an integral part of a total environmental breakdown. The Environmental Protection Agency's most valuable contribution to the

Excerpted from Task Force on the Environmental Problems of the Inner City, *Our Urban Environment and Our Most Endangered People: A Report to the Administrator of the Environmental Protection Agency* (Washington, DC: US Government Printing Office, 1971).

solutions of these problems lies in its ability to envision the interrelationship of these problems and deal with them in that light.

Cities share many of the problems faced by smaller communities and rural areas, but in the crowded urban environment they are compounded by those conditions which are unique to the city. City residents must breathe the emissions of suburban automobiles which travel in to work every morning, and travel out in the evening to escape the noise and dirt of the city. City children play in the streets over which the automobiles travel, inhaling the gases and dirt left behind. The alleys behind homes are havens for rats which feast on garbage set out for collection. The dirt found on streets and in the air has much greater concentrations of harmful particulate matter in the city than in the less dense suburban and rural areas.

Added together, these ecological conditions contribute to the unattractiveness of residence in the cities. Those who are able to move to cleaner suburban environments do so, taking with them valuable revenue sources and contributing vicariously to the decay of the cities. The residents left behind in the migration include a high percentage of those whose poverty inhibits their mobility. Discriminatory practices and the economics of poverty confine poor residents to certain high density areas within the city.

In general, high density poverty pockets suffer most from the dirt and inadequate sanitary services of the city. Slums are plagued by rats because garbage is allowed to stand uncollected in unsanitary alleys for longer periods of time than in the more affluent neighborhoods. Homes in the poorer areas frequently have dilapidated pipes and sanitary facilities which attract insects and rodents into the very rooms in which people eat and sleep. Insecticides are sprayed to combat the pests but also may have a harmful effect on the human residents who breathe and otherwise come in contact with these chemicals. Lead-based paint chipping off walls is a potential source of danger to children or anyone else who might repeatedly ingest this harmful matter, which can cause lead-poisoning.

The fulfillment of civil rights responsibilities is one approach to alleviating the burdensome environmental problems of the poor. By strict enforcement of the provisions of Title VI of the Civil Rights Act of 1964, the Environmental Protection Agency will ensure that all sectors of a community which receive the benefits of our grants are serviced by our projects. Executive Order 11246 requires that recipients of our financial assistance and contractors with whom we do business affirmatively demonstrate that they do not discriminate on the grounds of race or color in the hiring of employees who work on EPA projects. Within the Agency, there is a vigorous affirmative action plan to provide equal employment opportunity for all citizens seeking employment with EPA as well as for all those working in the Agency.

Even greater efforts are required for the future if social problems are to be alleviated. The Environmental Protection Agency must take a close look at its role in urban life, the nature and extent of the problems and the impact of remedies. Information gathering and analysis and research efforts must be considered on a broad scale of inter-related problems and solutions in a framework of complex, far-reaching social issues.

To date, most efforts have been compensatory, palliative measures to correct problems created by the environmental mismanagement of the past. We must explore preventative measures for the future. Even more importantly, we must devise programs to enhance the quality of life for the urban poor and to involve them in those programs. Bold, creative ideas must be generated and we must not be reluctant to experiment.

We must listen not only to the advice of technical experts but also to those who are most affected by the plight of the urban environment. No one person or agency can single-handedly solve the vast urban problems but each can play a part in assuring that, in the future, our cities will be pleasant and healthy for all who chose to live in an urban environment. . . .

ONE ENVIRONMENT UNEQUALLY SHARED—A NARRATIVE

By Summer Interns: Linda Bryant and Tony Collins

MS (Mr. Suburbanite) is concerned about pollution. He remembers his childhood days spent swimming in the stream near his home. Today, his kids cannot play in the river which runs through their suburban community because 20 miles up stream a large factory pollutes the water. Instead, his children must swim in the pool at the club nearby. Luckily, the kids can enjoy fresh lake water at camp and can go to the seashore during family vacations. Thus, they are still able to experience the thrill of jumping off rocks and diving for shells that cannot be simulated in a chlorinated pool.

Every morning, Mr. Suburbanite wakes up in the fresh air-conditioned atmosphere of his bedroom. The air outside his home is fresh, too, and full of the smells of trees, flowers, and grass, a sharp contrast to the air outside of his downtown office. Driving down the expressway on his way to work, MS notices the difference in spite of the air-conditioning in his car. He is annoyed by the foul smell and sickening sight of polluted air. Once downtown, he finds it unpleasant even to walk the streets at lunchtime. Waiting on the corner is noisy, and the annoyance is aggravated by the fumes created by passing buses and cars. After the shortest exposure to the sights, sounds, and smells of the city street, his air-conditioned office becomes an oasis by comparison. Rush hour traffic is a trying experience, but MS justifies subjecting himself to it since it means he doesn't have to live with the unpleasantness of the city 24-hours a day, and more importantly, neither do his kids.

Arriving home in the evening is like stepping into another world. Settling down with the evening paper on the patio overlooking the mowed lawn and well-tended garden dispels all the annoyances of the day in the hot, dirty city.

Just a few blocks off the expressway MS travels over twice a day is the home of MI (Mr. Inner City). He awakens every morning without noticing the habitual fumes and sounds from the automobiles of commuters. MI's children, too, awaken to the sounds and smells of traffic coming in the windows left open to cool their bedrooms at night. During the day, they play in the streets over which the cars travel and on which are left the dangerous residue[s] of automotive emissions. MI's children cannot swim in the river that flows through the city park, nor do they go away to summer camp or to an ocean cottage in the hottest months. The community swimming pool is many blocks away, and on hot days, there is standing room only. Jumping off of rocks and diving for shells will never be part of their childhood memories.

MI worries about the dirty and unsafe surroundings his children are forced to play in, but not as much as he worries about how to keep them fed and in good health. Little does he know how harmful many things in their surroundings are. He is unaware of the deleterious effects which pesticides may have on them in the long run. He is concerned with protecting the children from harmful rodent and insect bites. He is unaware of the need for new pipes and new paint to decrease the possibility of lead poisoning. He is concerned with buying food and clothing to satisfy immediate needs.

MI tries to earn enough money to provide the basics for his family. He lacks training because he had to go to work at a young age to help support his brothers and sisters. As a result, he has never been given a job which provides training or opportunity for advancement and he cannot afford to go back to school. Nor can he afford to participate in a low paying job training program when higher wages are needed in the here and now, rather than at the end of a long training period. He is always among the first to be laid off. He sometimes is forced into having to buy the family's groceries with food stamps. At such times, he suffers not only limited income, but a feeling of helplessness as well. It is hard to maintain self-confidence or to gain a sense of self-importance under such conditions.

Coming home at night is not a relief for MI. The city must be tolerated 24-hours a day. Some of his neighbors try to escape by deadening their awareness of the environment. MI feels such escape is not possible for him; he must try to stay well. He does not realize his life expectancy is seven years less than that of his suburban counterpart. The rest of his family has not been as fortunate. The children have been bitten by rats and cut on broken glass while playing in the back alley, but the street is worse because of the traffic. The parks have broken playground equipment which no one ever repairs and the ground is covered with old cans, broken bottles and other debris which is rarely, if ever, removed by municipal maintenance crews. This contrasts sharply with the well manicured parks in the downtown and other more affluent areas of the city. The world his kids grow up in is dirty, unhealthy and often unpleasant, but MI cannot afford to move elsewhere. His children are aware of how the world treats their father. Their own experience in unpleasant surroundings, compounded by the poor quality of their schools, and general discrimination dim their outlook on the world, and any prospects for a happy future.

JOHN H. WHITE

CHICAGO GHETTO ON THE SOUTH SIDE, 1974

John H. White, *Chicago Ghetto on the South Side*, May 1974, NARA, RG 412:
Records of the Environmental Protection Agency, 1944–2006, DOCUMERICA:
The Environmental Protection Agency's Program to Photographically Docu-
ment Subjects of Environmental Concern, compiled 1972–1977, NWDNS-412
-DA-13768.

DON COOMBS

"THE [SIERRA] CLUB LOOKS AT ITSELF," 1972

When you have 140,000 members, spread across the country and a little beyond, "knowing thyself" is both a desirable and a difficult thing to accomplish.

In this case the difficulty was surmounted by conducting a national membership survey in the latter half of 1971, with professional planning and lots of volunteer help. Some of the most interesting results are presented here, with the hope that they will be of value to Club leaders across the country. . . .

Who belongs?

First of all, most members haven't belonged for long. About half the members had belonged for two years or less when the survey was made, while only nine percent had belonged more than 12 years. This is the natural result of the Club's great growth in the last few years.

About 46 percent of the members are less than 35 years old, with 11 percent under 20. Some 62 percent are men, 38 percent women.

About 19 percent of members are students, with 18 percent teachers, 12 percent homemakers and 11 percent managers and executives. . . . [T]he next largest categories of occupation are lawyers, doctors, dentists etc. (8 percent), other professionals (7 percent), and clerical and blue-collar workers (7 percent). . . .

Excerpted from Don Coombs, "The Club Looks at Itself," *Sierra Club Bulletin,* September 11, 1972.

Is the Club an elitist group?

At this point we should consider whether the Sierra Club is an elitist group, in the bad sense of the word. The average member has much more education and a "more professional" job than the average U.S. citizen. But two big points should be made:

1) Nobody attends conservation meetings or goes on outings or sends in his dues who is an "average member"; averages are statistical, but members are real and individual, and the Club does have members of all descriptions and backgrounds.

2) If the Club doesn't seek special and selfish privileges for its members, and if it actively attempts to broaden its membership base, being called elite isn't exactly a stinging criticism. . . .

Should the Club concern itself with the conservation problems of such special groups as the urban poor and ethnic minorities?

The balance of sentiment was against the Club so involving itself.

About 40 percent strongly disagreed with such a proposal, while 15 percent strongly agreed. But the younger the member, the less he opposed such involvement. Although 58 percent of all members either strongly or "somewhat" opposed such involvement, only 46 percent of those under 35 were opposed, and only 43 percent of those under 25. Members from households whose main wage earners were managers or executives tended to be more opposed to such involvement, while members from households whose main wage earners were students, clerical or blue-collar workers or "other professionals" were less opposed.

TOXICS, WARREN COUNTY, AND THE DOCUMENTATION OF ENVIRONMENTAL DISPARITIES

Beginning in the late 1970s, events in the small, working-class community in Niagara Falls, New York, known as Love Canal, brought to a crescendo a decade of national conversations about how to safely dispose of toxic chemicals. The community had been built on top of an old industrial canal, which the Hooker Chemical Company had filled with some 43 million pounds of toxic chemical waste before covering it with a layer of clay and selling it, in 1952, to the local school board. A strange black sludge began seeping into area basements by the early 1970s, and residents began to suffer a range of unusual maladies. In 1978, the state ordered 240 families to evacuate. The unfolding disaster received national attention, and residents created a variety of media-friendly yard signs, such as the two shown here, as part of a larger effort to pressure Congress into acting. It did so on December 11, 1980, by passing the Comprehensive Environmental Response, Compensation, and Liability Act (CERCLA), more commonly known as Superfund. In the third document, Senator Robert T. Stafford (R-Vt.) explains why Superfund was needed.

When protests over the opening of a toxic waste landfill erupted in Warren County, North Carolina, in September 1982—as part of a cleanup that would get Superfund financing in 1983—the press quickly picked up the story. "The state's decision to dump the toxic wastes in sparsely populated Warren County has set off a continuing struggle over disposal of the soil," reported the *New York Times* six days after the protests began, reflecting broader national coverage. "Civil rights leaders joined the protests after residents charged that the state chose the site because the county is predominantly black."[1]

The next five documents, all photographs of the protests, include the iconic image of the struggle: protesters lying in the middle of a highway to block dump trucks from carrying PCB-laced soil to the new landfill. Following the photos of the protests are the lyrics to "A Warren County PCB Protest Song," which participants sang during the protests.

The events in Warren County resulted in, among other things, a series of broader investigations into protesters' central claim: that the poor, African American county had been targeted to play host to the PCB landfill precisely because it was poor and African American. The first major study, the federal General Accounting Office's report of June 1, 1983, found a disproportionate "correlation between the location of hazardous waste landfills and the racial and economic status of the surrounding communities."

The next document, a consulting firm's report titled "Political Difficulties Facing Waste-to-Energy Conversion Plant Siting," was prepared in 1984 for the California Waste Management Board (CWMB).[2] The report is notable for its central recommendation: that those seeking to site polluting facilities should use demographic analysis to identify "neighborhoods least likely to express opposition." This recommendation seemed to illustrate, in a single phrase, the truth of one of EJ activists' key claims.

The next document is an excerpt from the United Church of Christ's bombshell report, "Toxic Wastes and Race in the United States" (1987), the first study to validate the findings of the small-scale 1983 GAO report on a national level. Studying both hazardous wastes and "uncontrolled toxic waste sites," it found "a striking relationship between the location of commercial hazardous waste facilities and race," and was able to document "the widespread presence of uncontrolled toxic waste sites in racial and ethnic communities throughout the United States." (The next document, a map from the report, illustrates this point.) In addition to giving new life to the national conversation about environmental inequalities that activists in Warren County had started, the report spurred further in-depth study of the geographical relationships among race, class, and exposure to toxic pollution.

The final document in this section, an excerpt from Marianne Lavelle and Marcia Coyle's "Unequal Protection" (1992), applied a legal lens to "the racial divide in environmental law." Did the government enforce environmental laws and regulations evenly in different communities? Their findings suggested otherwise.

NOTES

1   "150 PCB Protesters Arrested," *New York Times*, September 21, 1982, A10.
2   Although the report's title page indicates that it was prepared "for California Waste Management Board," there is no documentary evidence that the Board ever accepted the report or adopted its recommendations. Its current successor agency, CalRecycle, "disavows any association with it" and embraces "the need to incorporate environmental justice principles into community and State decision-making" (personal correspondence with author, June 12, 2107).

PENELOPE PLOUGHMAN

PROTEST SIGNS IN FRONT YARD
LOVE CANAL 99TH STREET HOME, 1978

Protest Signs in Front Yard Love Canal 99th Street Home. Photo by Penelope D.
Ploughman, © 1978, all rights reserved. Courtesy University Archives, University at Buffalo, State University of New York.

Protest Sign: Danger, Dioxin Kills, c. 1980. Courtesy University Archives, University at Buffalo, State University of New York.

ROBERT T. STAFFORD

"WHY SUPERFUND WAS NEEDED," 1981

The country has waited a long time for the Superfund law dealing with chemical poisons in the environment. What we have now is, in my judgment, the major preventative health law passed by the Congress in the past four years.

Together with the other members of the Senate Committee on Environment and Public Works, I worked on this legislation for nearly three years. I will not say that it was a labor of love, because the process was trying. We were beset with problems at nearly every turn.

But it has been a three-year trial well worth it. Eighty percent of the American people wanted some legislation. That sentiment was reflected in the Senate, where 24 Senators joined as sponsors of the legislation. And, judging from what we know, those concerns are well founded. The Surgeon General of the United States considers toxic chemicals to pose the major threat to health in the United States for the decade of the 1980's.

Modern chemical technology has produced miracles that have greatly improved this Nation's standard of living. But the increased generation of hazardous substances associated with these new products has proved to be a serious threat to our Nation's public health and environment.

The legacy of past haphazard disposal of chemical wastes and the continuing danger of spills and other releases of dangerous chemicals pose what many call the most serious health and environmental challenges of the decade. Chemical spills capable of inflicting environmental harm occur about 3,500 times each year, and an estimated $65 million

Excerpted from Robert T. Stafford, "Why Superfund Was Needed," *EPA Journal 7* (June 1981): 9–10.

to $260 million is needed to clean them up. More than 2,000 dumpsites containing hazardous chemicals are believed by the Environmental Protection Agency to pose threats to the public health. The cost of containing their contents is estimated to be an average of $3.6 million per site.

PERVASIVE CHEMICALS

The acceptance of man-made chemicals to the extent that they are hardly recognized as such anymore has become a fact of daily life in the United States. We are dependent on synthetic chemicals for health, livelihood, housing, transportation, food, and for our funerals.

But within recent years, there has been a realization that what is our meat may also be our poison. Here are some examples:

- In a report dated March 1980, the Library of Congress concluded that damages to natural resources of the United States because of toxic chemicals were "substantial and enduring." The report identified damaged resources ranging from all five of the Great Lakes to the aquifer underlying the San Joaquin Valley, possibly the richest agricultural area in the United States.
- In a report to the President of the United States, the Toxic Substances Strategy Committee concluded that the cancer death rate in the United States had increased sharply and that "occupational exposure to carcinogens is believed to be a factor in more than 20 percent of all cases of cancer."
- In a report released in the spring of 1980 by the Congressional Office of Technology Assessment, agricultural losses because of chemical contamination were placed at $283 million. The report said the value was based on economic data from only six of the 50 States and was therefore "likely to be a gross underestimation of the actual costs."
- In 1979, the total production of chemicals in the United States was 565 billion pounds. Of this amount, 347 billion pounds was of chemicals officially classified by the United States Government as hazardous. Production growth was increasing at a rate of 7.6 percent in 1979. At that rate, production will double in 10 years.

This is not to say that chemicals are necessarily bad. On the contrary, they have contributed mightily to American prosperity. We rely increasingly on them because of this contribution which they made to American life in a changing and sometimes hostile world. In fact, most chemicals are benign. Only a small number of them cause cancer, birth defects, or other illnesses. But the fact remains that, small though the relative number of these dangerous chemicals may be, they can cause terrible damage when set loose on the public. Moreover, because we do use these substances in such a large volume, the number of incidents involving them has increased dramatically in the recent past.

EPA SURVEY

Using existing documentation, the Environmental Protection Agency identified some 250 hazardous waste sites involving damages or significant threats of damages. Among the reported incidents were 27 sites associated with actual damages to health (kidneys, cancer, mutations, aborted pregnancies, etc.), 32 sites which have resulted in the closure of public and private drinking water wells, 130 sites with contaminated groundwaters and 74 sites where natural habitats have been damaged and are adversely affecting indigenous species.

The preliminary findings of a joint States/EPA survey of pits, ponds, and lagoons used to treat, store, and dispose of liquid wastes identify 11,000 industrial sites with 25,000 such surface impoundments. At least one-half of the sites are believed to contain hazardous wastes. The survey found that virtually no monitoring of groundwater was being conducted and that 30 percent of the impoundments, or 2,455 of the 8,221 sites assessed, are unlined, overlie usable groundwater aquifers, and have intervening soils which would freely allow liquid wastes to escape into groundwater. . . .

The Surgeon General of the United States, in a report to the Senate Committee on Environment and Public Works, said that, in his opinion, toxic chemicals posed a major threat to public health in the United States. There is not one adult American who does not carry body burdens of one or several of these substances, many of which have now been removed from the market because of their dangers.

What I have just described is the scope of the toxics problem in the United States. The scope is not just of inactive hazardous waste disposal sites, as tragic as Love Canal may be. Nor is the scope confined to accidental spills into rivers, as disastrous as they may be. The problem is just as broad as the benefit.

I am not suggesting, nor have the members of my Committee suggested, that chemicals be banned. What we have proposed through legislation is that we reduce the number of people who may become victims of chemical poisoning incidents.

LEGISLATIVE HISTORY

For three years, the Senate worked on a bill that would respond to emergencies caused by chemical poisons, and to seek to discourage the release of those chemicals into the environment. In many ways, the Senate bill was analogous to the natural disaster assistance programs we have enacted into law. When those natural disaster assistance laws were enacted, no one suggested that we should respond to floods, but not to earthquakes.

It makes no more sense to make that kind of distinction when dealing with chemical emergencies than it does when dealing with natural emergencies.

There is simply no good reason for us to respond to one type of release of a poison, but not another. The test should not be whether poison was released into river water rather than into well water; or by toxic waste buried in the ground rather than toxic waste discharged to the ground. The test should be whether the poison was released. I assure you that the victim does not care to make those distinctions, nor should we.

JENNY LABALME

ANTI-PCB PROTESTS IN WARREN COUNTY, NORTH CAROLINA, 1982

From Jenny Labalme, *A Road to Walk: A Struggle for Environmental Justice* (Durham, NC: Regulator Press, 1987).

"A WARREN COUNTY PCB
PROTEST SONG," 1982

To "Come by Here My Lord" (Kum-by-ah)

Well, Warren County has some PCBs;
They're from the governor; he does what he please.
But we will dump Jim Hunt before too long.
Oh, Lord, come along.

We've got a road to walk; it's mighty steep too.
But one thing that we know is true,
Let history not be repeated,
A people united will never be defeated.

The way we're walking is dark and long,
But while we're marching we'll sing our song.
Give us faith, Lord, when we can't see.
Oh, Lord, come by me.

Our good old earth we've got to guard and share;
We've got to keep her safe and free from care,
And that means standing up for what is right.
We'll fight the poison with all our might.

"A Warren County PCB Protest Song," in Jenny Labalme, *A Road to Walk: A Struggle for Environmental Justice* (Durham, NC: Regulator Press, 1987).

We won't stop, oh Lord, we'll barely rest.
We're committed 'cause the truth is our test.
We have righteousness on our side;
Those poison devils had better hide.

Some folks think we'll never win,
That toxic waste is a deadly sin,
But we ain't gonna let nobody turn us around.
We once were lost, but now we're found.

"SITING OF HAZARDOUS WASTE LANDFILLS AND THEIR CORRELATION WITH RACIAL AND ECONOMIC STATUS OF SURROUNDING COMMUNITIES," 1983

The Honorable James J. Florio
Chairman, Subcommittee on Commerce,
    Transportation and Tourism
Committee on Energy and Commerce
House of Representatives

The Honorable Walter E. Fauntroy
House of Representatives

By letter dated December 16, 1982, you requested us to determine the correlation between the location of hazardous waste landfills and the racial and economic status of the surrounding communities. As agreed with your offices, we focused our review on offsite landfills—those not part of or contiguous to an industrial facility—found in the eight southeastern States comprising the Environmental Protection Agency's (EPA's) Region IV....

We found that:

— There are four offsite hazardous waste landfills in Regions IV's eight States. Blacks make up the majority of the population in three of the four communities where the landfills are located. At

---

Excerpted from General Accounting Office, "Siting of Hazardous Waste Landfills and Their Correlation with Racial and Economic Status of Surrounding Communities" (Washington, DC: US General Accounting Office, 1983).

least 26 percent of the population in all four communities have income below the poverty level and most of this population is Black.

— The determination of where a hazardous waste landfill will be located is currently a State responsibility. Federal regulations, effective in January 1983, require that selected sites meet minimal location standards. EPA has just begun its review process to determine if sites meet these standards.

— Federal legislation requires public participation in the hazardous waste landfill permit process except for the approval of disposal for polychlorinated biphenyls (PCBs), which are regulated under separate legislation that does not provide for public participation. Because of delays in issuing final regulations three of the four landfills in Region IV have not yet undergone the final permit process where public participation is required. The fourth is a PCB landfill and even though not subject to Federal requirements, had undergone this process. Only one site in the Nation (in Region VI) has been granted a final hazardous waste landfill permit and had been subjected to the public participation process. . . .

RACIAL AND ECONOMIC DATA

Based on 1980 census data at three of the four sites—Chemical Waste Management, Industrial Chemical Company, and the Warren County PCB Landfill—the majority of the population in census areas (areas within a county such as a township or subdivision) where the landfills are located is Black. Also, at all four sites the Black population in the surrounding census areas has a lower mean income than the mean income for all races combined and represents the majority of those below poverty level (the poverty level was $7,412 for a family of four in the 1980 census).

[signed]

J. Dexter Peach
Director

1980 CENSUS POPULATION, INCOME, AND POVERTY DATA FOR CENSUS AREAS WHERE LANDFILLS ARE LOCATED

Landfill	Population Number	Percent Black	Mean family income All races	Blacks	Population below poverty level Number	Percent	Percent Black
Chemical Waste Mgmt.	626	90	$11,198	$10,752	265	42	100
SCA Services	849	38	16,371	6,781	260	31	100
Industrial Chemical Co.	728	52	18,996	12,941	188	26	92
Warren County PCB Landfill	804	66	10,367	9,285	256	32	90

CERRELL ASSOCIATES

POLITICAL DIFFICULTIES FACING WASTE-TO-ENERGY CONVERSION PLANT SITING, 1984

INTRODUCTION

. . . People tend to view Waste-to-Energy projects in the same light as any waste disposal facility, and they simply do not want a "dump" nearby. Any type of waste facility will pose some aesthetic problems to those who live close to the facility. However, the community as a whole will receive significant economic and environmental benefits from a Waste-to- Energy facility. The issue becomes a dilemma: while the benefits to society in general are evident, the costs of the proposed facility to its neighbors almost always appear greater.

The focus of this study is on the people who live close to any of California's proposed Waste-to- Energy facilities, and their host communities. What are the issues raised against Waste-to-Energy projects? Who in the community objects most vociferously? And who objects least? And, finally, what decisions can be made in selecting a site that encourage community acceptance of the project? . . .

NATURE OF PUBLIC OPPOSITION

. . . The complaints of the public against Waste-to-Energy facilities have been used with varying emphases to delay, modify, or prevent the siting

---

Excerpted from Cerrell Associates, J. Stephen Powell, and California Waste Management Board, "Political Difficulties Facing Waste-to-Energy Conversion Plant Siting" (Cerrell Associates, 1984).

of virtually all major projects that affect the public directly. According to the California survey, only three of California's 29 Waste-to-Energy projects that managers have declared as primarily public-owned facilities have successfully progressed into the siting phase of the project, gaining at least passive community acceptance. Additionally, there are 11 project proposals that plan to serve the general public but are privately owned. Of these, two units appear to be successfully entering the siting phase, and one unit is currently operating. Although the privately-owned facilities have a somewhat better track record in avoiding public opposition, it is because the private enterprises tend to be considerably smaller than the public projects. . . .

WHO CARES? THE PEOPLE WHO FIGHT FACILITY SITINGS

A demographic picture of the types of communities and the types of people that are most likely and least likely to oppose a Waste-to-Energy project would be invaluable to an effective siting program. A great deal of time, resources, and planning could be saved and political problems avoided, if people who are resentful and people who are amenable to Waste-to-Energy projects could be identified before selecting a site. If this information was available, facilities could be placed in areas, if technically feasible, where people do not find them so offensive. . . .

Personality Profile

Independent studies on public opposition to waste management facilities have painted a very clear personality profile of those most likely and least likely to oppose facility sitings (see Appendix C).

The kind of person who is most likely to oppose the siting of a major facility is young or middle aged, college educated, and liberal. For the purposes of this analysis, liberal specifically designates a welfare state orientation in political philosophy. The person least likely to oppose a facility is older, has a high school education or less, and adheres to a conservative, free market orientation. . . .

Demographic Picture

Constructing a demographic profile of the locale surrounding a proposed Waste-to-Energy site as well as the community at large serves two fundamental purposes in the siting process. The first purpose is to assist in selecting a site that offers the least potential of generating public opposition. The second purpose is to identify the affected groups of people, and to tailor a community acceptance program specifically to these groups. . . .

A thorough demographic picture should take into account the size of the proposed Waste-to-Energy facility, its economic benefits and costs, the markets for the facility's waste-disposal and energy-producing services, the nature and spirit of the community, including any previous favorable or unfavorable experiences shared by the community and facility proponents, the extent of industrialization at the proposed site, the proximity of commercial and residential areas, and a personality profile of those living nearest the facility, especially the residents' educational level, age, and political ideology.

SITE SELECTION CRITERIA

Selecting an appropriate site for a Waste-to-Energy facility is a difficult task of finding a workable balance between numerous criteria. There are a wide array of technical requirements for a viable site, such as proximity of a fuel source, accessibility of resources, and an adequate transportation infrastructure. There are physical requirements that must be met, including sufficient acreage and geologic suitability. There are also environmental regulations, and the problem of securing adequate financing.

The above criteria tend to emphasize engineering criteria. Since the 1970s, political criteria have become every bit as important in determining the outcome of a project as engineering factors. The introduction of political criteria significantly complicates the task for the simple reason that political criteria often are at odds with engineering concerns. The best site in terms of financial feasibility and geologic suitability may very well be the most troublesome politically. . . .

Political Criteria

There are several political criteria that should be considered by facility proponents in evaluating initial sites prior to public involvement. . . .

Community History

It is important to take a good, hard look at the recent history of potential host communities. Case histories can reveal much about the community's needs, character, and spirit. A history favorable to industrial growth is a reassuring factor. Contrarily, a history of environmental activism, especially against major facilities, could be indicative of an antigrowth sentiment. Furthermore, the recent existence of environmental activist groups implies a community spirit that can swiftly and effectively turn into an organized movement. . . .

Personality Profile

Certain types of people are likely to participate in politics, either by virtue of their issue awareness or their financial resources, or both. Members of middle or higher socioeconomic strata (a composite index of level of education, occupational prestige, and income) are more likely to organize into effective groups to express their political interests and views. All socioeconomic groupings tend to resent the nearby siting of major facilities, but the middle and upper socioeconomic strata possess better resources to effectuate their opposition. Middle and higher socioeconomic strata neighborhoods should not fall at least within the one-mile and five-mile radii of the proposed site.

As shown in Appendix C, although environmental concerns cut across all subgroups, people with a college education, young or middle-aged, and liberal in philosophy are most likely to organize opposition to the siting of a major facility. Older people, people with a high school education or less, and those who adhere to a free market orientation are least likely to oppose a facility. A thorough demographic study of the residential clusters falling within the radii would reveal the characteristics of the inhabitants in terms of the above features, as well as the features of secondary importance—namely, party affiliation, community involvement, and occupation. Technically feasible sites could then be rated in accordance to the composition of the nearby residential clusters, weighing the "strong personality indicators" of opposition greater than the secondary features.

A personality profile can help identify the residential clusters most likely to oppose a Waste-to-Energy facility. It should be kept in mind however, that adverse sentiments tend to cross subgroups, and that the most important determinant motivating a person to action is the proximity of the project. There is a strong possibility of public opposition to the siting of such facilities regardless of educational level and social class among those who live within one mile of the project. Remoteness within the first radius is most important in managing community acceptance, which can then be accentuated by the "least resistant" personality profile. . . .

CONCLUSIONS

. . . A personality profile of those who are most likely to support and oppose Waste-to-Energy projects provides a valuable working framework for project proponents. Candidate sites can be suggested partly on the basis of neighborhoods least likely to express opposition—older, conservative, and lower socioeconomic neighborhoods. Meanwhile, the people most likely to express opposition to a Waste-to-Energy project— residents in the vicinity, liberal, and higher educated persons—can be targeted in a public participation program and public relations campaign. . . .

The siting of major Waste-to-Energy projects will probably always remain a difficult task. But many of the sources of opposition are unnecessary at best; and many others can be alleviated. With the proper political considerations, there is no reason that these projects should have such a poor track record in gaining community acceptance.

UNITED CHURCH OF CHRIST

"TOXIC WASTES AND RACE IN THE UNITED STATES," 1987

EXECUTIVE SUMMARY

Recently, there has been unprecedented national concern over the problem of hazardous wastes. This concern has been focused upon the adverse environmental and health effects of toxic chemicals and other hazardous substances emanating from operating hazardous waste treatment, storage and disposal facilities as well as thousands of abandoned waste sites. Efforts to address this issue, however, have largely ignored the specific concerns of African Americans, Hispanic Americans, Asian Americans, Pacific Islanders and Native Americans. Unfortunately, racial and ethnic Americans are far more likely to be unknowing victims of exposure to such substances.

Public policies ushered in by the Reagan Administration signaled a reduction of domestic programs to monitor the environment and protect public health. Reduction of efforts to protect public health is especially disturbing in light of the many citizens who unknowingly may be exposed to substances emanating from hazardous waste sites. According to a December 1986 U.S. General Accounting Office (GAO) report, the U.S. Environmental Protection Agency (EPA) "does not know if it has identified 90 percent of the potentially hazardous wastes or only 10 percent."

Excerpted from United Church of Christ, "Toxic Wastes and Race in the United States: A National Report on the Racial and Socio-Economic Characteristics of Communities with Hazardous Waste Sites" (New York: Public Data Access, 1987). Reprinted by permission of the United Church of Christ, www .ucc.org. All rights reserved.

Issues surrounding the siting of hazardous waste facilities in racial and ethnic communities gained national prominence in 1982. The Commission for Racial Justice joined ranks with residents of predominantly Black and poor Warren County, North Carolina, in opposing the establishment of a polychlorinated biphenyl (PCB) disposal landfill. This opposition culminated in a nonviolent civil disobedience campaign and more than 500 arrests. As a result of the protests in Warren County, the GAO studied the racial and socio-economic status of communities surrounding four landfills in southeastern United States. It found that Blacks comprised the majority of the population in three of the four communities studied.

Previous to the Warren County demonstrations, racial and ethnic communities had been marginally involved with issues of hazardous wastes. One reason for this can be traced to the nature of the environmental movement which has historically been white middle and upper-class in its orientation. This does not mean, however, that racial and ethnic communities do not care about the quality of their environment and its effect on their lives. Throughout the course of the Commission for Racial Justice's involvement with issues of hazardous wastes and environmental pollution, we have found numerous grassroots racial and ethnic groups actively seeking to deal with this problem in their communities.

Racial and ethnic communities have been and continue to be beset by poverty, unemployment and problems related to poor housing, education and health. These communities cannot afford the luxury of being primarily concerned about the quality of their environment when confronted by a plethora of pressing problems related to their day-to-day survival. Within this context, racial and ethnic communities become particularly vulnerable to those who advocate the siting of a hazardous waste facility as an avenue for employment and economic development. Thus, proposals that economic incentives be offered to mitigate local opposition to the establishment of new hazardous waste facilities raise disturbing social policy questions.

Having observed these developments, the United Church of Christ Commission for Racial Justice decided, in 1986, to conduct extensive research on the relationship between the location of sites containing hazardous wastes and the racial and socio-economic characteristics of persons living in close proximity to those sites. The Commission for Racial Justice employed Public Data Access, Inc., a New York-based research firm, to assist in these investigations. It was hoped that these studies would lead, for the first time, to a comprehensive national analysis of the relationship between hazardous wastes and racial and ethnic communities.

"Hazardous wastes" is the term used by the EPA to define by-products of industrial production which present particularly troublesome health and environmental problems. Newly generated hazardous wastes must be managed in an approved "facility," which is defined by the EPA as any land and structures thereon which are used for treating, storing or disposing of hazardous wastes (TSD facility). Such facilities may include landfills, surface impoundments or incinerators. A "commercial" facility is defined as any facility (public or private) which accepts hazardous wastes from a third party for a fee or other remuneration.

"Uncontrolled toxic waste sites" refer to closed and abandoned sites on the EPA's list of sites which pose a present and potential threat to human health and the environment. The problem of human exposure to uncontrolled hazardous wastes is national in its scope. By 1985, the EPA had inventoried approximately 20,000 uncontrolled sites containing hazardous wastes across the nation. The potential health problems associated with the existence of these sites is highlighted by the fact that approximately 75 percent of U.S. cities derive their water supplies, in total or in part, from groundwater.

Major Findings

This report presents findings from two cross-sectional studies on demographic patterns associated with (1) commercial hazardous waste facilities and (2) uncontrolled toxic waste sites. The first was an analytical study which revealed a striking relationship between the location of commercial hazardous waste facilities and race. The second was a descriptive study which documented the widespread presence of uncontrolled toxic waste sites in racial and ethnic communities throughout the United States. Among the many findings that emerged from these studies, the following are most important:

Demographic Characteristics of Communities with Commercial Hazardous Waste Facilities

— Race proved to be the most significant among variables tested in association with the location of commercial hazardous waste facilities. This represented a consistent national pattern.

— Communities with the greatest number of commercial hazardous waste facilities had the highest composition of racial and ethnic residents. In communities with two or more facilities or one of the nation's five largest landfills, the average minority percentage of the population* was more than three times that of communities without facilities (38 percent vs. 12 percent).

— In communities with one commercial hazardous waste facility, the average minority percentage of the population was twice the average minority percentage of the population in communities without such facilities (24 percent vs. 12 percent).

— Although socio-economic status appeared to play an important role in the location of commercial hazardous waste facilities, race still proved to be more significant. This remained true after the study controlled for urbanization and regional differences. Incomes and home values were substantially lower when communities with commercial facilities were compared to communities in the surrounding counties without facilities.

— Three out of the five largest commercial hazardous waste landfills in the United States were located in predominantly Black[†] or Hispanic communities. These three landfills accounted for 40 percent of the total estimated commercial landfill capacity in the nation.

---

* In this report, "minority percentage of the population" was used as a measure of "race."
[†] In this report, the terminology used to describe various racial and ethnic populations was based on categories defined by the U.S. Bureau of the Census: Blacks, Hispanics, Asian/Pacific Islanders and American Indians.

Demographic Characteristics of Communities
with Uncontrolled Toxic Waste Sites

— Three out of every five Black and Hispanic Americans lived in communities with uncontrolled toxic waste sites.

— More than 15 million Blacks lived in communities with one or more uncontrolled toxic waste sites.

— More than 8 million Hispanics lived in communities with one or more uncontrolled toxic waste sites.

— Blacks were heavily over-represented in the populations of metropolitan areas with the largest number of uncontrolled toxic waste sites. These areas include:

Memphis, TN (173 sites)	Cleveland, OH (106 sites)
St. Louis, MO (160 sites)	Chicago, IL (103 sites)
Houston, TX (152 sites)	Atlanta, GA (94 sites)

— Los Angeles, California had more Hispanics living in communities with uncontrolled toxic waste sites than any other metropolitan area in the United States.

— Approximately half of all Asian/Pacific Islanders and American Indians lived in communities with uncontrolled toxic waste sites.

— Overall, the presence of uncontrolled toxic waste sites was highly pervasive. More than half of the total population in the United States resided in communities with uncontrolled toxic waste sites.

Major Conclusions and Recommendations

The findings of the analytical study on the location of commercial hazardous waste facilities suggest the existence of clear patterns which show that communities with greater minority percentages of the population are more likely to be the sites of such facilities. The possibility that these patterns resulted by chance is virtually impossible,* strongly suggesting that some underlying factor or factors, which are related to race, played a role in the location of commercial hazardous waste facilities. Therefore, the Commission for Racial Justice concludes that, indeed, race has been a factor in the location of commercial hazardous waste facilities in the United States.

The findings of the descriptive study on the location of uncontrolled toxic waste sites suggest an inordinate concentration of such sites in Black and Hispanic communities, particularly in urban areas. This situation reveals that the issue of race is an important factor in describing the problem of uncontrolled toxic waste sites. We, therefore, conclude that the cleanup of uncontrolled toxic waste sites in Black and Hispanic communities in the United States should be given the highest possible priority.

These findings expose a serious void in present government programs addressing racial and ethnic concerns in this area. This report, therefore, strongly urges the formation of necessary offices and task forces by federal, state and local governments to fill this void. Among the many recommendations of this report, we call special attention to the following:

— We urge the President of the United States to issue an executive order mandating federal agencies to consider the impact of current policies and regulations on racial and ethnic communities.

— We urge the formation of an Office of Hazardous Wastes and Racial and Ethnic Affairs by the U.S. Environmental Protection Agency. This office should insure that racial and ethnic concerns regarding hazardous wastes, such as the cleanup of uncontrolled sites, are adequately addressed. In addition, we urge the EPA to establish a National Advisory Council on Racial and Ethnic Concerns.

* All of the national findings were found to be statistically significant with 99.99 percent confidence (that is, findings with a probability of less than 1 in 10,000 that they occurred by chance).

— We urge state governments to evaluate and make appropriate revisions in their criteria for the siting of new hazardous waste facilities to adequately take into account the racial and socioeconomic characteristics of potential host communities.

— We urge the U.S. Conference of Mayors, the National Conference of Black Mayors and the National League of Cities to convene a national conference to address these issues from a municipal perspective.

— We urge civil rights and political organizations to gear up voter registration campaigns as a means to further empower racial and ethnic communities to effectively respond to hazardous waste issues and to place hazardous wastes in racial and ethnic communities at the top of state and national legislative agendas.

— We urge local communities to initiate education and action programs around racial and ethnic concerns regarding hazardous wastes.

We also call for a series of additional actions. Of paramount importance are further epidemiological and demographic research and the provision of information on hazardous wastes to racial and ethnic communities.

This report firmly concludes that hazardous wastes in Black, Hispanic and other racial and ethnic communities should be made a priority issue at all levels of government. This issue is not currently at the forefront of the nation's attention. Therefore, concerned citizens and policy-makers, who are cognizant of this growing national problem, must make this a priority concern.

UNITED CHURCH OF CHRIST

"FIFTY METROPOLITAN AREAS WITH GREATEST NUMBER OF BLACKS LIVING IN COMMUNITIES WITH UNCONTROLLED TOXIC WASTE SITES," 1987

FIGURE A-1

FIFTY METROPOLITAN AREAS WITH GREATEST NUMBER OF
BLACKS LIVING IN COMMUNITIES WITH UNCONTROLLED TOXIC WASTE SITES

Source: U.S. Bureau of the Census
U.S. EPA Comprehensive Environmental Response,
Compensation and Liability Act Information System

Note: Large numbers denote EPA Regions

From United Church of Christ, "Toxic Wastes and Race in the United States: A National Report on the Racial and Socio-Economic Characteristics of Communities with Hazardous Waste Sites" (New York: Public Data Access, 1987), Appendix A, Figure A-1. Reprinted by permission of the United Church of Christ, www.ucc.org. All rights reserved.

149

MARIANNE LAVELLE AND MARCIA COYLE

"UNEQUAL PROTECTION," 1992

In a comprehensive analysis of every U.S. environmental lawsuit concluded in the past seven years, the NLJ found penalties against pollution
law violators in minority areas are lower than those imposed for violations in largely white areas. In an analysis of every residential toxic
waste site in the 12-year-old Superfund program, the NLJ also discovered the government takes longer to address hazards in minority communities, and it accepts solutions less stringent than those recommended
by the scientific community.

This racial imbalance, the investigation found, often occurs whether
the community is wealthy or poor.

Since 1982, activists with ties to both the civil rights and environmental movements have been pressing their case for "environmental justice"
before the U.S. Congress and the Environmental Protection Agency.
Using an increasing body of scientific study, they have shown that
minorities bear the brunt of the nation's most dangerous pollution.

But The National Law Journal's investigation for the first time scru-
tinized how the federal government's policies of dealing with polluters
during the past decade have contributed to the racial imbalance.

The life-threatening consequences of these policies are visible in the
day-to-day struggles of minority communities throughout the country.

Excerpted from Marianne Lavelle and Marcia Coyle, "Unequal Protection:
The Racial Divide In Environmental Law," *National Law Journal* 15, no. 3 (1992):
S2. *Reprinted and excerpted with permission from the September 21, 1992 edition of
The National Law Journal* © *1992 ALM Media Properties, LLC. All rights reserved.
Further duplication without permission is prohibited. ALMReprints.com—877-257-
3382—reprints@alm.com.*

These communities feel they are victims three times over—first by polluters, then the government, and finally the legal system.

Black families in South Chicago wonder whether the rampant disease among them springs from the 50 abandoned factory dumps that circle their public housing project, and why the federal government won't help them. In Tacoma, Wash., where paper mills and other industrial polluters ruined the salmon streams and way of life of a Native American tribe, the government never included the tribe in assessing the pollution's impact on residents' health. And, nine years after an Hispanic neighborhood in Tucson, Ariz., poisoned by chemical-infested water, drew federal attention to its problems, nothing has been done to stop the migration of contamination as it creeps underground.

From communities like these across the country has emerged the contour of a new civil rights frontier—a movement against what the activists charge is pervasive "environmental racism." Whether pushing the edges of constitutional law or shaming the environmental establishment into opening up its own white-dominated boards and membership, this movement calls not for "equity" in the face of pollution, but for prevention and equal protection.

The following are key National Law Journal findings, gathered over an eight-month period, and based on a computer-assisted analysis of census data, the civil court case docket of the Environmental Protection Agency, and the agency's own record of performance at 1,177 Superfund toxic waste sites:

- Penalties under hazardous waste laws at sites having the greatest white population were about 500 percent higher than penalties at sites with the greatest minority population. Hazardous waste, meanwhile, is the type of pollution experts say is most concentrated in minority communities.
- For all the federal environmental laws aimed at protecting citizens from air, water and waste pollution, penalties in white communities were 46 percent higher than in minority communities.
- Under the giant Superfund cleanup program, abandoned hazardous waste sites in minority areas take 20 percent longer to be placed on the national priority action list than those in white areas.

- In more than half of the 10 autonomous regions that administer EPA programs around the country, action on cleanup at Superfund sites begins from 12 percent to 42 percent later at minority sites than at white sites.
- At the minority sites, the EPA chooses "containment," the capping or walling off of a hazardous dump site, 7 percent more frequently than the cleanup method preferred under the law, permanent "treatment," to eliminate the waste or rid it of its toxins. At white sites, the EPA orders treatment 22 percent more often than containment.

A RACIST IMBALANCE

EPA lawyers, while declining to respond directly to The National Law Journal's analysis, say they carry out the law, case by case, on the basis of the science, the size and legal complications particular to each toxic waste site or illegal pollution case.

"Environmental equity is serious business for this agency," says Scott Fulton, EPA deputy assistant administrator for enforcement. "We want to guarantee that no segment of society is bearing a disproportionate amount of the consequences of pollution."

But activists who have been working in communities inundated by waste say that the hundreds of seemingly race-neutral decisions in the science and politics of environmental enforcement have created a racist imbalance. Through neglect, not intent, they say minorities are stranded on isolated islands of pollution in the midst of the nation that produced the first, most sophisticated environmental protection laws on earth.

"People say decisions are made based on risk assessment and science," says Prof. Robert D. Bullard, a sociologist at the University of California, Riverside, who has been studying environmental racism for 14 years. "The science may be present, but when it comes to implementation and policy, a lot of decisions appear to be based on the politics of what's appropriate for that community. And low-income and minority communities are not given the same priority, nor do they see the same speed at which something is perceived as a danger and a threat."

Many activists argue the result has been a less safe environment for all citizens, as polluters' use of politically weak minority communities creates a gateway for disposal of wastes that will ultimately affect the larger environment. The lead particles that rise in West Dallas fall on Dallas, they point out, as the chemical stew that starts near slums on the Mississippi ends in the fishing source of the Gulf, and the South Chicago dumps threaten the grand reservoir of the Midwest, Lake Michigan. . . .

That is why the most hopeful of "environmental justice" advocates believe that if they can force federal leaders to factor in race and poverty in making decisions, it could revolutionize and improve the law.

"This issue has the power to change the fundamental assumptions of environmental protection," says Charles Lee, director of the United Church of Christ's special project on toxic injustice, which did groundbreaking research on the issue in 1987. . . .

A NEW MOVEMENT

The movement against environmental racism began to coalesce a decade ago with a church-led protest by black residents against a toxic landfill in North Carolina that led to 500 arrests.

Minority community leaders today in towns like Wallace, La., and Moss Point, Miss., have taken up the fight, standing firm against two of the most reviled of pollution threats—a hazardous waste burner and a paper factory—that want to set up shop in their backyards. They hope to build upon the attempts that have been made since 1979 to use the law and the courts to mete out "environmental justice," as groundbreaking and as difficult an effort as the first equal protection cases that outlawed school segregation 40 years ago.

"This is the cutting edge of a new civil rights struggle," says Wade Henderson, director of the Washington office of the NAACP. "For our organization, it is a new and important area of activity."

It has been a difficult struggle, however, for communities that bear all the other historical disadvantages of racism, such as lack of education and money. That's why some community organizers are aiming to create a new civil rights movement that will link the money, contacts and legal know-how of the big national environmental groups with the grassroots people who are tackling local problems.

But at the same time, the nation's handful of mainstream green groups have been criticized roundly for their role in shaping the 22-year history of environmental law—a story of progress that nevertheless has left behind groups without a strong voice or scientific know-how.

Prof. Richard J. Lazarus of Washington University School of Law in St. Louis uses the example of the lobbying frenzy around the Clean Air Act of 1990 as a process that has excluded some of the people, urban minorities, who suffer from toxic air pollution the most. . . .

[T]he environmental racism charge has troubled the conscience of a movement accustomed to thinking of itself as progressive. "The fact is that all environmental statutes . . . pick winners and losers," he says. "They pick between problems, because there aren't enough resources to deal with all problems. And certain solutions redistribute risks, the most obvious example being that when you move a hazardous dump, one location is gaining and one is losing."

In the environmental game, Professor Lazarus argues, minority communities have been the biggest losers.

ASSESSING PENALTIES

The most striking imbalance between whites and minorities in The National Law Journal's analysis of the EPA's enforcement effort was a 506 percent disparity in fines under the Resource Conservation and Recovery Act [RCRA]—the 13-year-old law intended to assure the safe handling and disposal of hazardous waste. The average fine in the areas with the greatest white population was $335,566, compared to $55,318 in the areas with the greatest minority population.

"This particular statistic is probably the most telling," says Arthur Wiley Ray, senior attorney for Baltimore Gas & Electric Co. Mr. Ray, who left the EPA in 1990, says he spent much energy during his 10 years in government urging the agency to heed the environmental racism issue.

RCRA cases, he says, target active toxic dump sites. And in the view of minority communities, "That's where the problem is," he says. "They don't put those dumps on Rodeo Drive; they put them across the tracks."

In fact, the landmark 1987 United Church of Christ study, "Toxic Wastes and Race," found that communities that had two or more active hazardous waste plants or major landfills had three times as many minorities as communities without such facilities.

The other type of case in which minority areas also saw far lower fines than white areas was in the 28 cases brought using multiple law charges that the EPA has concluded during the past seven years. In those, fines were 306 percent higher in white than in minority areas, $239,000 compared to $59,429. . . .

SUPERFUND DELAYS

Community activism gave birth to the most ambitious environmental program in the world, Superfund, and many believe that progress in this 12-year-old program still requires the political access and financial resources so scarce in minority communities.

The Law Journal's investigation of the EPA's Superfund program shows that for the sites with the most minorities, it took an average of 5.6 years from the date a toxic dump was discovered to place it on a Superfund list. That's 20 percent longer than the 4.7 years it took for the sites with the highest white population.

EPA officials respond that the pace of action in the Superfund program depends upon how long it takes to study the hazards and assess the risk to people at hazardous waste sites. Urban sites may have a more complex mix of pollutants that therefore take longer to study. On the other hand, the officials say, a rural site may be many miles wide and therefore may take a much longer time to assess.

Richard J. Guimond, deputy assistant administrator of the EPA's office of solid waste and emergency response, which manages Superfund, says he cannot draw conclusions from the Law Journal's analysis. He says the EPA is attempting to study whether there is a disparate impact on minority communities in Superfund by comparing toxic sites that are similar in makeup. "We realize in some cases we don't have all the information that would enable us to fully conclude whether there are inequities as an artifact of the way things operate in society, what might be the reasons, and the best ways to deal with them," he says.

Latinos who live near a lead smelter site in West Dallas are suing the EPA, charging environmental racism was the reason they could not gain Superfund status for their toxic sites. Similar complaints arise among blacks who live near abandoned steel plants in Chicago and from an Hispanic community near an Air Force plant in Tucson, who saw no action or slow action on their problems in the Superfund program. All three of these communities complained of a high incidence of cancer, lupus, nerve damage and birth defects, but lacking money and expertise, they feel saddled with the burden of proving the link between disease and the toxics. . . .

POLITICAL CLOUT HELPS

The EPA says it is a simplification to judge its decisions at sites strictly by whether containment or treatment is chosen, (although many studies by industry, environmental groups and the government itself have done so). Mr. Guimond says that the EPA acts immediately at every site to remove unstable canisters and other materials that are considered an imminent threat to health.

In the Superfund decision-making realm, the EPA argues that its decisions are based on the science of particular sites, not on race.

But in a program as massive and costly as Superfund, political clout certainly does help a community to get solutions. Unfortunately, environmental justice activists argue, white communities usually have been better able to wield this access than minority communities. A classic illustration is the difference in the treatment of two heavily polluted neighborhoods whose plights won the attention of Congress: a black middle-class neighborhood of homeowners in Texarkana, Texas, and a white trailer park in Globe, Ariz.

One scholar, Prof. Paul Mohai of the University of Michigan School of Natural Resources, says that this difference stems from the classic effects of racism in U.S. society. Minorities continue to be underrepresented at every level of government and on the boards of polluting companies, he points out. And housing discrimination prohibits minorities from escaping their pollution problems, he says. Classic social science studies have shown that minorities, especially blacks, live in segregated enclaves in the United States, even as their level of income and education increases.

That's why activists like Ms. Ferris of the National Wildlife Federation are asking the EPA to begin to take into account disparate racial impact in addition to the scientific analysis the agency makes in its decisions. This would be analogous to the Reagan-era directives that now require federal agencies to consider the cost to industry with every decision.

The Rev. Ben Chavis, executive director of the United Church of Christ's Commission on Racial Justice and a founder of the environmental justice movement, agrees that the EPA needs to rethink how it does business. "So much of the methodology of the last 12 years in environmental protection has been risk-assessment and therefore risk-management, and too little attention has been paid to equal enforcement of the law," he says. . . .

"Cancer Alleys serve as a reminder that the issue of the environment for us is an issue of life and death," he says. "There is a sense of urgency and wanting to ensure there will be no more Cancer Alleys, or Columbia, Mississippi, or South Side Chicagos.

"In each one of these areas," he says, "people are fighting back. Even in the worst situations, glimmers of hope emerge, because people are uniting—uniting across racial lines and socio-economic lines—and the common demand is for environmental justice."

BUILDING THE MOVEMENT

As researchers documented evidence supporting the claim that poor and minority populations shouldered disproportionate environmental burdens, activists began to build a full-fledged environmental justice movement. Strong local and regional groups slowly began to develop national and even international reach. The first six documents all represent early local and regional EJ organizations. One fertile region for activism came in Louisiana's so-called "Cancer Alley," which stretched roughly one hundred miles along the Mississippi River from Baton Rouge to New Orleans, where oil refineries and chemical plants produced close to one-eighth of the nation's hazardous waste. A number of organizations there embraced EJ work in the 1980s, including the Gulf Coast Tenants Organization, the Local 4-620 branch of the Oil, Chemical and Atomic Workers (OCAW) Union, and the Louisiana Toxics Project (LTP), a coalition of different activist groups. The first two documents, both photos from the nine-day-long, LTP-sponsored "Great Louisiana Toxics March" in November 1988, helped push EJ issues onto the state's political agenda.

The third document, a photo taken during a protest against New York City's North River Sewage Treatment Plant in 1988, shows Peggy Shepard and Chuck Sutton, founders (with Vernice Miller-Travis) of West Harlem Environmental Action (WE ACT). As the city's first EJ organization, WE ACT went on to play an influential role both locally and nationally, serving as a model of effective organization, coalition building, agenda setting, and strategic thinking.

The fourth document is a March 1990 letter from the SouthWest Organizing Project (SWOP) to the leaders of the Group of Ten environmental organizations. Sent from a leading EJ organization and signed by more than a hundred leaders of color, the letter publicly challenged mainstream environmentalists to address environmental problems that disproportionately affected people of color and to provide a more substantial role for people of color in decision-making processes and leadership positions. The fifth document, a political cartoon published by the Panos Institute, which played an important role in organizing national conversations about EJ in the early 1990s, lampoons the failures of mainstream environmentalists to address the pressing environmental problems in minority communities. The sixth document, the "Unifying Principles" of the Indigenous Environmental Network, was adopted in 1991 at the organization's second annual meeting, where leaders and activists from tribes across the nation gathered to discuss questions of environmental justice.

The next three documents all originated in the First National People of Color Environmental Leadership Summit, held in October 1991 in Washington, DC, which helped establish EJ as a truly national movement by convening over three hundred leaders of color from across the country to discuss the environmental problems confronting their communities. The first, an excerpt from the opening press conference, reflects the summit's tone and concerns. The second, Dana Alston's response to consecutive speeches by the executive directors of two Group of Ten organizations—the Sierra Club and the Natural Resources Defense Council—insisted that people of color had gathered to speak for themselves, not to react to mainstream environmentalism. It is also in this speech that Alston voiced her influential definition of the environment as "where we live, where we work and where we play." The third document, "Principles of Environmental Justice," which the conference produced after intense deliberation, helped galvanize the movement and has become the touchstone statement of its vision and principles.

As EJ became a truly national movement, federal officials took note. Toward the end of George H. W. Bush's presidency, the EPA administrator, William K. Reilly, pushed back against charges of environmental racism and unequal protection, describing his creation of an Environmental Equity Workgroup and arguing that the most intractable problems, like the "sad legacies of inherited poverty and discrimination," were beyond the capacity of the EPA to address. The next year, toward the end of President Bill Clinton's first year in office, the *Los Angeles Times* published a wide-ranging article, reproduced here, describing the new administration's "determined effort" to confront EJ issues more directly than its predecessor had. The Clinton administration made good on this promise on February 16, 1994, when Clinton signed Executive Order 12898. This order, excerpted here, directed all federal agencies to incorporate environmental justice into their mission "by identifying and addressing, as appropriate, disproportionately high adverse human health or environmental effects of its programs, policies, and activities on minority and low-income populations."

As the EJ movement gained attention at the federal level in the 1990s, it exhibited other notable characteristics. For example, EJ activism proved an unusually fertile arena for leadership by women of color, as the EJ scholar Dorceta Taylor illustrates in the next document, a topic that continues to attract significant scholarly attention. In addition, as the final three documents show, international issues and collaborations all grew within the EJ movement during the 1990s. The first, "Standing on Principle," sketches the growth of international relationships and commitments, beginning with the decision by a group of leaders from the First National People of Color Environmental Leadership Summit to travel in 1992 to the Earth Summit in Rio de Janeiro, Brazil. The second document, the Jemez Principles for Democratic Organizing, was issued during a meeting hosted by the Southwest Network for Environmental and Economic Justice in December 1996, which focused on responding to the challenges of globalization and trade. The third, excerpted from a 1997 report by Public Citizen, focuses on the environmental burdens that the North American Free Trade Agreement placed on minority populations along the US-Mexico border.

SAM KITTNER

THE GREAT LOUISIANA TOXICS MARCH, 1988

Sam Kittner, *The Great Louisiana Toxics March, 1988*, kittner.com/environmental
_documentary.php.

PEGGY SHEPARD AND CHUCK SUTTON PROTEST NEW YORK CITY'S NORTH RIVER SEWAGE TREATMENT PLANT, 1988

Image courtesy of WE ACT for Environmental Justice.

"LETTER TO BIG TEN ENVIRONMENTAL GROUPS," MARCH 16, 1990

Jay D. Hair, President
National Wildlife Federation

Dear Mr. Hair:

We are writing this letter in the belief that through dialogue and mutual strategizing we can create a global environmental movement that protects us all.

We are artists, writers, academics, students, activists, representatives of churches, unions, and community organizations writing you to express our concerns about the role of your organization and other national environmental groups in communities of people of color in the Southwest.

For centuries, people of color in our region have been subjected to racist and genocidal practices including the theft of lands and water, the murder of innocent people, and the degradation of our environment. Mining companies extract minerals leaving economically depressed communities and poisoned soil and water. The U.S. military takes lands for weapons production, testing and storage, contaminating surrounding communities and placing minority workers in the most highly radioactive and toxic worksites. Industrial and municipal dumps are intentionally placed in communities of

SouthWest Organizing Project, "Letter to Big Ten Environmental Groups," March 16, 1990, available online at www.ejnet.org/ej/swop.pdf. Used with permission.

color, disrupting our cultural lifestyle and threatening our communities' futures. Workers in the fields are dying and babies are born disfigured as a result of pesticide spraying.

Although environmental organizations calling themselves the "Group of Ten" often claim to represent our interests, in observing your activities it has become clear to us that your organizations play an equal role in the disruption of our communities. There is a clear lack of accountability by the Group of Ten environmental organizations towards Third World communities in the Southwest, in the United States as a whole, and internationally.

Your organizations continue to support and promote policies which emphasize the clean-up and preservation of the environment on the backs of working people in general and people of color in particular. In the name of eliminating environmental hazards at any cost, across the country industrial and other economic activities which employ us are being shut down, curtailed or prevented while our survival needs and cultures are ignored. We suffer from the end results of these actions, but are never full participants in the decision-making which leads to them.

These are a few examples which we have witnessed of the lack of accountability by the Group of Ten:

- Legislation was passed in December, 1987 to annex lands to form El Malpais National Monument in New Mexico. 13,000 acres were considered to be the ancestral holdings of the Pueblo of Acoma. "Conservation" groups such as the Sierra Club and the Wilderness Society supported the bill in complete disregard for the cultural heritage of the Acoma people.
- Legislation is also being proposed to form the Albuquerque Petroglyph National Monument; 6,500 acres of escarpment that would include rock drawings carved centuries ago by Indian and Chicano peoples. Part of the land is within the boundaries of the Atrisco Land Grant, owned by Chicano heirs. The Atrisco Land Rights Council, an advocacy group for the heirs is opposing complete sale of the lands and is trying to assure that the heirs rights are recognized and preserved. Opposing the interests of the heirs is the Friends of the Albuquerque Petroglyphs. Members of this group

also work in conjunction with the Sierra Club. Recently, the Trust for Public Lands, another conservation group, has proposed to buy the lands for the monument.

- The Nature Conservancy, National Audubon Society, and others are opposing the grazing of sheep on the Humphries and Sargent Wildlife areas by a local, highly successful economic development project run by Chicanos in Northern New Mexico, one of the most economically depressed areas in the United States. Due to the encroachment of major tourism development companies in the area and consequent loss of private pastoral land historically controlled by local Chicanos, this grazing is considered essential to the continued viability of the project. Despite the fact that this grazing is considered by many to be an ecologically sound practice, these environmental organizations have chosen to "shoot from the hip" in their response to this proposed activity and are opposing the reasoned alternative of those who have lived in the region for hundreds of years.
- Organizations such as the National Wildlife Federation have been involved in exchanges where Third World countries will sign over lands (debt-for-nature swaps) to conservation groups in exchange for creditors agreeing to erase a portion of that country's debt. In other cases the debt is purchased at reduced rates; the creditors can then write it off. This not only raises the specter of conservation groups now being "creditors" to Third World countries, but legitimizes the debt itself through the further expropriation of Third World Resources. The question arises whether such deals are in the long term economic interests of both the countries involved and of the people living on the land.
- The lack of people of color in decision-making positions in your organizations such as executive staff and board positions is also reflective of your histories of racist and exclusionary practices. Racism is a root cause of your inaction around addressing environmental problems in our communities.
- Group of Ten organizations are being supported by corporations such as ARCO, British Petroleum, Chemical Bank, GTE, General Electric, Dupont, Dow Chemical, Exxon, IBM, Coca Cola, and

Waste Management, Incorporated. Several of these companies are known polluters whose disregard for the safety and well-being of workers has resulted in the deaths of many people of color. It is impossible for you to represent us in issues of our own survival when you are accountable to these interests. Such accountability leads you to pursue a corporate strategy towards the resolution of the environmental crisis, when what is needed is a people's strategy which fully involves those who have historically been without power in this society.

Comments have been made by representatives of major national environmental organizations to the effect that only in the recent past have people of color begun to realize the impacts of environmental contamination. We have been involved in environmental struggles for many years and we have not needed the Group of Ten environmental organizations to tell us that these problems have existed.

We again call upon you to cease operations in communities of color within 60 days, until you have hired leaders from those communities to the extent that they make up between 35–40 percent of your entire staff. We are asking that Third World leaders be hired at all levels of your operations.

Although some Group of Ten organizations have sent general information on the people of color within their staffs and Boards of Directors, the information has been insufficient. Again we request a comprehensive and specific listing of your staff of non-European descent, their tenure, salary ranges, and classification (clerical, administrative, professional, etc.). Also provide a list of communities of color with whom you provide services or Third World communities in which you have organizing drives or campaigns, and contacts in those communities.

Finally, we call upon your organization to cease fundraising operations in communities of color within 60 days until a meeting is held with you including representatives of our choice. Once your organization responds to these requests you will be invited to confer with other national leaders on the poisoning of United States Third World communities.

Please send all materials and information to:

Richard Moore, Co-Director
Southwest Organizing Project
1114 7th Street NW
Albuquerque, NM 87102
Phone: (505) 247-8832

It is our sincere hope that we be able to have a frank and open dialogue with your organization and other national environmental organizations. It is our opinion that people of color in the United States and throughout the world are clearly endangered species. Issues of environmental destruction are issues of our immediate and long term survival. We hope that we can soon work with your organization in helping to assure the safety and well-being of all peoples.

Sincerely,

[103 signatories]

MARK GUTIERREZ

FROM ONE EARTH DAY TO THE NEXT, 1990

Mark Gutierrez, *From One Earth Day to the Next*, in "We Speak for Ourselves: Social Justice, Race and Environment," ed. Dana Alston (Washington, DC: Panos Institute, 1990), 22. Used with permission.

"UNIFYING PRINCIPLES," 1991

The Indigenous Peoples of the Americas have lived for over 500 years in confrontation with an immigrant society that holds an opposing world view. As a result we are now facing an environmental crisis which threatens the survival of all natural life.

We believe in unified action, sharing of information, and working together with mutual respect. We recognize we must assert our sovereignty and jurisdictional rights through the application of our traditional laws and recognizing our traditional forms of leadership of our indigenous nations. We stand on principles of empowering and supporting each other to take direct, informed action and affect our ability to protect our lands from contamination and exploitation. By attempting to fulfill our responsibility to defend our mother earth we are assuring the survival of our unborn generations.

The members of IEN are unified in our recognition that the traditional teachings, lifestyles, spirituality, cultures and leadership of our people as well as the survival of our future generations, are entirely dependent upon our respectful relationship with the natural world and our responsibility to the sacred principles given to us by the creator.

Indigenous Environmental Network, "Unifying Principles," Second Annual Protecting Mother Earth Gathering, near the sacred Bear Butte, South Dakota, 1991, www.ienearth.org/about.

FIRST NATIONAL PEOPLE OF COLOR ENVIRONMENTAL LEADERSHIP SUMMIT PRESS CONFERENCE, OCTOBER 24, 1991

OPENING STATEMENTS

Rose Marie Augustine
President, Tucsonians for a Clean Environment, Tucson, Arizona

I come from Tucson, Arizona. I am President of Tucsonians for a Clean Environment. My community is 85 percent Latino. In Tucson, 30 square miles have been designated Superfund, where 47,000 people have been contaminated by drinking contaminated water. The water was contaminated by one of this country's major defense contractors, Hughes Tool Company.

We bathed in and we drank the water for over 30 years. In 1981 the EPA came in and designated Tucson a Superfund site. We didn't know anything about what had happened to us for five years, until a newspaper reporter did an investigative report and we saw the article that came out in the paper. It was a series of articles. We were never informed

Rose Marie Augustine et al., "Press Conference, Thursday, October 24, 1991, 11:00 A.M.," in *The First National People of Color Environmental Leadership Summit, Proceedings*, ed. Charles Lee (New York: United Church of Christ, 1992), 1–4. Reprinted by permission of the United Church of Christ, www.ucc.org. All rights reserved.

what happens to people who drink contaminated water. We knew that there was a large population in our area that was suffering. We were suffering a lot of cancers, and we thought, "My God, what's happening here?"

My neighbors, my friends, my family have suffered greatly. I have lupus; my husband has bladder cancer; my son has a rare form of muscular dystrophy. My first grandchild was born dead. My aunt died of cancer. That's four generations that we [have] seen in our family. My neighbors recently had a child who had the chicken pox. His mother thought that he was having effects from the chicken pox, but they found out that he had lymphoma. We have mothers who had children born with heart-valve defects. I had one mother tell me that she had three of her children die, and one of them died in her arms. She was asking me, "Could this be an effect from TCE (trichloroethylene)?"

We have noticed, by speaking with the women in the community, that the women are the ones that are suffering the greatest. I am not saying that the men don't suffer, but the women are the ones that have to take care of the illness. When someone has a cancer, they are the ones that have to take care of the family members; they are the ones that have to take care of the children when they are sick; they are the ones that are left. When the husbands can no longer stand the expense of the medical care and the illnesses, they are left with their children, and to take care of them.

Our community has suffered a lot. Our government has done nothing to help us. And we have a lot of fear in the neighborhood. We have a lot of concerns, and we have a lot of anger. And that is why I am here today. Tucson is not the only community that is experiencing these problems. We have communities throughout the country that are experiencing our problems. I am here today because I cannot do anything alone. In Tucson we have been fighting this for 10 years now, and I am hoping that by coming here the government will pay attention to what is happening to us. I think that if we stand together, we will become stronger. And we need one another.

Benjamin F. Chavis, Jr.
Executive Director, United Church of Christ
Commission for Racial Justice, Cleveland, Ohio

We wanted to begin this press conference with Rose Marie Augustine's story, because that is the reason why the First National People of Color Environmental Leadership Summit is being convened. Her story can be repeated in thousands of communities throughout this nation. We have come to Washington, D.C. to catch the attention of the President and the Government, and all forces that have contributed to our sister's and her community's suffering and pain.

Native American, African American, Latino American and Asian Pacific American delegates to the First National People of Color Environmental Leadership Summit will be arriving here today from every state in the nation, along with delegates from Canada, Puerto Rico, the Marshall Islands, Central America and Africa. The convening of this Leadership Summit has the potential to reshape and redefine the environmental movement.

The United Church of Christ Commission for Racial Justice is pleased to sponsor this historic Leadership Summit on one of the most critical issues of our time. Environmental racism is both a national and international problem. While our focus will primarily be on the environmental crisis in people of color communities throughout the United States, we are profoundly aware of the relationship between the U.S. domestic policies and foreign policies on the environment.

Environmental racism is racial discrimination in environmental policy making and the enforcement of regulation and laws, the deliberate targeting of people of color communities for toxic waste facilities, the official sanctioning of a life threatening presence of poisons and pollutants in our communities, and the history of excluding people of color from the leadership of the environmental movement.

The issue of environmental injustice in our communities has become an issue of life and death. We believe that there is a direct correlation between the disproportionate presence of toxic facilities and pollutants and the increase of infant mortality, birth defects, cancer, and respiratory illnesses in people of color communities. This insidious form of institutionalized racism must be challenged, and it must be stopped.

It is our intention to build an effective multiracial environmental movement with the capacity to transform the political landscape of this nation around these issues.

It is our intention to expose the blatant refusal of the United States Environmental Protection Agency to enforce equally this nation's environmental laws in regard to the well documented national pattern of environmental injustice in people of color communities. In other words, there is no equal justice under the law in terms of environmental protection.

It is our intention to challenge every member of the United States Congress to respond legislatively, and with their oversight authority, to the particularities of environmental injustice in all communities, but especially to the genocidal character of environmental racism in people of color communities.

It is our intention to say clearly to President George Bush: You have failed to keep your promise to use your good office for making the protection of the environment a national priority. It appears to us that the Bush Administration has had a greater commitment to protect the petrochemical industry and other large corporate interests rather than the environment.

It is our intention to call upon the Nuclear Regulatory Commission to ban permanently the storage or disposal of nuclear waste in Native American lands and communities. We are opposed to any attempts to export toxic wastes from the United States to people of color communities in Third World countries.

The living pain of Rose Marie Augustine, and of all of those women and children in her community of Tucson, Arizona, is not an isolated phenomenon. But their reality of suffering has been experienced by people of color throughout this nation. Our cup has run over, and we assembled here to join hands with all of the Rose Marie Augustines, who are valiantly standing up to this injustice.

Gail Small
Executive Director, Native Action, Lame Deer, Montana

I am a member of the Northern Cheyenne Indian tribe from Lame Deer, Montana. My Cheyenne name is Nisseyot, which means "Woman Standing in the Timber." I have traveled a long way to be here, to give you an understanding of the sacredness of the land. My tribe is approximately 6,000 people. Our territory is 500,000 acres of aboriginal ancestral homeland in southeastern Montana. Along with our Sioux and Arapaho allies, we defeated the United States Government in a military victory known as the Custer Battle.

Today, however, we are still fighting for our lands. We are still fighting for our reservations, the Chicano communities and black communities. My reservation today is being surrounded by major coal strip mining. The largest coal strip mine in America is 15 miles from Lame Deer, Montana. The coal is being used to fuel the cities of America: Los Angeles, Seattle, Minneapolis, etc. Major coal strip mining surrounding our ancestral homeland, the land which our people died for and are still fighting for today. The environmental laws which this country passes do not protect our lands and our people of color.

It has been 500 years now since Columbus arrived in our world—500 years of colonization and oppression. "Conquer the Indians, conquer the land" is the white man's way of thinking. As human beings today, we must reestablish our spiritual connections to the sacredness of our Mother Earth. In order to do this, America's way of thinking must be challenged.

Our lands, our communities are being poisoned by white America's garbage. Indian reservations, black, Chicano, and Asian communities are becoming the dumping grounds for America. It must stop. As people of color today, we are challenging America's thinking, the economic thinking which poisons our people and our land.

Toney Anaya
Governor, State of New Mexico (1983–87),
Santa Fe, New Mexico

I am a former Governor of New Mexico, a state that today is the first majority minority state. We are now principally Hispanic American and Native American, with a good population of other people of color as well. My background in the environmental movement is not new-found. As with most people of color, we feel that we probably were the original environmentalists. With most people of color, the environment is something to which we have a profound spiritual attachment, where we have always respected and shown a deep love and attraction to the land, the air and the water.

In the past we have had to spend all of our time dealing with day to day issues, like putting food on the table, and perhaps addressing some of the environmental issues in another context: the context of human rights and civil rights, employment, and so on. But as we look around, we recognize that we have been disproportionately impacted by the adverse effects of the environmental policies of this country, to which this Summit will be addressing itself. We find that we have been disproportionately impacted in the effects on our health, our very life, much less our livelihood, and we see the damage inflicted on the land, in the air and the water that we have always held so cherished in our lives.

We want to play a substantive role in the future debate. Some of us have been able to play some role in the past. When I served as governor, for example, I was also chairman of the National Governors' Association Subcommittee on the Environment, and sought to bring my fellow governors more aggressively into the national debate on some of these issues. I also sought to bring us into the international debate, particularly to look at the environmental implications of our industrial policies. But whatever opportunities we have had, they have been limited and minimal in the past.

We are not looking for solutions today that would lock anybody out; we are looking for a way in which all of us can be involved in the process, and try to help find the solutions. We are looking, for example, to come up with a technology and the political will to insure that we force the polluters (the industrial plants, the military establishment and others) to detoxify at the point of production. We must stop producing toxins in the first place. We must find a more responsible way to dispose of toxic wastes where you just simply can't avoid producing them. We are not asking that you take it out of people of color neighborhoods and put it in white Anglo neighborhoods; we are saying it should not be in anybody's neighborhood—we all have to work together.

We are here in a responsible fashion, we are here to empower ourselves, so that we will have a greater voice to play, and through that, to help our government and our policy makers to find solutions. And, if need be, we are here to give them the political will to enforce those solutions.

Co-Chair Syngman Rhee, President, National Council of Churches was in transit from Louisville, Kentucky.

Other persons in attendance were Dana Alston, Panos Institute (Washington, D.C.); Pat Bryant, Gulf Coast Tenants Organization (New Orleans, Louisiana); Robert D. Bullard, University of California at Riverside (Riverside, California); Donna Chavis, Center for Community Action (Pembroke, North Carolina); and Richard Moore, SouthWest Organizing Project (Albuquerque, New Mexico).

DANA ALSTON

"MOVING BEYOND THE BARRIERS," 1991

Our movement is not a reaction to the environmental movement. We have come here to define for ourselves the issues of the ecology and the environment. We have to speak these truths that we know from our lives to those participants and observers whom we have invited here to join us. We have come for you to hear our understandings from our mouths directly, so there will be no confusion and no misunderstandings.

ENVIRONMENTALISM AND
THE CRITICAL ISSUES OF OUR TIME

For us, the issues of the environment do not stand alone by themselves. They are not narrowly defined. Our vision of the environment is woven into an overall framework of social, racial and economic justice. It is deeply rooted in our cultures and our spirituality. It is based in a long tradition and understanding and respect for the natural world. The environment, for us, is where we live, where we work and where we play.

The environment affords us the platform to address the critical issues of our time: questions of militarism and defense policy; religious freedom; cultural survival; energy and sustainable development; the future of our cities; transportation; housing; land and sovereignty rights; self-determination; and employment. We can go on and on.

We understand nuclear development and militarism. Native people die at every single level of nuclear development from the mining of

---

Excerpted from Dana Alston, "Moving beyond the Barriers," in *The First National People of Color Environmental Leadership Summit, Proceedings*, ed. Charles Lee (New York: United Church of Christ, 1992), 103–6. Reprinted by permission of the United Church of Christ, www.ucc.org. All rights reserved.

uranium at the beginning of the process to the processing of nuclear material. The Havasupai have told us about their struggle with uranium mining. The Native Americans for a Clean Environment have spoken about Sequoia Fuels.

We understand underground nuclear testing and its environmental and health impacts from the Western Shoshone. We know about the ultimate end of this nuclear process, i.e., the targeting of Native land for the disposal of nuclear wastes. We understand the issues of transportation. We all saw the earthquake in San Francisco and we saw the highway entrance ramp collapse. That highway goes through the middle of a black community. We all know where all the highways go through around the cities in this country; they go through our communities. So the Clean Air Alternative Coalition in the Bay Area has built a multiracial movement to deal with where they are going to rebuild that highway.

We know these things from our daily lives. We know the issue of the environment is a housing issue. We know what Marjorie Moore has told us—we realize that black and Latino children . . . have been poisoned by lead. But the media didn't want to talk about that too much, until they found out that white children also had lead poisoning.

We know about how racism works in this country. We have heard the delegates about the boycott of Levi Strauss and how Latino women have been crippled by making Docker Jeans. When they were so crippled and they couldn't work anymore, the company closes down with no notice. The workers come back from Christmas vacation to find out that they don't have a job. After asking the company before Christmas, "Are you going to close?" They were told, "Oh, no." So the women went out and bought Christmas presents, bought the trees, celebrated the holidays with their family, only to come back from the Christmas holiday to their gift—a pink slip. And that company then moves where? To Latin America, where they cripple and poison there.

"THE PRINCIPLES OF ENVIRONMENTAL JUSTICE," 1991

PREAMBLE

WE, THE PEOPLE OF COLOR, gathered together at this multinational People of Color Environmental Leadership Summit, to begin to build a national and international movement of all peoples of color to fight the destruction and taking of our lands and communities, do hereby re-establish our spiritual interdependence to the sacredness of our Mother Earth; to respect and celebrate each of our cultures, languages and beliefs about the natural world and our roles in healing ourselves; to ensure environmental justice; to promote economic alternatives which would contribute to the development of environmentally safe livelihoods; and, to secure our political, economic and cultural liberation that has been denied for over 500 years of colonization and oppression, resulting in the poisoning of our communities and land and the genocide of our peoples, do affirm and adopt these Principles of Environmental Justice:

1. *Environmental justice* affirms the sacredness of Mother Earth, ecological unity and the interdependence of all species, and the right to be free from ecological destruction.

"The Principles of Environmental Justice," adopted at the People of Color Environmental Leadership Summit, October 27, 1991, Washington, DC. (Simultaneously published in Spanish as "Principios para la justicia ambiental.") Reprinted by permission of the United Church of Christ, www.ucc.org. All rights reserved.

2. *Environmental justice* demands that public policy be based on mutual respect and justice for all peoples, free from any form of discrimination or bias.

3. *Environmental justice* mandates the right to ethical, balanced and responsible uses of land and renewable resources in the interest of a sustainable planet for humans and other living things.

4. *Environmental justice* calls for universal protection from nuclear testing, extraction, production and disposal of toxic/hazardous wastes and poisons and nuclear testing that threaten the fundamental right to clean air, land, water, and food.

5. *Environmental justice* affirms the fundamental right to political, economic, cultural and environmental self-determination of all peoples.

6. *Environmental justice* demands the cessation of the production of all toxins, hazardous wastes, and radioactive materials, and that all past and current producers be held strictly accountable to the people for detoxification and the containment at the point of production.

7. *Environmental justice* demands the right to participate as equal partners at every level of decision-making, including needs assessment, planning, implementation, enforcement and evaluation.

8. *Environmental justice* affirms the right of all workers to a safe and healthy work environment, without being forced to choose between an unsafe livelihood and unemployment. It also affirms the right of those who work at home to be free from environmental hazards.

9. *Environmental justice* protects the right of victims of environmental injustice to receive full compensation and reparations for damages as well as quality health care.

10. *Environmental justice* considers governmental acts of environmental injustice a violation of international law, the Universal Declaration On Human Rights, and the United Nations Convention on Genocide.

11. *Environmental justice* must recognize a special legal and natural relationship of Native Peoples to the U.S. government through treaties, agreements, compacts, and covenants affirming sovereignty and self-determination.

12. *Environmental justice* affirms the need for urban and rural ecological policies to clean up and rebuild our cities and rural areas in balance

with nature, honoring the cultural integrity of all our communities, and providing fair access for all to the full range of resources.

13. *Environmental justice* calls for the strict enforcement of principles of informed consent, and a halt to the testing of experimental reproductive and medical procedures and vaccinations on people of color.

14. *Environmental justice* opposes the destructive operations of multinational corporations.

15. *Environmental justice* opposes military occupation, repression and exploitation of lands, peoples and cultures, and other life forms.

16. *Environmental justice* calls for the education of present and future generations which emphasizes social and environmental issues, based on our experience and an appreciation of our diverse cultural perspectives.

17. *Environmental justice* requires that we, as individuals, make personal and consumer choices to consume as little of Mother Earth's resources and to produce as little waste as possible; and make the conscious decision to challenge and reprioritize our lifestyles to ensure the health of the natural world for present and future generations.

WILLIAM K. REILLY

"ENVIRONMENTAL EQUITY," 1992

I have a certain idea about environmental protection: It is about *all* of us: it benefits *all* of us. In fact, it improves our health, defends our natural systems, and involves us in the humanly defining enterprise of stewardship. That's why talk of environmental racism at EPA and charges that the Agency's efforts pay less regard to the environments of poor people infuriate me. I am determined to get to the bottom of these charges, to refute or respond to them.

At its core, environmental equity means fairness. It speaks to the impartiality that should guide the application of laws designed to protect the health of human beings and the productivity of ecological systems on which all human activity, economic activity included, depends. It is emerging as an issue because studies are showing that certain groups of Americans may disproportionately suffer the burdens of pollution. And it is emerging because across America people of color are forging a constituency to put this issue squarely on the national agenda.

The debate surrounding equity is deeply rooted in American history, for our tradition suggests, as Alexander Hamilton stated, "that every individual of the community at large has an equal right to the protection of government." Despite notable gaps between ideal and practice, this principle continues to undergird our notions of proper governance.

A conference in Michigan and a report by the United Church of Christ raised my concern about the equity issue. They indicated that certain waste facilities tended to be sited disproportionately in poor and minority communities. I formed an Environmental Equity Workgroup,

Excerpted from William K. Reilly, "Environmental Equity: EPA's Position," *EPA Journal* 18, no. 1 (April 1992): 18–22.

comprised of 40 professionals from across the Agency who were tasked with assessing the evidence that racial minorities and low-income communities are exposed to higher environmental risks than the population at large. I also wanted to know: What could EPA do to address any disparities that were identified?

It was already clear that EPA had entered a pivotal period in our history, a time of transformation, formidable challenges, fresh directions. The concept of risk—its assessment and management—is a pervasive theme. This follows more than two decades of doggedly pursuing an improved environment. The United States has spent approximately $1.5 trillion to attack contamination of the air, water, land, and food supply, registering, in many cases, substantial progress and more than a few triumphs. No other country comes close to this record.

In one of my first actions as Administrator, I asked EPA's Science Advisory Board (SAB) to suggest ways to improve the process of identifying, assessing, and comparing multiple risks. The SAB report, published in 1990 and entitled *Reducing Risk: Setting Priorities and Strategies for Environmental Protection*, urges EPA to target the most promising opportunities for reducing the most serious risks to human health and the environment. The health risks emphasized in the report include ambient air pollution; exposure to dangerous chemicals, especially workplace exposure; indoor air pollution; and contamination of drinking water, particularly by lead.

Risk is central to equity, and the Environmental Equity Workgroup started with some basic questions: How is environmental risk distributed across population groups?' How have EPA programs addressed differential risks in the past? How can we do so in the future? . . .

In 1982, a demonstration against the siting of a polychlorinated biphenyl (PCB) landfill in predominantly black Warren County, North Carolina, became a watershed in the movement to link environmental issues with social justice. In response to the protests, Representative Walter Fauntroy (DC) requested the General Accounting Office (GAO) to investigate the race and income dimensions of locating dangerous and dirty facilities. Answer: Blacks were disproportionately represented in three of the four sites that were surveyed.

By January 1990, the debate over environmental equity had progressed sufficiently for the University of Michigan's School of Natural

Resources to hold a conference on the relationship between race and the incidence of environmental hazards. In its aftermath, a group of social scientists and civil rights leaders informally joined together as the Michigan Coalition. It was the arguments of this group that prompted me to create the Environmental Equity Workgroup.

At EPA, our approach to environmental equity is drawing on three interwoven strands: the Agency's strengthened relationship with minority academic institutions; ambitious goals we have for hiring many more racial minorities in policy and decision-making positions at the Agency; and plans to address the distribution and management of environmental risk. Prior to the workgroup's appointment, EPA had developed specific programs to increase employment opportunities and reach out to minority academic institutions. The workgroup, consequently, focused on the distribution of risks.

In my charge to this workgroup, I emphasized EPA's basic goal of making certain that the consequences of environmental pollution should not be borne unequally by any segment of the population. EPA has a responsibility to identify such risks and target our scarce resources to address them.

The workgroup's draft report has now been published. It found that data on the incidence of health effects among different race and income groupings are poor—with one notable exception, lead poisoning. A much higher percentage of African American children have unacceptably high levels of lead in their blood. Moreover, our analyses suggested, some low-income and minority communities may experience greater exposure to other pollutants.

Using what data are available, then, the task force on environmental equity has turned up only one instance of environmental contamination that correlates with race: high blood lead in African American children.

Income levels are a somewhat clearer case, although again data from systematic studies are lacking. Property values and rentals are generally higher in less polluted areas. Supply and demand EPA cannot reverse. But we can improve the overall quality of air in cities.

What about poor rural areas? A March 1990 study by Clean Sites, Inc., a private nonprofit group, identified 470 rural poor counties in the United States. Although 15 percent of all counties in the United States are rural and poor, these counties contain only 4 percent of the total sites contaminated by hazardous waste, 2 percent of the active hazard-ous waste storage and treatment facilities, and 2 percent of the nation's Superfund sites. The study concluded that when Superfund sites are identified in rural poor counties, they receive about the same level of federal attention as Superfund sites nationally.

EPA's workgroup on environmental equity made several recommen-dations to elevate and improve the Agency's response to environmental equity issues. Informed decisions about environmental equity require a better database, one that should provide an objective basis for assess-ment of risks by income and race. The Agency should also move to integrate considerations of equity in risk assessment. EPA should employ creative measures to address equity issues and target high-risk populations. Mechanisms should be established to ensure that equity is incorporated into long-term planning. Finally, the Agency must sig-nificantly improve its ability to communicate with racial minority and low-income communities.

EPA alone cannot correct whatever imbalance has developed in the application of environmental protection. By way of example, while the Agency sets technology standards for what comes out the stacks, or what type of liner must be used to protect ground water, the siting of landfills and incinerators is largely the function of private firms, state regulators, and local zoning boards. Addressing equity issues will need the concerted efforts of state and local governments and of the private sector, as well. . . .

It is also undeniable that minorities usually benefit from—are, indeed, sometimes the chief beneficiaries of—more general efforts to protect the environment. New pesticide regulations, for example, will soon be in effect to protect farm workers and others exposed to these compounds from unsafe uses and storage practices. In 1991, we issued a final rule reducing the amount of lead in drinking water, with the highest risks being targeted for treatment first. We expect that neuro-logical threats to over 20 million children will be reduced and that about 100,000 additional children will avoid detrimental effects. This year, EPA will propose banning lead solder and limiting lead in plumb-ing fixtures. We also expect to propose tightening the national ambient air quality standard for lead in the atmosphere. . . .

Failures to achieve perfect equity in environmental matters are woven, along with other threads of triumph and defeat, into the full tapestry of American history. They are, in fact symptomatic of larger patterns of industrial growth and neglect and of sad legacies of inherited poverty and discrimination. It will take time and hard work to mend the fabric. Restrained by resources, jurisdiction, and knowledge, a government agency is necessarily limited in its capacity to affect larger cultural and social trends. Yet, within its domain, an agency of the United States government—situated as it is in long traditions of governance that compel close attention to questions of equity—must make every possible effort to redress obvious wrongs. At EPA, although we have just begun, we are well begun.

MELISSA HEALY

"ADMINISTRATION JOINS FIGHT FOR 'ENVIRONMENTAL JUSTICE' POLLUTION," 1993

Her neighborhood is not a very friendly place, especially if you like to breathe.

Even on brisk, breezy days, the fumes from more than a dozen major factories ringing Florence Robinson's middle-class subdivision burn the sinuses and tickle the throat and sometime sicken the stomach. On still, sultry days—and there are many of those—the fumes darken the air and cause respiratory problems for Robinson and many others who live nearby.

Like most of her neighbors in this stretch of America called "Cancer Alley," Florence Robinson is African American. A biology professor at Southern University, she sees a connection between the color of her skin and the degraded state of the air she breathes.

"We couldn't even vote when the planning for most of this was taking place," said Robinson as she drove past the fuming industrial hulks that line Baton Rouge's curiously named Scenic Highway. "Those decisions were made when we were disenfranchised. And we were deliberately denied the opportunity to voice our opinions. That's environmental racism."

Now, Robinson and minority communities throughout the nation are fighting back. And they have found an ally in the Clinton Administration, which has embraced the issue officials call "environmental justice."

In October, the Administration quietly handed minority communities a potentially powerful new tool to fight the introduction of hazardous materials sites in their neighborhoods. Breaking new legal ground, the Administration agreed to investigate two civil rights complaints from largely minority communities in Louisiana and Mississippi, which charged that the proposed siting of new plants in their midst was racially biased.

The decision marks the first time that the federal government has encouraged the use of the 1964 Civil Rights Act in community environmental battles, although the nation's courts traditionally have been wary of such efforts. Administration officials said that the move is a measure of their commitment to rectifying environmental injustices.

The White House is also preparing an executive order, expected to be signed by President Clinton next month, that would make the issue of environmental justice a factor in all federal decisions. The Environmental Protection Agency, where "environmental equity" initiatives simmered at a low level during the presidencies of Ronald Reagan and George Bush, has seized upon the issue with a combination of religious zeal and bureaucratic attention to detail.

"It's clear that low-income and minority communities have been asked to bear a disproportionate burden of this country's industrial lifestyle," EPA Administrator Carol Browner said in an interview. "They're angry and rightfully so. To solve this, we have got to incorporate environmental justice concerns into everything we do."

Pressed by Browner, who invokes the environmental justice issue on virtually all of her nationwide stops, the EPA is preparing initiatives that would attack the issue by refining its rhetoric, its enforcement mechanisms and its technical regulations.

The EPA is expected to review its regulations so that they better protect minorities from exposure to potentially harmful substances such as cancer-causing PCBs found in fish. Current EPA standards typically use white men as the models for studies that establish a population's average exposure to such hazards. The agency now wants to take account of how much fish is consumed by minority populations, including poor blacks living in the rural South.

The Administration's fervor has heartened minority leaders such as Benjamin Chavis, head of the National Assn. for the Advancement of Colored People, who first chronicled the issue in a 1987 study titled "Toxic Wastes and Race."

That nationwide survey of census and federal environmental data established for the first time that communities with large minority populations—even relatively prosperous ones—were far more likely to have hazardous waste facilities and other pollution-producing industries in their midst than were communities where minorities were not overrepresented.

A more recent investigation published by the National Law Journal in 1992 concluded that polluters based in minority areas were fined less stiffly than those in communities with the greatest white populations. It also found that clean-ups of toxic waste sites took longer and were less thorough for dumps in minority areas than in heavily white communities.

Some of the nation's traditional environmental groups, whose overwhelmingly white leaders and membership have been seen as distant from the concerns of poor and urban minorities, are starting to take notice. The Sierra Club and the Natural Resources Defense Council, in particular, have begun to address the problem. But for most other groups, the inclusion of minorities and their concerns has been a fitful process.

The Clinton Administration, by comparison, is making a determined effort. In a speech last week, Vice President Al Gore made clear that the Administration saw a clear pattern of race discrimination in the distribution of American environmental hazards ranging from air and water pollution to lead paint to Superfund clean-up sites.

"Those who are less able to defend themselves, those who have less economic and political power within the larger community are those most often taken advantage of and victimized with a disproportionate quantity of hazardous waste and pollution and the harmful and unwanted byproducts of production," Gore told African American church leaders in Washington. "It is time for this nation to respond to this crisis . . . and we are beginning to respond."

The Administration's newfound concern is likely to make its earliest and most dramatic impact in legislative efforts to reform the clean-up of Superfund sites, many of which are in the heart of urban neighbor-hoods with large minority populations. At a Superfund site in Cleve-land last month, Browner told city leaders that the Administration wanted to open the process by which abandoned toxic waste sites are identified and cleaned, allowing communities to help shape the course of the clean-ups.

Drawing from a recurrent Clinton Administration theme, Browner added that future Superfund clean-ups should aim to return contami-nated sites to productive uses and train local community members in environmental cleanup techniques, putting them to work in their neighborhoods. Administration officials are promising that minority communities near Superfund sites in places such as Cleveland, Chicago and Detroit soon will begin to see the employment benefits of the pro-gram's $1.5-billion pool of federal funding.

Those principles are also getting a test in Washington, where lead paint in crumbling inner-city buildings has become a hot environmen-tal justice issue.

Lead poisoning from pipes, paints and soil affects 44% of urban black children in the nation. It can cause brain damage and nervous system disorders. In a predominantly black Washington neighbor-hood, the EPA—working with the Housing and Urban Development Department—is funding a pilot program in which unemployed resi-dents have been trained in lead abatement.

"You're talking about giving people access to the decision-making process about what happens in their communities and neighborhoods, bringing them in on the front end, giving them significant informa-tion," said Browner. Clinton Administration officials contend that they are hobbled in dealing with one of the other central complaints of envi-ronmental justice activists—the concentration of dangerous industries in and around neighborhoods of color.

In communities such as Baton Rouge, EPA officials said, they have scant legal right to intervene because individual plants operate over-whelmingly within federal standards for pollution emissions—even though collectively, the plants can cause serious pollution problems. Moreover, granting of industrial sites is largely the responsibility of states and localities.

Several miles to the south of Baton Rouge, the tiny towns of Carville and St. Gabriel are charging environmental racism in the proposed siting of a new hazardous waste facility in their midst. Carville and St. Gabriel, low-income communities founded by freed slaves and still more than three-quarters black, sit in the shadows of 10 major chemical facilities, most of which belch fumes and handle hazardous materials every day.

The Louisiana Department of Environmental Quality, which must grant the new facility a license to operate there, has indicated that it favors the idea. When the state office called a public hearing at which hundreds of citizens passionately opposed the plant, the official running the meeting sought the help of state troopers to shut it down.

"The personnel of the state of Louisiana are disproportionately white men and they're operating like a giant Ku Klux Klan," said Pat Bryant, who heads the Gulf Coast Tenants Organization. "We had qualified people to put into Louisiana's Department of Environmental Quality, but they put the white men in charge. And white men consistently make the decision to put the poisons on us. The environment is just a new lynch-post for them."

EPA regulations being drafted would press state agencies to consider the environmental impact of high concentrations of industries or "multiple contaminant loading" in deciding whether to grant operating licenses to companies seeking to locate plants in minority communities.

But Clinton Administration officials conceded that their most effective course may be coaxing states and industries to cooperate voluntarily. The EPA in the past has collected no data that would allow federal or state governments to recognize when the concentration of potential sources of pollution in a given community has reached unfair and potentially dangerous levels. Officials said the agency is seeking such data.

"Frequently it is enough to say, 'Hey, this is going on,' and try to encourage voluntary efforts that will address the problem," said one Clinton environmental adviser. "It may well be that—by sensitizing companies to the issue of multiple-contaminant loading and letting them know that the government takes this seriously and wants it addressed—we might be able to accomplish this voluntarily."

The Administration's willingness to broker voluntary measures with industry has not pleased traditional environmental groups and it is not clear that the increasingly active environmental justice community will be satisfied with a policy of exhortation and rhetoric. Bryant, of the Gulf Coast Tenants Organization, is wary, saying that new laws as well as new attention will be necessary to reverse decades of environmental racism.

"We've had far more contact at a policy level with the EPA than we had under the last two Administrations," he said. "But the fruit of that is not quite clear. We see the possibilities of some changes but we're not quite sure what that means."

WILLIAM J. CLINTON

EXECUTIVE ORDER 12898, FEBRUARY 16, 1994

FEDERAL ACTIONS TO ADDRESS ENVIRONMENTAL JUSTICE IN
MINORITY POPULATIONS AND LOW-INCOME POPULATIONS

By the authority vested in me as President by the Constitution and the laws of the United States of America, it is hereby ordered as follows:

Section 1-1. Implementation.

1-101. *Agency Responsibilities.* To the greatest extent practicable and permitted by law, and consistent with the principles set forth in the report on the National Performance Review, each Federal agency shall make achieving environmental justice part of its mission by identifying and addressing, as appropriate, disproportionately high and adverse human health or environmental effects of its programs, policies, and activities on minority populations and low-income populations in the United States and its territories and possessions, the District of Columbia, the Commonwealth of Puerto Rico, and the Commonwealth of the Mariana islands.

1-102. *Creation of an Interagency Working Group on Environmental Justice.* (a) Within 3 months of the date of this order, the Administrator of the Environmental Protection Agency ("Administrator") or the

---

Excerpted from William J. Clinton, "Executive Order 12898: Federal Actions to Address Environmental Justice in Minority Populations and Low-Income Populations," February 16, 1994.

Administrator's designee shall convene an Interagency Federal Working Group on Environmental Justice ("Working- Group"). . . . The Working Group shall report to the President through the Deputy Assistant to the President for Environmental Policy and the Assistant to the President for Domestic Policy.

(b) The Working Group shall: (1) provide guidance to Federal agencies on criteria for identifying disproportionately high and adverse human health or environmental effects on minority populations and low-income populations;

(2) coordinate with, provide guidance to, and serve as a clearinghouse for, each Federal agency as it develops an environmental justice strategy as required by section 1-103 of this order, in order to ensure that the administration, interpretation and enforcement of programs, activities and policies are undertaken in a consistent manner;

(3) assist in coordinating research by, and stimulating cooperation among, the Environmental Protection Agency, the Department of Health and Human Services, the Department of Housing and Urban Development, and other agencies conducting research or other activities in accordance with section 3-3 of this order;

(4) assist in coordinating data collection, required by this order;

(5) examine existing data and studies on environmental justice;

(6) hold public meetings [as] required in section 5-502(d) of this order; and

(7) develop interagency model projects on environmental justice that evidence cooperation among Federal agencies.

1-103. *Development of Agency Strategies.* (a) Except as provided in section 6-605 of this order, each Federal agency shall develop an agency-wide environmental justice strategy, as set forth in subsections (b)–(e) of this section that identifies and addresses disproportionately high and adverse human health or environmental effects of its programs, policies, and activities on minority populations and low-income populations. The environmental justice strategy shall list programs, policies, planning and public participation processes, enforcement, and/or rulemakings related to human health or the environment that should be revised to, at a minimum: (1) promote enforcement of all health and environmental statutes in areas with minority populations and low-income populations; (2) ensure greater public participation; (3) improve research and data collection relating to the health of and environment of minority populations and low-income populations; and (4) identify differential patterns of consumption of natural resources among minority populations and low-income populations. In addition, the environmental justice strategy shall include, where appropriate, a timetable for undertaking identified revisions and consideration of economic and social implications of the revisions. . . .

1-104. *Reports to The President.* Within 14 months of the date of this order, the Working Group shall submit to the President, through the Office of the Deputy Assistant to the President for Environmental Policy and the Office of the Assistant to the President for Domestic Policy, a report that describes the implementation of this order, and includes the final environmental justice strategies described in section 1-103(e) of this order.

Sec. 2-2. Federal Agency Responsibilities for Federal Programs.

Each Federal agency shall conduct its programs, policies, and activities that substantially affect human health or the environment, in a manner that ensures that such programs, policies, and activities do not have the effect of excluding persons (including populations) from participation in, denying persons (including populations) the benefits of, or subjecting persons (including populations) to discrimination under, such programs, policies, and activities, because of their race, Color, or national origin.

Sec. 3-3. Research, Data Collection, and Analysis

3-301. *Human Health and Environmental Research and Analysis.* (a) Environmental human health research, whenever practicable and appropriate, shall include diverse segments of the population in epidemiological and clinical studies, including segments at high risk from environmental hazards, such as minority populations, low-income populations and workers who may be exposed to substantial environmental hazards.

(b) Environmental human health analyses, whenever practicable and appropriate, shall identify multiple and cumulative exposures.

(c) Federal agencies shall provide minority populations and low-income populations the opportunity to comment on the development and design of research strategies undertaken pursuant to this order.

3-302. *Human Health and Environmental Data Collection and Analysis.* To the extent permitted by existing law, including the Privacy Act, as amended (5 U.S.C. section 552a): (a) each federal agency, whenever practicable and appropriate, shall collect, maintain, and analyze information assessing and comparing environmental and human health risks borne by populations identified by race, national origin, or income. To the extent practical and appropriate, Federal agencies shall use this information to determine whether their programs, policies, and activities have disproportionately high and adverse human health or environmental effects on minority populations and low-income populations;

(b) In connection with the development and implementation of agency strategies in section 1-103 of this order, each Federal agency, whenever practicable and appropriate, shall collect, maintain and analyze information on the race, national origin, income level, and other readily accessible and appropriate information for areas surrounding facilities or sites expected to have substantial environmental, human health, or economic effect on the surrounding populations, when such facilities or sites become the subject of a substantial Federal environmental administrative or judicial action. Such information shall be made available to the public unless prohibited by law. . . .

William J. Clinton

DORCETA E. TAYLOR

"WOMEN OF COLOR, ENVIRONMENTAL JUSTICE, AND ECOFEMINISM," 1997

WOMEN OF COLOR AND THE ENVIRONMENTAL MOVEMENT

The role of women of color in the environmental justice movement cannot be understated. In no other sector of the environmental movement (not even in the more progressive or radical sectors) can one find such high percentages of women of color occupying positions as founders and leaders of organizations, workshop and conference organizers, researchers, strategists, lawyers, academics, policymakers, community organizers, and environmental educators. As table 6 shows, 49% of 205 people-of-color environmental justice groups had women as founders, presidents, or chief contact persons. In twenty-two of the thirty-nine jurisdictions listed, more than 50 percent of the groups had women leaders. A similar analysis in Malaspina et al. (1993) shows that 59 percent of the environmental justice groups profiled were led by women, many of whom were women of color. Similarly, about 48 percent of the delegates attending the People of Color Environmental Leadership Summit were women of color.[1]

Excerpted from Dorceta E. Taylor, "Women of Color, Environmental Justice, and Ecofeminism," in *Ecofeminism: Women, Culture, Nature*, ed. Karen J. Warren and Nisvan Erkal (Bloomington: Indiana University Press, 1997), 38–81 (excerpt pp. 58–60).

1 By contrast, a similar analysis of the gender and leadership in traditional environmental organizations revealed that 27 percent of the leadership positions in 1,083 groups were held by women.

TABLE 6. GENDER AND LEADERSHIP IN ENVIRONMENTAL GROUPS OF COLOR

Jurisdiction	No. of Groups	% Women Leaders
Alabama	3	33
Alaska	2	0
Arizona	5	40
Arkansas	1	0
California	30	57
Colorado	4	67
District of Columbia	8	50
Florida	2	100
Georgia	4	75
Idaho	3	33
Illinois	4	75
Kansas	2	50
Louisiana	4	75
Maine	1	0
Maryland	3	67
Michigan	1	0
Minnesota	1	0
Mississippi	3	100
Missouri	2	50
Montana	3	100
Nebraska	3	0
Nevada	6	17
New Jersey	3	67
New Mexico	21	48
New York	7	14
North Carolina	9	67
Ohio	7	57
Oklahoma	8	50
Oregon	4	0

(continued)

TABLE 6. (*continued*)

Jurisdiction	No. of Groups	% Women Leaders
Pennsylvania	2	100
Rhode Island	1	100
South Dakota	3	67
Tennessee	2	100
Texas	18	50
Virginia	3	100
Washington	8	13
Wisconsin	9	22
Puerto Rico	4	25
Quebec, Canada	1	100
Total (or average)	205	(49)

Source: *People of Color Environmental Groups Directory* (1992).

LUZ CLAUDIO

"STANDING ON PRINCIPLE"

Environmental justice was defined by Robert Bullard, director of the Environmental Justice Resource Center at Clark Atlanta University, in his seminal 1990 work *Dumping in Dixie: Race, Class, and Environmental Quality* as "the principle that all people and communities are entitled to equal protection of environmental and public health laws and regulations." In countries around the world, the concept of environmental justice can apply to communities where those at a perceived disadvantage—whether due to their race, ethnicity, socioeconomic status, immigration status, lack of land ownership, geographic isolation, formal education, occupational characteristics, political power, gender, or other characteristics—puts them at disproportionate risk for being exposed to environmental hazards. At a global scale, environmental justice can also be applied to scenarios such as industrialized countries exporting their wastes to developing nations.

In either case, "environmental and human rights have no boundaries, because pollution has no boundaries," says Heeten Kalan, director of the Global Environmental Health and Justice Fund of the New World Foundation in New York City. "Environmental justice organizations are starting to understand that they are working in a global context."

GLOBAL AWARENESS

The history of international efforts in environmental justice parallels the series of agreements and conventions held around the globe to

Excerpted from Luz Claudio, "Standing on Principle: The Global Push for Environmental Justice," *Environmental Health Perspectives* 115 (Oct. 2007): A501–A503, address environmental issues. Bullard recounts that during the 1992 Earth Summit in Rio de Janeiro, Brazil, there was not much official discussion about environmental justice in the context of human health. "Most of the official discussion centered around saving the Amazon and other ecosystems. Human health and urban centers were not considered part of the 'environment,'" he says.

However, Bullard and other U.S. environmental justice leaders had already met in Washington, DC, at the First National People of Color Environmental Leadership Summit a year earlier, where they drafted the Principles of Environmental Justice, a document to guide grassroots organizing. "When we went to Rio in 1992 we found that some groups had translated the Principles into Portuguese and were circulating the document to local community leaders at the summit," remembers Bullard.

Ten years later, during the World Summit on Sustainable Development held in Johannesburg, South Africa, the issue of environmental inequity was formally recognized by the leadership of the summit. "By the time we went to Johannesburg, environmental justice had really caught on across borders as part of the whole idea of sustainable development," says Bullard. Just two years earlier, the eight UN Millennium Development Goals that resulted from the UN Millennium Summit held in New York City had encompassed environmental sustainability as a goal that would require a reduction in inequality.

International organization around environmental justice issues takes several different forms. Broad networks of community-based organizations can work on different issues affecting the disenfranchised and come together on matters related to the environment. Other groups may organize a particular labor sector to improve worker health. On an international scale, community-based groups in different countries who find themselves fighting similar environmental problems can unite in order to synergize their efforts.

"The issue of globalization is one of common concern to the environmental justice movement in many developing countries," says

www.ncbi.nlm.nih.gov/pmc/articles/PMC2022674. Reproduced with permission from *Environmental Health Perspectives*.

Michelle DePass, program officer of the Environmental Justice and Healthy Communities Program at the Ford Foundation. Concerns about globalization can bring together a wide range of stakeholders including workers, academics, and community leaders for whom increased industrial development is a common denominator. . . .

GOING INTERNATIONAL

Upon interacting with each other, some organizations in the environmental justice movement across the globe are discovering that although each case has its own particular circumstances, there are many common experiences that can inform each other's struggles for environmental justice. For example, members of the Farmworker Association of Florida have been exchanging visits with citrus farmers in Brazil to trade ideas on how to address environmental justice issues. They found that some of their local circumstances were different, primarily the fact that in the United States most of the farmworkers are immigrants, whereas in Brazil they are mostly nationals. "This makes a huge difference since in Brazil [workers] have the right to unionize to seek better working conditions," says Tirso Moreno, general coordinator of the Farmworker Association of Florida.

Yet, during these exchanges, the workers from both countries discovered that they had been facing similar working conditions established by the same multinational agrobusiness companies. "Some of the information that we had [was of use to] the Brazilians and vice versa because many of these multinational companies are the same ones with different names," says Moreno. "That is why there is a lot more interest in collaborating internationally. While the details may be different in each country, the struggles are the same." . . .

The flow of information is highly bidirectional in the international environmental justice movement, providing models for both North-to-South as well as South-to-North exchange. For example, community-based organizations in the Philippines, where the government passed a national ban on incineration in 1999, are able to share with others around the world how they were able to achieve this in their country. And in Kenya, lawyers are required to train in environmental law through continuing education programs such as those managed by the

Institute for Law and Environmental Governance (ILEG). "In the United States, we can learn a lot from organizations like ILEG," says DePass, who is herself an environmental lawyer who will be leading a delegation of U.S. lawyers to visit ILEG for consultation on environmental justice strategies.

A COMMON CAUSE

Increasingly, due to globalization and the advance of multinational corporations, communities around the world find they are fighting the same battles. One such example began in Diamond, a black community in Norco, Louisiana, which is home to 130 petrochemical facilities, incinerators, and landfills in what is known by some as the Chemical Corridor and by others as Cancer Alley. There, a local school teacher named Margie Richard and other neighbors founded Concerned Citizens of Norco in 1990 and began demanding that Shell Corporation, the owner of the nearby petrochemical facilities, take responsibility for its pollution by relocating affected residents to a cleaner area.

To achieve this, the group engaged in highly visible campaigns at the state, national, and international levels, culminating with Richard's presentation in 2001 at the international headquarters of Royal/Dutch Shell in the Netherlands. Shell agreed to relocate those in the community who wished to leave the area and to reduce its emissions by 30%. This unprecedented victory won Richard the 2004 Goldman Environmental Prize (considered the Nobel Prize for environmental activism). With this increased visibility and recognition, Richard began traveling abroad to talk about the environmental justice movement and likening this experience to the wider issue of international human rights.

Communities in other parts of the world are now utilizing tactics similar to those used by Concerned Citizens of Norco. For example, Desmond D'Sa, a resident of South Durban, South Africa, and chairperson of the South Durban Community Environmental Alliance, has engaged the leadership of Shell Corporation directly to deal with environmental issues similar to those in Norco. Other communities in Texas, the Philippines, Nigeria, Brazil, Curaçao, and Russia have brought similar complaints to Shell's annual General Meetings. . . .

The global push for environmental justice can only be expected to grow—and the time for action is ripe. As Bullard summarizes, "if you live on the wrong side of the tracks and you are denied a good environment, then you need environmental justice. It is the same struggle everywhere."

"JEMEZ PRINCIPLES FOR DEMOCRATIC ORGANIZING," 1996

#1 BE INCLUSIVE

If we hope to achieve just societies that include all people in decision-making and assure that all people have an equitable share of the wealth and the work of this world, then we must work to build that kind of inclusiveness into our own movement in order to develop alternative policies and institutions to the treaties [and] policies under neoliberalism.

This requires more than tokenism, it cannot be achieved without diversity at the planning table, in staffing, and in coordination. It may delay achievement of other important goals, it will require discussion, hard work, patience, and advance planning. It may involve conflict, but through this conflict, we can learn better ways of working together. It's about building alternative institutions, movement building, and not compromising out in order to be accepted into the anti-globalization club.

#2 EMPHASIS ON BOTTOM-UP ORGANIZING

To succeed, it is important to reach out into new constituencies, and to reach within all levels of leadership and membership base of the orga-

Working Group Meeting on Globalization and Trade, "Jemez Principles for Democratic Organizing," hosted by Southwest Network for Environmental and Economic Justice, Jemez, New Mexico, December 1996, available online at www .ejnet.org/ej/jemez.pdf. Used with permission.

nizations that are already involved in our networks. We must be continually building and strengthening a base which provides our credibility, our strategies, mobilizations, leadership development, and the energy for the work we must do daily.

#3 LET PEOPLE SPEAK FOR THEMSELVES

We must be sure that relevant voices of people directly affected are heard. Ways must be provided for spokespersons to represent and be responsible to the affected constituencies. It is important for organizations to clarify their roles, and who they represent, and to assure accountability within our structures.

#4 WORK TOGETHER IN SOLIDARITY AND MUTUALITY

Groups working on similar issues with compatible visions should consciously act in solidarity, mutuality and support each other's work. In the long run, a more significant step is to incorporate the goals and values of other groups with your own work, in order to build strong relationships. For instance, in the long run, it is more important that labor unions and community economic development projects include the issue of environmental sustainability in their own strategies, rather than just lending support to the environmental organizations. So communications, strategies and resource sharing is critical, to help us see our connections and build on these.

#5 BUILD JUST RELATIONSHIPS AMONG OURSELVES

We need to treat each other with justice and respect, both on an individual and an organizational level, in this country and across borders. Defining and developing "just relationships" will be a process that won't happen overnight. It must include clarity about decision-making, sharing strategies, and resource distribution. There are clearly many skills necessary to succeed, and we need to determine the ways for those with different skills to coordinate and be accountable to one another.

#6 COMMITMENT TO SELF-TRANSFORMATION

As we change societies, we must change from operating on the mode of individualism to community-centeredness. We must "walk our talk." We must be the values that we say we're struggling for and we must be justice, be peace, be community.

"NAFTA'S BROKEN PROMISES," 1997

5. ENVIRONMENT

After the signing of the environmental side agreement, Administration officials claimed that NAFTA would lead to cleanup of serious
environmental problems along the U.S.-Mexico border and improved
environmental protection. In all three countries, NAFTA supporters
promised NAFTA would eliminate the incentive for factories to locate
in the Mexican border free trade zone where 2000 companies have
crowded without adequate facilities for treating toxic chemicals or
residential sewage. Instead, the work force of the maquila sector is up
60% in NAFTA's first three and one half years. Yet, none of the public
health and toxic waste problems that predated NAFTA have been significantly remedied, much less new environmental protection or
enforcement undertaken.

Public Citizen and its colleague Mexican citizen group, RMALC,
have thoroughly documented the deterioration of U.S.-Mexico border
environmental and health conditions under NAFTA in a January 1996
study. Conditions have deteriorated under NAFTA as documented by
specific, objective measures such as water quality, incidence of environ-
ment-related disease, toxic waste production and dumping rates.

On both sides of the border from Texas to California, tuberculosis
and hepatitis rates have continued to soar since NAFTA. Near Browns-
ville, Texas and Matamoros, Mexico, scores of babies have been born

---

Excerpted from "NAFTA's Broken Promises: The Cost to Texas of Our Failed
Experiment with NAFTA," Public Citizen Report (1997), www.citizen.org/naftas
-broken-promises-cost-texas-our-failed-experiment-nafta.

with deadly anencephaly, a defect resulting in an exposed or missing brain. Several new clusters of this tragic disease have started since NAFTA, including at Eagle Pass, Texas-Piedras Negras, Mexico. The world's highest rate of Lupus occurs in the Nogales, Arizona and Nogales, Sonora border area. Here factories producing and using toxic chemicals and solvents, and using unhealthy operations, such as lead smelters and glass factories that burn old tires as fuel, operate without environmental rules. Since NAFTA went into effect, rather than leaving the area, at least 150 new plants have opened. The Lupus rate in Nogales has continued to grow since NAFTA.

In a forthcoming report, Public Citizen further documents the failure of NAFTA's environmental institutions three and one half years into NAFTA. In sum, the NAFTA-created North American Development Bank [NADBank] has done little to further cleanup of the pre-NAFTA or post-NAFTA mess on the border. NADBank has not made a single actual loan in three and one half years of existence. It has only approved several million in loans or loan guarantees, with the most polluted towns unable to afford the Bank's market interest rates. If fully funded, the NADBank could provide $2 billion in loans. Yet in 1993, the Sierra Club had estimated that $20 billion would be necessary to fund essential border cleanup and infrastructure improvement. The North American Commission on Environmental Cooperation [CEC] has also done very little to improve enforcement of environmental law in the NAFTA countries. The CEC has not approved a single case requesting more than a factual review. Thus, not a single attempt to get this body to enforce environmental laws has been successful. Currently, the CEC is refusing to release a thorough report on NAFTA's impacts on the environment.

PART 3

THE ENVIRONMENT AND JUSTICE IN THE SUSTAINABILITY ERA

The environmental justice movement remained vibrant in the early twenty-first century. Grassroots coalitions continued to battle toxic exposure in minority neighborhoods, and the mainstream environmental movement became less exclusively white and more attuned to social justice. At the same time, EJ concerns gained some traction in environmental governance but fell short of the far-reaching transformations that advocates envisioned. In addition, as sustainability began to compete with environmentalism as a framework for thinking about environmental issues, the EJ movement built strong international networks and began to address environmental inequalities extending far beyond its earlier focus on landfills, incinerators, and exposure to toxins. A variety of new causes at the intersection of social justice issues and environmental issues began to attract sustained attention as well, including climate justice, food justice, and green-collar jobs.

INSTITUTIONAL LEGACIES

In contrast to the 1990s, which marked the increasing institutionalization of the EJ movement, much work in the first decade of the new century focused on translating those gains into new environmental decision-making structures. As the political winds began to blow in a new direction during George W. Bush's presidency, advocates worked to give affected communities a stronger voice and better tools to address their problems. In the first document, Richard Moore describes the efforts of the National Environmental Justice Advisory Council (NEJAC) to create structures and programs that would "lift up the voices of the grassroots" and prioritize "issues that people on the ground in our communities were facing." The second document, a memo from Christine Todd Whitman, appointed as EPA administrator after George W. Bush assumed office in 2001, signaled a shift in the EPA's emphasis. Rather than focusing special attention on those communities bearing the heaviest environmental burdens, Whitman signaled the EPA's intent to return to a more across-the-board approach to healthy environments, reminiscent of the EPA's emphasis on "environmental equity" during George H. W. Bush's administration.

The final five documents all reflect moments of self-assessment and regrouping as the movement matured. The first is a statement issued during the Second National People of Color Environmental Leadership Summit (Summit II), which convened in Washington, DC, in October 2002. These "Principles of Working Together" both identified and tried to find ways to resolve ongoing tensions between grassroots EJ groups and larger, better-resourced environmental organizations, especially as the latter attempted to embrace EJ work in a meaningful way. The second document, "Toxic Wastes and Race at Twenty," brought sophisticated analytical methods to bear on new data from the 2000 census, with the goal of assessing progress since the United Church of Christ's 1987 report. It found an even stronger spatial correlation between hazardous wastes and minority populations than the original report had found.

The third document, excerpted from a *High Country News* article, assesses the long-term impact of SWOP's 1990 letter to Group of Ten organizations by examining changes in the Sierra Club, one of the largest and best-known environmental organizations. In addition to gaining influence within mainstream environmental groups, EJ's fortunes also improved at the federal level during Barack Obama's presidency. The fourth document, an excerpt from "Plan EJ 2014" (2011), lays out the EPA's aggressive plan to incorporate EJ concerns into the full range of its operations. Yet aspirations did not always align with reality. The final document, for example, published by the Center for Public Integrity in 2015, charged the EPA with systematic failures to live up to the goals it had set for itself in "Plan EJ 2014."

RICHARD MOORE

"GOVERNMENT BY THE PEOPLE"

20 years ago, when I was appointed as one of the first members to the National Environmental Justice Advisory Council (NEJAC), I remember very clearly we decided that we wanted to make this a different type of government advisory council. The NEJAC was established by the EPA in order to obtain advice and recommendations from a diverse group of stakeholders involved in environmental justice. This was a big deal for the environmental justice community because it helped give legitimacy to the decades-long fight for the EJ movement. And so when the first board of the NEJAC convened we made a decision that we were going to make this advisory council truly representative of the people.

We wanted to lift up the voices of the grassroots, and make sure that the issues that were being addressed by the Council were the issues that people on the ground in our communities were facing. When we convened our first meetings, we made it clear to communities across the country that we were going to make sure that their voices would be heard. And sure enough, in those early meetings hundreds of concerned residents showed up to testify about the problems their communities were facing, and to hear what EPA and other Federal agencies were doing to address the disproportionate impacts that were happening across the country.

I remember the revelations that people had when they heard others from cities and towns far away talking about the same problems they were facing in their own backyards. It was transformative. The people

Richard Moore, "Government by the People: Looking Back at the NEJAC after 20 Years," *EPA Blog*, September 10, 2013, blog.epa.gov/blog/2013/09/government
-by-the-people-looking-back-at-the-nejac-after-20-years/.

in these meetings learned that the pollution in their neighborhoods wasn't an accident, it was happening everywhere and in some cases it was deliberate. More importantly, they also saw what types of solutions were being tested across the country to address these injustices.

From these public comments the Council also started forming recommendations to deal with the disproportionate pollution problems we were facing. We proposed to the EPA a grant program that specifically focused on providing financial support to benefit communities with environmental justice concerns. We also recommended EPA provide expert support to help give communities equal representation when controversial permits or government actions were being proposed. These recommendations were the foundations for the EJ Small Grants Program and the Technical Assistance Grants.

In 1995, the EPA and NEJAC cosponsored a series of dialogues across the country that provided an opportunity for environmental justice advocates and residents of impacted communities to give input on revitalization of abandoned properties called "brownfields." Out of these public dialogues, the NEJAC developed "The Search for Authentic Signs of Hope" report. A consistent theme throughout the report was the importance of seeking and including communities in decisions and planning. Taking these recommendations into consideration, EPA took a number of actions to improve its Brownfields program. For example, EPA agreed to create a Brownfields Job Training Grants Program, which now spends over $3 million annually in low income and minority communities.

When we first convened the NEJAC 20 years ago we didn't want to play by the rules. We wanted to make a new type of advisory council that would vigilantly fight for the rights of every resident to be heard by the government. Over the years the Council has elevated community concerns and made recommendations on many vitally important issues; from school air toxics monitoring and gulf coast restoration, to US/Mexico border issues and tribal consultation. Let's hope that the Council maintains that spirit, and continues to expand the conversation around environmentalism over the next 20 years.

CHRISTINE TODD WHITMAN

"MEMORANDUM," AUGUST 9, 2001

MEMORANDUM EPA MAIL

SUBJECT: EPA's Commitment to Environmental Justice

TO: Assistant Administrators
       General Counsel
       Inspector General
       Chief Financial Officer
       Associate Administrators
       Regional Administrators
       Office Directors

The Environmental Protection Agency has a firm commitment to the issue of environmental justice and its integration into all programs, policies, and activities, consistent with existing environmental laws and their implementing regulations.

The Agency defines environmental justice to mean the fair treatment of people of all races, cultures, and incomes with respect to the development, implementation, and enforcement of environmental laws and policies, and their meaningful involvement in the decision-making processes of the government. Among other things, this requires the following:

(a) Conducting our programs, policies, and activities that substantially affect human health and the environment in a manner that

---

Christine Todd Whitman, "Memorandum: EPA's Commitment to Environmental Justice," Environmental Protection Agency, August 9, 2001.

ensures the fair treatment of all people, including minority populations and/or low-income populations;

(b) Ensuring equal enforcement of protective environmental laws for all people, including minority populations and/or low-income populations;

(c) Ensuring greater public participation in the Agency's development and implementation of environmental regulations and policies; and

(d) Improving research and data collection for Agency programs relating to the health of, and the environment of all people, including minority populations and/or low-income populations.

In sum, environmental justice is the goal to be achieved for all communities and persons across this Nation. Environmental justice is achieved when everyone, regardless of race, culture, or income, enjoys the same degree of protection from environmental and health hazards and equal access to the decision-making process to have a healthy environment in which to live, learn, and work.

The purpose of this memorandum is to ensure your continued support and commitment in administering environmental laws and their implementing regulations to assure that environmental justice is, in fact, secured for all communities and persons. Environmental statutes provide many opportunities to address environmental risks and hazards in minority communities and/or low-income communities. Application of these existing statutory provisions is an important part of this Agency's effort to prevent those communities from being subject to disproportionately high and adverse impacts, and environmental effects.

In the National Environmental Policy Act of 1969 (NEPA), Congress could not have been any clearer when it stated that it shall be the continuing responsibility of the Federal government to assure for all Americans safe, healthful, productive and aesthetically and culturally pleasing surroundings.

Integration of environmental justice into the programs, policies, and activities via Headquarters/Regional Office Memoranda of Agreements and Regional Office/State Performance Partnership Agreements is an Agency priority. The Director of the Office of Environmental Justice, Barry E. Hill, and his staff are available to assist you. Barry Hill can be reached at (202) 564-2515.

I am positive that each of you will join me in working to secure environmental justice for all communities.

[signed]

Christine Todd Whitman

"PRINCIPLES OF WORKING TOGETHER," 2002

PREAMBLE

"WE, THE PEOPLE OF COLOR, gathered together at this multinational[, multiethnic] People of Color Environmental Leadership Summit, to begin to build a national and international movement of all peoples of color to fight the destruction and taking of our lands and communities, do hereby re-establish our spiritual interdependence to the sacredness of our Mother Earth; to respect and celebrate each of our cultures, languages and beliefs about the natural world and our roles in healing ourselves; to ensure environmental justice; to promote economic alternatives [and to support traditional cultural economics] which would contribute to the development of environmentally safe livelihoods; and, to secure our political, economic and cultural liberation that has been denied for over 500 years of colonization and oppression, resulting in the poisoning of our communities and [water, air,] land and the genocide of our peoples, to affirm and adopt these Principles of Environmental Justice."

Second People of Color Environmental Leadership Summit, "Principles of Working Together," October 26, 2002 (brackets in the original), available online at www.ejnet.org/ej/workingtogether.pdf.

First People of Color Leadership Summit
Principles of Environmental Justice
October 27, 1991

Principle One: Purpose

1.A.   The Principles of Working Together uphold the Principles of Environmental Justice . . . to eradicate environmental racism in our communities.

1.B.   The Principles of Working Together require local and regional empowered partnerships, inclusive of all.

1.C.   The Principles of Working Together call for continued influence on public policy to protect and sustain Mother Earth and our communities and also honor past promises and make amends for past injustices.

Principle Two: Core Values

2.A.   The Principles of Working Together commit us to working from the ground up, beginning with all grassroots workers, organizers and activists. We do not want to forget the struggle of the grassroots workers. This begins with all grassroots workers, organizers and activists.

2.B.   The Principles of Working Together recognize traditional knowledge and uphold the intellectual property rights of all peoples of color and Indigenous peoples.

2.C.   The Principles of Working Together reaffirm that as people of color we speak for ourselves. We have not chosen our struggle, we work together to overcome our common barriers, and resist our common foes.

2.D.   The Principles of Working Together bridge the gap among various levels of the movement through effective communication and strategic networking.

2.E.   The Principles of Working Together affirm the youth as full members in the environmental justice movement. As such, we commit resources to train and educate young people to sustain the groups and the movement into the future.

Principle Three: Building Relationships

3.A. The Principles of Working Together recognize that we need each other and we are stronger with each other. This Principle requires participation at every level without barriers and that the power of the movement is shared at every level.

3.B. The Principles of Working Together require members to cooperate with harmony, respect and trust—it must be genuine and sustained relationship-building. This demands cultural and language sensitivity.

3.C. The Principles of Working Together demand grassroots workers, organizers and activists set their own priorities when working with other professionals and institutions.

3.D. The Principles of Working Together recognize that community organizations have expertise and knowledge. Community organizations should seek out opportunities to work in partnerships with academic institutions, other grassroots organizations and environmental justice lawyers to build capacity through the resources of these entities.

Principle Four: Addressing Differences

4.A. The Principles of Working Together require affirmation of the value in diversity and the rejection of any form of racism, discrimination and oppression. To support each other completely, we must learn about our different cultural and political histories so that we can completely support each other in our movement inclusive of ages, classes, immigrants, indigenous peoples, undocumented workers, farm workers, genders, sexual orientations and education differences.

4.B. The Principles of Working Together require respect, cultural sensitivity, patience, time and a willingness to understand each other and a mutual sharing of knowledge.

4.C. The Principles of Working Together affirm the value in our diversity. If English is not the primary language, there must be effective translation for all participants.

Principle Five: Leadership

5.A. The Principles of Working Together demand shared power, community service, cooperation, and open and honest communication.

5.B. The Principles of Working Together demand that people from the outside should not come in and think that there is no leadership in the grassroots community. The people in the community should lead their own community and create legacy by teaching young people to be leaders.

5.C. The Principles of Working Together demand that people from grassroots organizations should lead the environmental justice movement.

5.D. The Principles of Working Together demand accountability to the people, responsibility to complete required work, maintain healthy partnerships with all groups.

Principle Six: Participation

6.A. The Principles of Working Together demand cultural sensitivity. This requires patience and time for each group to express their concerns and their concerns should be heard.

6.B. The Principles of Working Together require a culturally appropriate process.

6.C. The Principles of Working Together have a commitment to changing the process when the process is not meeting the needs of the people. The changes should be informed by the people's timely feedback and evaluation.

Principle Seven: Resolving Conflicts

7.A.   The Principles of Working Together encourage respectful discussion of our differences, willingness to understand, and the exploration of best possible solutions.

7.B.   The Principles of Working Together require that we learn and strengthen our cross-cultural communication skills so that we can develop effective and creative problem-solving skills. This Principle promotes respectful listening and dialogue.

7.C.   The Principles of Working Together affirm the value in learning strengthening mediation skills in diverse socio-economic and multicultural settings.

Principle Eight: Fundraising

8.A.   The Principles of Working Together recognize the need for expanding sustainable community based avenues for raising funds, such as building a donor base, membership dues, etc.

8.B.   The Principles of Working Together oppose funding from any organization impacting people of color and indigenous communities. In addition, the Principles oppose funding from any organization that is the current target of active boycotts, or other campaign activity generated by our allies.

8.C.   The Principles of Working Together encourage larger environmental justice organizations to help smaller, emerging environmental justice organizations gain access to funding resources. We encourage the sharing of funding resources and information with other organizations in need.

Principle Nine: Accountability

9.A.   The Principles of Working Together encourage all partners to abide by the shared agreements, including, but not limited to, oral and written agreements. Any changes or developments to agreements/actions need to be communicated to all who are affected and agreed upon.

9.B.   The Principles of Working Together encourage periodic evaluation and review of process to ensure accountability among all partners. Any violation of these agreements or any unprincipled actions that violate the EJ principles, either:

1. Must attempt to be resolved among the partners
2. Will end the partnership if not resolved AND
3. Will be raised to the larger EJ community

ROBERT D. BULLARD ET AL.

"TOXIC WASTES AND RACE AT TWENTY," 2007

EXECUTIVE SUMMARY

Introduction

In 1987, the United Church of Christ Commission for Racial Justice released its groundbreaking study *Toxic Wastes and Race in the United States*. The report was significant because it found race to be the most potent variable in predicting where commercial hazardous waste facilities were located in the U.S., more powerful than household income, the value of homes and the estimated amount of hazardous waste generated by industry.

This year, the United Church of Christ Justice and Witness Ministries commissioned a new report as part of the twentieth anniversary of the release of the 1987 report. The 2007 *Toxic Wastes and Race at Twenty* report uses 2000 census data. The report also chronicles important environmental justice milestones since 1987 and includes a collection of "impact" essays from environmental justice leaders on a range of topics. This new report also examines the environmental justice implications in post-Katrina New Orleans and uses the Dickson County (Tennessee) Landfill case, the "poster child" for environmental racism, to illustrate the deadly mix of waste and race.

226

Toxic Wastes and Race at Twenty is designed to facilitate renewed grassroots organizing and provide a catalyst for local, regional and national environmental justice public forums, discussion groups and policy changes in 2007 and beyond.

Approach

This new report includes the first national-level study to employ 2000 Census data and distance-based methods to a current database of commercial hazardous waste facilities to assess the extent of racial and socioeconomic disparities in facility locations in the U.S. Disparities are examined by region and state, and separate analyses are conducted for metropolitan areas, where most hazardous waste facilities are located.

Key Findings

The application of these new methods, which better determine where people live in relation to where hazardous sites are located, reveals that racial disparities in the distribution of hazardous wastes are greater than previously reported. In fact, these methods show that people of color make up the majority of those living in host neighborhoods within 3 kilometers (1.8 miles) of the nation's hazardous waste facilities. Racial and ethnic disparities are prevalent throughout the country.

National Disparities

More than nine million people (9,222,000) are estimated to live in circular host neighborhoods within 3 kilometers of the nation's 413 commercial hazardous waste facilities. More than 5.1 million people of color, including 2.5 million Hispanics or Latinos, 1.8 million African Americans, 616,000 Asians/Pacific Islanders and 62,000 Native Americans live in neighborhoods with one or more commercial hazardous waste facilities.

Host neighborhoods of commercial hazardous waste facilities are 56% people of color whereas non-host areas are 30% people of color. Percentages of African Americans, Hispanics/Latinos and Asians/ Pacific Islanders in host neighborhoods are 1.7, 2.3 and 1.8 times greater

(20% vs. 12%, 27% vs. 12%, and 6.7% vs. 3.6%), respectively. Poverty rates in the host neighborhoods are 1.5 times greater than non-host areas (18% vs. 12%)

Neighborhoods with Clustered Facilities

Neighborhoods with facilities clustered close together have higher percentages of people of color than those with non-clustered facilities (69% vs. 51%). Likewise, neighborhoods with clustered facilities have disproportionately high poverty rates. Because people of color and the poor are highly concentrated in neighborhoods with multiple facilities, they continue to be particularly vulnerable to the various negative impacts of hazardous waste facilities.

EPA Regional Disparities

Racial disparities for people of color as a whole exist in nine out of 10 U.S. EPA regions (all except Region 3). Disparities in people of color percentages between host neighborhoods and non-host areas are greatest in: Region 1, the Northeast (36% vs. 15%); Region 4, the southeast (54% vs. 30%); Region 5, the Midwest (53% vs. 19%); Region 6, the South, (63% vs. 42%); and Region 9, the southwest (80% vs. 49%). For Hispanics, African Americans and Asians/Pacific Islanders, statistically significant disparities exist in the majority or vast majority of EPA regions. The pattern of people of color being especially concentrated in areas where facilities are clustered is also geographically widespread throughout the country.

State Disparities

Forty of the 44 states (90%) with hazardous waste facilities have disproportionately high percentages of people of color in circular host neighborhoods within 3 kilometers of the facilities. States with the 10 largest differences in people of color percentages between host neighborhoods and non-host areas include (in descending order by the size of the differences): Michigan (66% vs. 19%), Nevada (79% vs. 33%), Kentucky (51% vs. 10%), Illinois (68% vs. 31%), Alabama (66% vs. 31%), Tennessee (54% vs. 20%), Washington (53% vs. 20%), Kansas (47% vs. 16%), Arkansas (52% vs. 21%) and California (81% vs. 51%). Thirty-five states have socioeconomic disparities, i.e., in poverty rates. In these states, the average poverty rate in host neighborhoods is 18% compared to 12% in non-host areas.

Metropolitan Disparities

In metropolitan areas, where four of every five hazardous waste facilities are located, people of color percentages in hazardous waste host neighborhoods are significantly greater than those in non-host areas (57% vs. 33%). Likewise, the nation's metropolitan areas show disparities in percentages of African Americans, Hispanics/Latinos and Asians/Pacific Islanders, 20% vs. 13%, 27% vs. 14% and 6.8% vs. 4.4%, respectively. Socioeconomic disparities exist between host neighborhoods and non-host areas, with poverty rates of 18% vs. 12%, respectively. One hundred and five of the 149 metropolitan areas with facilities (70%) have host neighborhoods with disproportionately high percentages of people of color, and 46 of these metro areas (31%) have majority people of color host neighborhoods.

Continuing Significance of Race

In 1987, Toxic Wastes and Race in the United States found race to be more important than socioeconomic status in predicting the location of the nation's commercial hazardous waste facilities. In 2007, our current study results show that race continues to be a significant and robust predictor of commercial hazardous waste facility locations when socioeconomic factors are taken into account.

Conclusions

Twenty years after the release of Toxic Wastes and Race, significant racial and socioeconomic disparities persist in the distribution of the nation's commercial hazardous waste facilities. Although the current assessment uses newer methods that better match where people and hazardous waste facilities are located, the conclusions are very much the same as they were in 1987.

Race matters. People of color and persons of low socioeconomic status are still disproportionately impacted and are particularly concentrated in neighborhoods and communities with the greatest number of facilities. Race continues to be an independent predictor of where hazardous wastes are located, and it is a stronger predictor than income, education and other socioeconomic indicators. People of color now comprise a majority in neighborhoods with commercial hazardous waste facilities, and much larger (more than two-thirds) majorities can be found in neighborhoods with clustered facilities. African Americans, Hispanics/ Latinos and Asian Americans/Pacific Islanders alike are disproportionately burdened by hazardous wastes in the U.S.

Place matters. People of color are particularly concentrated in neighborhoods and communities with the greatest number of hazardous waste facilities, a finding that directly parallels that of the original UCC report. This current appraisal also reveals that racial disparities are widespread throughout the country, whether one examines EPA regions, states or metropolitan areas, where the lion's share of facilities is located. Significant racial and socioeconomic disparities exist today despite the considerable societal attention to the problem noted in this report. These findings raise serious questions about the ability of current policies and institutions to adequately protect people of color and the poor from toxic threats.

Unequal protection places communities of color at special risk. Not only are people of color differentially impacted by toxic wastes and contamination, they can expect different responses from the government when it comes to remediation—as clearly seen in the two case studies in Post-Katrina New Orleans and in Dickson County, Tennessee. Thus, it does not appear that existing environmental, health and civil rights laws and local land use controls have been adequately applied or adapted to reducing health risks or mitigating various adverse impacts to families living in or near toxic "hot spots."

Polluting industries still follow the path of least resistance. For many industries it is a "race to the bottom," where land, labor and lives are cheap. It's about profits and the "bottom line." Environmental "sacrifice zones" are seen as the price of doing business. Vulnerable communities, populations and individuals often fall between the regulatory cracks. They are in many ways "invisible" communities. The environmental justice movement served to make these disenfranchised communities visible and vocal.

The current environmental protection apparatus is "broken" and needs to be "fixed." The current environmental protection system fails to provide equal protection to people of color and low-income communities. Various levels of government have been slow to respond to environmental health threats from toxic waste in communities of color. The mission of the United States Environmental Protection Agency (EPA) was never to address environmental policies and practices that result in unfair, unjust and inequitable outcomes. The impetus for change came from grassroots mobilization that views environmental protection as a basic right, not a privilege reserved for a few who can "vote with their feet" and escape from or fend off locally undesirable land uses—such as landfills, incinerators, chemical plants, refineries and other polluting facilities.

Slow government response to environmental contamination and toxic threats unnecessarily endangers the health of the most vulnerable populations in our society. Government officials have knowingly allowed people of color families near Superfund sites, other contaminated waste sites and polluting industrial facilities to be poisoned with lead, arsenic, dioxin, TCE, DDT, PCBs and a host of other deadly chemicals. Having the facts and failing to respond is explicitly discriminatory and tantamount to an immoral "human experiment."

Clearly, the environmental justice movement over the last two decades has made a difference in the lives of people of color and low-income communities that are overburdened with environmental pollution. After years of intense study, targeted research, public hearings, grassroots organizing, networking and movement building, environmental justice struggles have taken center stage. However, community leaders who have been on the front line for justice for decades know that the lethargic, and too often antagonistic, government response to environmental emergencies in their communities is not the exception but the general rule. They have come to understand that waiting for the government to respond can be hazardous to their health and the health of their communities.

In fact, the U.S. EPA, the governmental agency millions of Americans look to for protection, has mounted an all-out attack on environmental justice and environmental justice principles established in the early 1990s. Moreover, the agency has failed to implement the Environmental Justice Executive Order 12898 signed by President Bill Clinton in 1994 or adequately apply Title VI of the Civil Rights Act.

Recommendations

Many of the environmental injustice problems that disproportionately and adversely affect low-income and people of color communities could be eliminated if current environmental, health, housing, land use and civil rights laws were vigorously enforced in a nondiscriminatory way— without regard to race, color or national origin. Many of the environmental problems facing low-income persons and people of color are systemic and will require institutional change, including new legislation. We also recognize that government alone cannot solve these problems, but need the assistance of concerned individuals, groups and organizations from various walks of life. . . .

MARTY DURLIN

"THE SHOT HEARD ROUND THE WEST," 2010

THE SENDER: RICHARD MOORE CHALLENGES THE BIG GREENS

In March 1990, Richard Moore was the director of the SouthWest Organizing Project, a grassroots advocacy group in Albuquerque, N.M. Founded in 1980, SWOP spent the decade conducting voter-registration drives and organizing in neighborhoods contaminated by pollution.

The group had been remarkably successful in its efforts, and Moore was poised to make SWOP a household name, at least in the mainstream environmental community.

So Moore and his colleagues sent out what came to be known as the "SWOP letter." Signed by 100 cultural, arts, community and religious leaders—all people of color—and addressed to the directors of the Big 10 conservation groups, the letter charged the organizations with a history of "racist and exclusionary practices," a lack of in-house diversity, and an all-around failure to support environmental justice efforts.

"That letter caught everybody in the mainstream environmental movement off guard," says The Wilderness Society's president, Bill Meadows. "I'm not sure people knew how to respond. Diversity became a pretty serious issue in the green community—the letter raised the level of awareness and concern. . . . "

Excerpted from Marty Durlin, "The Shot Heard Round the West: What Resulted from Activists' 1990 Challenge to the Big Greens," *High Country News* (hcn.org), February 1, 2010.

ONE RECIPIENT'S REACTION: MICHAEL FISCHER
OF THE SIERRA CLUB TAKES THE LEAD

Sierra Club Director Michael Fischer was sitting in his office on the third story of a brick building in San Francisco's Tenderloin district the day the SWOP letter arrived.

"My initial reaction was irritation and resentment. . . . I'd never heard of Richard Moore—he'd never talked to me. Did I feel the charges against me were justified? Hell, no. But applicable to the Sierra Club, yes," says Fischer, who currently directs the San Francisco–based Consultative Group on Biological Diversity, which facilitates grants for environmental groups.

Fischer had been executive director of the Sierra Club for three years. He was committed to civil rights—he'd fasted with Cesar Chavez to protest the treatment of farmworkers, wearing Chavez's mother's wooden cross around his neck. He believed the environmental movement was flawed because it consisted almost exclusively of white middle-class Americans like himself, and he was trying to convince his reluctant board of directors to create grants for communities of color fighting toxic waste dumps and uranium mining. One Sierra Club board member—so upset at Fischer's efforts that he was "trembling"— had complained, "We're a conservation group, and you're trying to turn us into a social welfare organization!"

Once he moved past his initial reaction, Fischer realized that the SWOP letter had given him "a tool to fan the flame."

He attended the first People of Color Environmental Leadership Summit in 1991 in Washington, D.C.—a landmark gathering where activists created the 17 principles of environmental justice that underlie the movement. Fischer found himself one of the few "people of pallor" in a room full of 650 environmentalists. He'd never encountered that situation before, and he was excited and a bit stunned to see the level of commitment to the things he really cared about. . . .

At the Sierra Club's centennial in 1992—flanked by Native American activist Winona LaDuke and civil rights leader Chavis—Fischer called for a "friendly takeover" of the Sierra Club by people of color. The alternative, he said, was for the Club to "remain a middle-class group of backpackers, overwhelmingly white in membership, program and agenda—and thus condemned to losing influence in an increasingly multicultural country. . . . The struggle for environmental justice in this country and around the globe must be the primary goal of the Sierra Club during its second century. . . ."

TWENTY YEARS LATER: LESLIE FIELDS FINDS A CALLING IN ENVIRONMENTAL JUSTICE

"You have to decide to make the investment," says African-American attorney Leslie Fields, who directs the Sierra Club's environmental justice program, with an annual budget of about $1 million. Although other big greens have also changed the way they work, the Sierra Club is the only one with a substantial environmental justice staff. "We have done the most, I have to say," says Fields. "I wouldn't be here if I didn't believe that."

Fields came to environmental justice through her commitment to civil rights. After graduating from Georgetown Law School in Washington, D.C., and working for the National Association for the Advancement of Colored People for a few years, she moved to Texas to become a legislative counsel on environment, health and safety. In 1992, she spent a week researching the Texas Clean Air Act in order to fight a synthetic rubber plant across the street from an elementary school "filled with black and Latino kids. It was ghastly. The kids were sick, everyone's got an inhaler. . . . "

To learn more about environmental issues, she began attending the local chapter of the Sierra Club. She enjoyed the work—battling landfills, refineries, effluent in streams, lead and nuclear waste—and was eventually hired by the Texas Commission on Environmental Equity. Later, she worked for Friends of the Earth, where she fought Shell and Chevron from Nigeria to Ghana: "the same issues, the same companies bedeviling the same kinds of people."

In 2004, she got the job with the Sierra Club. Fields, who is also a law professor at Howard University, directs her staff from Washington, D.C. In Flagstaff—the only Western outpost—Andy Bessler and Robert Tohe work to preserve tribal sacred sites, protect water sources, halt further uranium mining and clean up its legacy. Meanwhile, in New Orleans, Darryl Malek-Wiley works on restoring wetlands, fighting illegal dumping, and cleaning up the 150 petrochemical facilities and refineries between Baton Rouge and New Orleans. Other offices are based in El Paso, Detroit, Memphis, Minneapolis, Charleston and Puerto Rico.

"Our prime directive is to work at the community's request. And these initiatives are created by the communities and the local Sierra Club chapters," Fields says.

But what if the community itself is divided? In September, the Hopi Tribal Council voted unanimously to (symbolically) ban the Sierra Club, the National Parks Conservation Association, the Natural Resources Defense Council and the Grand Canyon Trust from Hopi land. The council charged the groups with depriving the tribe of "markets for its coal resources" because of their role in shutting down the Mohave Generating Station, which purchased Black Mesa coal from the Hopi tribe. Navajo Nation President Joe Shirley Jr. followed suit. On the surface, it seemed like a classic example of a local community defying outside special interests. But in fact, many of the leaders of the anti-coal movement are themselves Hopi or Navajo, and have long accused the coal mines and power plants of environmental injustice.

It just shows "how tough these issues are," says Sierra Club staffer Bessler. "The Sierra Club doesn't tiptoe around the tough issues. People need to know the intricacies of the problems where there are no easy answers."

"When you work with communities, you can only support and inform, and get their voices heard in the decision-making process," says Tohe, a Navajo and longtime community organizer. "If you bring their voices to the table, that's the best thing you can do, and your time is well-spent."

The Sierra Club won a big EJ victory with the 2008 closing of the Asarco copper smelter in Texas, which released lead, arsenic and cadmium into El Paso and across the border into Juarez—a bi-national effort that took many people years to accomplish, says Fields. The Flagstaff EJ staff also worked hard on a proposal to create a green economy in Navajoland, approved by the tribal council in July of 2009.

Fields is building on the work of Robert Bullard, African-American author of the groundbreaking 1990 book on environmental justice, *Dumping in Dixie*. He and other scholars had to "invent our methodology along the way, showing this is not an isolated case about one community, this is institutional" as they created a body of scholarly work to measure environmental racism.

The Environmental Protection Agency—now headed by Lisa Jackson, an African-American—announced last summer that it would consider the disproportionate impact of hazardous waste recycling plants on people of color, a situation that has actually worsened over the past 20 years, according to a study by Bullard and others released by the United Church of Christ in 2007.

"Environmental justice is in the lexicon, but we're making it up as we go along," says Fields. "It's changing and you can be changing it. It's messy and unstructured, relentless and global. It's really a different animal from 20 years ago, but the systemic stuff remains. People have to get sued to change; that's part of the process."

ENVIRONMENTAL PROTECTION AGENCY

"PLAN EJ 2014," 2011

EXECUTIVE SUMMARY

In January 2010, Administrator Lisa P. Jackson made Expanding the Conversation on Environmentalism and Working for Environmental Justice an Agency priority. This priority was incorporated into the U.S. Environmental Protection Agency's (EPA) Strategic Plan for 2011–2015. To implement this priority, EPA developed Plan EJ 2014 as the Agency's roadmap for integrating environmental justice into its programs, policies, and activities. This priority recognizes that Title VI of the Civil Rights Act and EPA's civil rights program is a critical component in advancing environmental justice.

Plan EJ 2014, which is meant to mark the 20th anniversary of the signing of Executive Order 12898 on environmental justice, is EPA's overarching strategy for advancing environmental justice. It seeks to:

- Protect the environment and health in overburdened communities.
- Empower communities to take action to improve their health and environment.
- Establish partnerships with local, state, tribal, and federal governments and organizations to achieve healthy and sustainable communities.

From Environmental Protection Agency, "Plan EJ 2014" (Washington, DC: Environmental Protection Agency, September 2011.

In July 2010, EPA introduced Plan EJ 2014 as a concept for public comment and initiated the development of implementation plans. This product is the culmination of nearly a year's effort by EPA programs and regions, as well as engagement with stakeholders, to develop nine implementation plans with the goals, strategies, deliverables, and milestones outlined herein. Plan EJ 2014 has three major sections: Cross-Agency Focus Areas, Tools Development Areas, and Program Initiatives. The following summaries outline the implementation plans for Plan EJ 2014's five Cross-Agency Focus Areas and four Tools Development Areas.

Cross-Agency Focus Areas

Incorporating Environmental Justice into Rulemaking

GOAL

To more effectively protect human health and the environment for overburdened populations by developing and implementing guidance on incorporating environmental justice into EPA's rulemaking process.

STRATEGIES

1. Finalize the *Interim Guidance on Considering Environmental Justice During the Development of an Action.*
2. Facilitate and monitor implementation of guidance on incorporating environmental justice into rulemaking.
3. Develop technical guidance on how to conduct environmental justice assessments of rulemaking activities.

Considering Environmental Justice in Permitting

GOAL

To enable overburdened communities to have full and meaningful access to the permitting process and to develop permits that address environmental justice issues to the greatest extent practicable under existing environmental laws.

STRATEGIES

1. Develop tools that will enhance the ability of overburdened communities to participate fully and meaningfully in the permitting process.

2. Concurrent with Strategy 1, develop tools to assist permitting authorities to meaningfully address environmental justice in permitting decisions.
3. Implement these tools at EPA and work with others to do the same.

Advancing Environmental Justice through Compliance and Enforcement

GOAL
To fully integrate consideration of environmental justice concerns into the planning and implementation of the Office of Enforcement and Compliance Assurance's (OECA) program strategies, case targeting strategies, and development of remedies in enforcement actions to benefit overburdened communities.

STRATEGIES
1. Advance environmental justice goals through selection and implementation of National Enforcement Initiatives.
2. Advance environmental justice goals through targeting and development of compliance and enforcement actions.
3. Enhance use of enforcement and compliance tools to advance environmental justice goals in regional geographic initiatives to address the needs of overburdened communities.
4. Seek appropriate remedies in enforcement actions to benefit overburdened communities and address environmental justice concerns.
5. Enhance communication with affected communities and the public regarding environmental justice concerns and the distribution and benefits of enforcement actions, as appropriate.

Supporting Community-Based Action Programs

GOAL
To strengthen community-based programs to engage overburdened communities and build partnerships that promote healthy, sustainable, and green communities.

STRATEGIES
1. Advance environmental justice principles by building strong state and tribal partnerships through the National Environmental Per-

formance Partnership System (NEPPS) and the National Program Manager (NPM) guidance.

2. Identify scalable and replicable elements of successful Agency community-based programs and align multiple EPA programs to more fully address the needs of overburdened communities.

3. Promote an integrated One EPA presence to better engage communities in the Agency's work to protect human health and the environment.

4. Foster community-based programs modeled on the Community Action for a Renewed Environment (CARE) principles.

5. Explore how EPA funding, policies, and programs can inform or help decision makers to maximize benefits and minimize adverse impacts when considering current land uses in decision making, planning, siting, and permitting.

6. Promote equitable development opportunities for all communities.

Fostering Administration-Wide Action on Environmental Justice

GOAL

To facilitate the active involvement of all federal agencies in implementing Executive Order 12898 by minimizing and mitigating disproportionate, negative impacts while fostering environmental, public health, and economic benefits for overburdened communities.

STRATEGIES

1. Assist other federal agencies in integrating environmental justice in their programs, policies, and activities.

2. Work with other federal agencies to strengthen use of interagency legal tools, i.e., National Environmental Policy Act and Title VI of the Civil Rights Act of 1964.

3. Foster healthy and sustainable communities, with an emphasis on equitable development and place-based initiatives.

4. Strengthen community access to federal agencies.

Tools Development Areas

Science

GOAL

To substantially support and conduct research that employs participatory principles and integrates social and physical sciences aimed at understanding and illuminating solutions to environmental and health inequalities among overburdened populations and communities in the United States. All Agency decisions will make use of the information, data, and analytic tools produced.

STRATEGIES

1. Apply integrated transdisciplinary and community-based participatory research approaches with a focus on addressing multi-media, cumulative impacts and equity in environmental health and environmental conditions.

2. Incorporate perspectives from community-based organizations and community leaders into EPA research agendas and engage in collaborative partnerships with them on science and research to address environmental justice.

3. Leverage partnerships with other federal agencies on issues of research, policy, and action to address health disparities.

4. Build and strengthen the technical capacity of Agency scientists on conducting research and related science activities in partnership with impacted communities and translating research results to inform change.

5. Build and strengthen technical capacity of community-based organizations and community environmental justice and health leaders to address environmental health disparities and environmental sustainability issues.

Law

GOAL

To provide legal assistance to EPA policy makers and other Agency decision makers to advance their environmental justice objectives.

Provide legal support to each Plan EJ 2014 cross-Agency Focus Area workgroup.

Information

GOAL

To develop a more integrated, comprehensive, efficient, and nationally consistent approach for collecting, maintaining, and using geospatial information relevant to potentially overburdened communities.

STRATEGIES

1. Develop EPA's GeoPlatform.
2. Develop a nationally consistent environmental justice screening tool.
3. Incorporate appropriate elements of the environmental justice screening tool into the GeoPlatform.

Resources

GRANTS AND TECHNICAL ASSISTANCE GOAL

To develop an efficient and effective system for delivering financial and technical assistance to communities to empower them to improve their health and environment.

STRATEGIES

1. Increase transparency and efficiency in providing community-based grant opportunities.
2. Improve delivery of technical assistance to communities.
3. Strengthen grants training for communities.
4. Improve community awareness of grant competition process.
5. Revise grant policies that are unduly restrictive.
6. Encourage legal and program offices to dialog on community-based grant opportunities.
7. Improve timeliness of Brownfields Grant Awards.

WORKFORCE DIVERSITY GOAL

To achieve an inclusive work environment by developing an efficient system for the outreach and recruitment of potential employees.

1. Increase the diverse pool of qualified applicants.
2. Operate under an integrated One EPA approach for recruitment and outreach.

Program Initiatives

Program Initiatives will focus on specific EPA programs. Many existing EPA programs actively pursue environmental justice goals or produce benefits for overburdened communities. Examples of such initiatives include: Community Engagement Initiative (Office of Solid Waste and Emergency Response), Urban Waters (Office of Water), National Enforcement Initiatives (Office of Enforcement and Compliance Assurance), Air Toxics Rules (Office of Air and Radiation), and the U.S. Mexico Border Program (Office of International and Tribal Affairs). Over the next year, EPA will designate at least one initiative per appropriate program for inclusion in Plan EJ 2014. In this way, many existing EPA initiatives can be tailored to better integrate environmental justice and produce greater benefits for overburdened communities.

Civil Rights

One effort already under way is implementing Administrator Jackson's priority to improve EPA's civil rights program. Complying with EPA's statutory civil rights obligations is a critical part of our efforts to advance environmental justice. Administrator Jackson has made improving EPA's civil rights program a priority. As part of this effort, EPA is pursuing long overdue, vigorous, robust, and effective implementation of Title VI of the Civil Rights Act of 1964 and other nondiscrimination statutes. EPA is committed to protecting people from discrimination based on race, color, or national origin in programs or activities that receive EPA's financial assistance.

Conclusion

Through Plan EJ 2014, EPA intends to develop a suite of tools to integrate environmental justice and civil rights into its programs, policies, and activities. It seeks to build stronger relationships with communities overburdened by environmental and health hazards and build partnerships that improve conditions in such communities. In 2014, EPA will make an assessment of its progress in achieving the goals of Plan EJ 2014. Based on this assessment, EPA will produce a report on the accomplishments, lessons learned, challenges, and next steps for continuing the Agency's efforts to make environmental justice an integral part of every decision.

KRISTEN LOMBARDI, TALIA BUFORD, AND RONNIE GREENE

"ENVIRONMENTAL JUSTICE, DENIED," 2015

The invasion of sewer flies moved residents of University Place subdivision to turn to the U.S. Environmental Protection Agency for help.
Darting from a neighboring sewage plant, the flies descended upon the
mostly African-American neighborhood in Baton Rouge, Louisiana,
with such regularity that one resident posted this warning sign: *Beware
of attack fly.*

In 2009, residents grew so sickened by the flies, odors and pollution
emanating from the city's North Wastewater Treatment Plant that they
sought out the federal agency that has touted the importance of tackling environmental racism.

"The citizens of University Place Subdivision are still suffering
through the dreadful, unhealthy, and downright shameful conditions
forced upon this community," wrote Gregory Mitchell, whose mother,
Mamie, erected that attack-fly warning atop her home, in a complaint
filed with the EPA's Office of Civil Rights.

A little-known niche within the EPA, the civil-rights office has one
mission: to ensure agencies that get EPA funding—like the city of Baton
Rouge—not act in a discriminatory manner. The mandate comes from
Title VI of the federal Civil Rights Act of 1964, a sweeping law prohibiting racial discrimination by those receiving federal financial assistance.
Experts say the provision presents a significant legal tool for combating
environmental injustice.

Excerpted from Kristen Lombardi, Talia Buford, and Ronnie Greene, "Environmental Justice, Denied: Environmental Racism Persists, and the EPA Is One
Reason Why," Center for Public Integrity, August 3, 2015, www.publicintegrity
.org/2015/08/03/17668/environmental-racism-persists-and-epa-one-reason-why.

Time and again, however, communities of color living in the shadows of sewage plants, incinerators, steel mills, landfills and other industrial facilities across the country—from Baton Rouge to Syracuse, Phoenix to Chapel Hill—have found their claims denied by the EPAs civil-rights office, an investigation by the Center for Public Integrity and NBC News shows. In its 22-year history of processing environmental discrimination complaints, the office has never once made a formal finding of a Title VI violation.

Months after receiving the Baton Rouge community's Title VI complaint, the office rejected it. Investigators declined to examine the claim that the city had violated the civil rights of black property owners around the North plant, citing a pending lawsuit filed by residents against the city.

In 2010, Mitchell and neighbors again turned to the EPA and, again, the agency said no. Settling their lawsuit later that year, the residents logged a third complaint charging the city had discriminated against them. This time, the EPA rejected it on another technicality—it was "not timely."

By 2012, they had returned to the EPA a fourth time, only to get a fourth rejection. Few communities have been rebuffed more than Baton Rouge. The distinction has left residents like Mitchell feeling as though regulators "say something to blow you off and just forget about it."

"Under the EPA's civil-rights division," he said, "nothing is done."

A PATTERN OF REJECTION

The Baton Rouge case is extreme but not unique. The Center filed a Freedom of Information Act request seeking every Title VI complaint submitted to the office, and every resolution of those complaints, since the mid-1990s. The agency produced records representing most of the complaints handled in that time, but not all. The records, consisting of thousands of pages of documents, cover 265 Title VI cases and stretch from 1996 to mid-2013.

The records reveal a striking pattern: More than nine of every 10 times communities have turned to it for help, the civil-rights office has either rejected or dismissed their Title VI complaints. In the majority, the office rejected claims without pursuing investigations. On the few occasions that it did, it dismissed cases more often than it proposed sanctions or remedies. Records show the office has failed to execute its authority to investigate claims even when it has reason to believe discrimination could be occurring, such as in Baton Rouge.

Of the cases reviewed by the Center, the EPA:

- Rejected 162 without investigation;
- Dismissed 52 upon investigation;
- Referred 14 to other agencies, including the departments of Justice, Health and Human Services and Transportation;
- Resolved 12 with voluntary or informal agreements;
- Accepted 13 for investigations that remain open today, the oldest begun in 1996. . . .

Asked about this record, the EPA did not dispute the Center's findings. Instead, the head of the EPA's civil-rights office, Velveta Golightly-Howell, declined to discuss cases prior to her tenure, which began in February 2014. In a half-hour telephone interview with the Center and NBC News, she stressed that the EPA is committed to "making a visible difference in communities," and is "making a lot of strides" to improve its Title VI enforcement.

"It is important to note that 'finding a formal Title VI violation' is not the ultimate objective as [a] civil rights office," Golightly-Howell said in a written response to follow-up questions. "The most important objective is to bring about prompt and effective resolution of cases in order to address discrimination issues as quickly and thoroughly as possible."

She acknowledged that "there have been some problems in the past" processing Title VI complaints.

"We cannot focus on the past because there's nothing we can do about it," she said. "We can, however . . . focus on the present and the future, and that's what we're doing."

To advocates, the EPA's pattern of denials, delays and dismissals speaks louder than the agency's words—from not only Golightly-Howell, but also Administrator Gina McCarthy, who in March gave the keynote address at a national conference on environmental justice, in Washington, D.C. Throughout her 20-minute speech, the administrator touted how the agency has promoted environmental justice in disadvantaged communities across the country. Not once did she mention the agency's civil-rights office.

Listening to McCarthy's speech, Richard Moore, an advocate from New Mexico, said, "You have to put the proof in the pudding. At the end of the day, we see no major activity taking place through [the agency's] Office of Civil Rights."

SEARING CRITIQUES

The dysfunction has been well known to EPA officials for years. Auditors and advocates alike have criticized the agency's civil-rights office for such systemic failures as compiling a lengthy backlog, having an opaque complaint process and misconstruing a key legal standard. In the past decade, reviewers, internal and external, have offered critiques.

One of the most damning was a 2011 Deloitte Consulting report that concluded the office "has not adequately adjudicated Title VI complaints."

The EPA moved slowly to process complaints, Deloitte found. "Only 6% of the 247 Title VI complaints [reviewed by Deloitte] have been accepted or dismissed within the Agency 20-day time limit," the audit stated. The backlog of cases stretched back a decade, to 2001.

The report depicted an office in turmoil. Managers had little ability to track employee performance. Record keeping was spotty. The civil-rights program took few steps to tap into EPA's larger resources, and connect with state environmental agencies—a lack of outreach that left it operating in an insular fashion.

The result: An office that appeared more ceremonial than meaningful, with communities left in the lurch.

Since Golightly-Howell joined the office last year, she said, the focus has been on "creating a robust and revitalized civil rights enforcement program."

In the years following the Deloitte audit, the office has taken steps to address its findings—tackling its massive backlog, for instance, and issuing two agency-wide orders to create what she called a "model" civil rights program. . . .

For communities, the changes have meant little.

That has been true, for example, for residents of the Rogers Road–Eubanks Road neighborhood, in Chapel Hill, North Carolina, whose case has been stuck in the EPA's Title VI complaint pipeline for eight years now.

The historically African-American neighborhood is the site of an expansive county solid-waste landfill and transfer station collecting auto parts, biological waste, transformers—"you name it," said Robert Lee Campbell, of the Rogers-Eubanks Neighborhood Association. In 2007, the association filed a Title VI complaint alleging that local government agencies discriminated against the adjacent black property owners, first siting the landfill there, and then not providing such basic amenities as water and sewer services. It followed up with a 2011 addendum of allegations to bolster its case.

It took nearly a year for residents to hear from the EPA's civil-rights office, which in 2008 and again in 2011 requested more information. Over the years, Campbell recalled his association and its lawyers sending the agency 12 two-pound boxes of documentation. They fielded occasional phone calls from an ever-rotating roster of agency investigators.

"We were always getting, 'We're still looking into the complaint,'" said Campbell, who has lived 2,500 feet from the dump site since the 1970s. "Not a whole lot about what they were going to do to help us."

By 2013, the EPA had denied some of the residents' claims on procedural grounds, but not all. The agency accepted the amended complaint for investigation almost a year after the county, responding to residents' decades-old political activism, shuttered the landfill. In its place the county has installed trash-disposal operations handling yard debris and electronics waste, along with a recycling center.

Today, the case is languishing on the agency's current list of 17 open investigations.

"We have no idea what's happening," said Mark Dorosin, of the University of North Carolina's Center for Civil Rights, which has handled the complaint. "It's been very frustrating."

CONTINUING EJ ACTIVISM

Traditional EJ battles against the unequal exposure of poor and minority populations to toxics and other environmental burdens continued during the Obama presidency. The first two documents are photos from California's San Joaquin Valley, part of the highly productive agricultural area of California known as the Central Valley. The valley contains one of the poorest populations in the United States, as well as a significant number of environmental health problems tied to industrial agricultural production. The first image was taken in Buttonwillow, a working-class Latino community that hosts one of the state's three toxic waste dumps. It captures a scene that appears frequently in EJ struggles: a playground in a so-called fence-line community, located immediately next to facilities that pose an environmental threat. The second image, of an activist's T-shirt, is part of a campaign against the unusually high rates of childhood asthma afflicting children in the San Joaquin Valley.

The final three documents originate in two high-profile EJ battles that received sustained press coverage during the Obama presidency: protests over an oil pipeline project in Standing Rock, North Dakota, and a public health crisis caused by lead-contaminated water in Flint, Michigan. The first document, a meme that circulated on the internet during struggles over the Dakota Access Pipeline (DAPL) project in 2016, questions the integrity of a siting process that appeared to heed the objections of white residents while ignoring those of Native Americans. The second document is excerpted from a transcript of a reporter's live coverage of DAPL protests on Labor Day weekend 2016, during which private security guards working for the pipeline company used pepper spray and attack dogs to disperse protesters. The final document, Brian Bienkowski's essay in *Environmental Health News*, ponders the lessons of Flint and Standing Rock in light of the EJ movement's successes, and alongside the growing tendency among contemporary environmentalists to embrace social justice issues.

TRACY PERKINS

BUTTONWILLOW PARK, CA, JANUARY 30, 2009

Tracy Perkins, *Buttonwillow Park*, CA, January 30, 2009, from Voices from the Valley, accessed June 8, 2017, www.voicesfromthevalley.org/photos/#23.

TRACY PERKINS

WASCO, CA, JANUARY 30, 2009

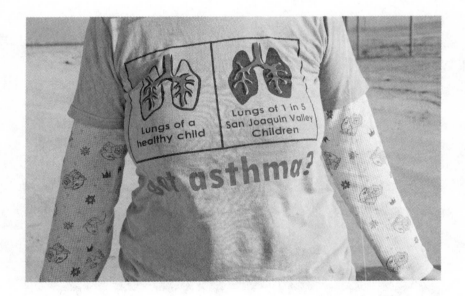

Tracy Perkins, *Wasco, CA, January 30, 2009*, from *Voices from the Valley*, accessed
June 8, 2017, www.voicesfromthevalley.org/photos/#17.

Reminder that DAPL was re-routed through Standing Rock because Bismarck's residents feared it could poison their drinking water.

The Sioux are literally being forced at gunpoint to accept ecological risks that North Dakota's white residents refused.

Author unknown, online meme on #NoDAPL, 2016.

AMY GOODMAN

"UNLICENSED #DAPL GUARDS ATTACKED WATER PROTECTORS WITH DOGS & PEPPER SPRAY," 2016

AMY GOODMAN: Many across the United States are celebrating this Thanksgiving holiday. But many Native Americans observe it as a National Day of Mourning, marking the genocide against their communities and the theft of their land. We'll spend today looking at the standoff at Standing Rock in North Dakota, the struggle against the $3.8 billion Dakota Access pipeline that's galvanized the largest resistance movement of Native Americans in decades. . . .

We begin with our report [from] Labor Day weekend. It was Saturday, September 3rd, when unlicensed Dakota Access security guards attacked water protectors trying to defend a sacred tribal burial site from destruction. . . .

People have gone through the fence—men, women and children. The bulldozers are still going. And they're yelling at the men in hard hats. One man in a hard hat threw one of the protesters down. And they're marching over the dirt mounds. Some of the security have dogs.

The six bulldozers are pulling back right now. People are marching forward in their tracks. There are men, women and children. More security trucks are pulling up. There are some protesters on

Excerpted from Amy Goodman, "Standing Rock Special: Unlicensed #DAPL Guards Attacked Water Protectors with Dogs & Pepper Spray," *Democracy Now!*, November 24, 2016, www.democracynow.org/2016/11/24/standing_rock_special_unlicensed_dapl_guards. Used with permission horseback. Hundreds of people are coming from the main camp. They're climbing up the tracks left by the bulldozers—six, at least, I've counted, that are now receding.

Protesters advance as far as a small wooden bridge. Security unleashes one of the dogs, which attacks two of the Native Americans' horses.

Security has some kind of gas. People are being pepper-sprayed.

WATER PROTECTORS: We are not leaving! We are not leaving! We are not leaving! We are not leaving! We are not leaving! We are not leaving! We are not leaving! We are not leaving! We are not leaving!

AMY GOODMAN: Sir, [I'm a] reporter from New York. What are you spraying people with?

SECURITY MAN: I didn't spray anything, ma'am.

AMY GOODMAN: But what is that?

WATER PROTECTOR 7: This guy just maced me in the face right now. Amy Goodman, this guy maced me in the face. . . . Look, it's all over my sunglasses. Just maced me in the face. Dog bit him right now.

VICTOR PUERTAS: Throwed the dog on me. This [bleep] throwed the dog on me. Look at this. Look at this. You throwed the dog on me. No, you did it on purpose, man.

AMY GOODMAN: Let me see. Let me see.

VICTOR PUERTAS: Over there, with that dog. I was like walking. Throwed the dog on me and straight, even without any warning. You know? Look at this. Look at this.

AMY GOODMAN: That dog bit you?

VICTOR PUERTAS: Yeah, the dog did it, you know? Look at this. It's there. It's all bleeding.

AMY GOODMAN: Ma'am, your dog just bit this protester. Your dog just bit that protester. Are you telling the dogs to bite the protesters?

WATER PROTECTOR 8: She keeps siccing them after people.

AMY GOODMAN: The dog has blood in its nose and its mouth.

WATER PROTECTOR 8: And she's still standing here threatening us. . . .

AMY GOODMAN: Why are you letting their—her dog go after the protesters? It's covered in blood!

WATER PROTECTOR 11: Stop!

AMY GOODMAN: One of the pipeline's security men unleashes a dog into the crowd. . . .

AMY GOODMAN: After the protesters said that the dog was bloody from biting them, they then pulled the dogs away, and now pickup truck by pickup truck is pulling away. We'll see what happens. The protesters are moving in to ensure that the security leaves. Let's go check on this woman. What happened?

REYNA CROW: Just a lot of mace, and the sweat was dripping it into— it was—the sweat was making it run down into my eyes. I had my glasses on, and that spared me the brunt of it, but then the sweat started putting it in.

AMY GOODMAN: How are you doing?

REYNA CROW: I'm great!

AMY GOODMAN: What's your name?

REYNA CROW: Reyna Crow.

AMY GOODMAN: And what do you think you've accomplished today?

REYNA CROW: I hope we've accomplished letting Enbridge know that the people of this nation and the people of this world, tribal or otherwise, have withdrawn their social license to pollute water, and that they need to find an honest, nonviolent way to make a living. . . .

AMY GOODMAN: Do you feel like you won today?

WATER PROTECTOR 19: We win every day when we stand in unity. We stand, and we fight.

BRIAN BIENKOWSKI

"2017 AND BEYOND: JUSTICE JUMPING GENRES," *ENVIRONMENTAL HEALTH NEWS*

There I was in a mid-March snowstorm riding shotgun in a truck heading south through the Crow reservation in Montana. I made a stupid comment to break the silence: "Man, there is nothing out there."

Crow member and my guide for the day, Emery Three Irons, politely corrected me: "There's a lot out there."

I saw an empty vastness. Three Irons saw a landscape of history and culture, and all of the splendor and pain attached to both.

Reviewing the year's news, I was reminded of this. With partisan publications, herd journalism and narrow-minded newsfeeds, it's easy to miss big, important developments on environmental issues—both good and bad.

Let's avoid being like me in the foothills of the Pryor Mountains. Survey the landscape. Avoid the urge to break the silence until there's something worth saying.

The most poignant stories of solution and struggle in 2016 were from those who too often shoulder the largest share of environmental harm—poor and minority communities.

It started with lead poisoning and government failure in Flint—a story that's still unfolding.

Flint prompted journalists from across the country to take a look at lead poisoning and water in their own communities—it turns out Flint is everywhere. St. Louis. East Chicago. Baltimore.

Brian Bienkowski, "2017 and Beyond: Justice Jumping Genres," *Environmental Health News*, December 28, 2016, www.environmentalhealthnews.org/ehs/news /2016/dec/environmental-justice-in-review-standing-rock-flint-trump-energy -justice.

Poor, often minority, communities are still poisoned by a toxic directly linked to criminal behavior and reduced IQs.

While Flint—a majority-black city that never regained its footing after the recession—is text book environmental injustice, the problematic intersection of pollution, poverty and people of color can be much more complex and multi-faceted.

Food insecurity and toxics are combining to hamper development in poor children. Drought is crushing small farmers in developing countries, the food source and economic backbone of their communities. Fossil fuel reliance continues to touch every aspect of our lives: the health of our lungs and farms, the stability of our economy and international relations.

But there are Native Americans camping in snow, bucking development on sacred land by exercising sovereignty, however ill defined it may be. Communities are pushing for—and building—small-scale, resilient energy systems, connecting people to their power in new and exciting ways.

People are providing healthy, necessary amounts of food to those in need, taking aim at waste, and seeking agriculture done without corporate stranglehold.

Activists tackling racial, criminal and labor injustice realize that dirty air, tainted water and poverty cannot be disentangled from economic and political marginalization.

Every day we at Environmental Health News and The Daily Climate compile the day's top environmental health and climate change news (and distribute it via free daily and weekly newsletters . . .).

We fill blanks in coverage with reporting of our own. Our small team aggregates around the clock, aggregating almost 30,000 stories this year alone.

We found more than 2,200 stories this year dealing with climate and environmental justice. While not an exhaustive collection of every environmental story, this represents a doubling of such stories from a year prior.

For 2017, experts say, expect the push for environmental justice to center more around the issue's intersections with racial, economic and environmental equality.

Campaigns for all three overlapped this year: As our economy stratified more starkly into haves and have-nots—and often ignores pollution and health costs in the name of progress—we've seen calls to restructure.

"Our failure to address environmental justice crosses many boundaries," said Sylvia Hood Washington, an environmental epidemiologist and editor of the *Environmental Justice* journal.

"Movements are merging and addressing multiple issues," she said. "Safe housing, police brutality, violence against children, inadequate housing, exposure to substances that cause learning disability. . . . All of these issues are important and must embrace environmental health science."

We began to see this in 2016. The Sierra Club came out in strong support of the Fight for Fifteen movement, a protest for low wage workers to make $15-an-hour. "Low wage jobs are some of the most environmentally hazardous jobs there are, especially when workers lack union representation. We need livable wages because we can't break a glass ceiling we can't reach," wrote Aaron Mair, president of the Sierra Club's board of directors.

Groups such as National People's Action have made clean energy a key point of their agenda, which aims for a more just economy. The New Economy Coalition and Our Power Campaign are pushing clean energy and other green jobs in conjunction with job training and opportunities for people to live healthy, both physically and financially.

As Trump takes office and fills key cabinet posts with mostly men who disavow climate science and promote fossil fuel development, it's worth noting this movement is coming from the ground up.

Even the large environmental organizations aren't driving the agenda, said Susan Casey-Lefkowitz, chief program officer with the Natural Resources Defense Council.

"We're seeing a harkening back to an early time, fighting for environmental rights, not just in the hands of environmental organizations, but every community that cares about air and water and health," said Casey-Lefkowitz.

David Pellow, a professor of environmental studies at University of California, Santa Barbara, said the Black Lives Matter movement is a great example: "They haven't necessarily passed laws but they've changed the conversation."

The Movement for Black Lives, which includes more than 50 groups including Black Lives Matter, released a platform in August that called for divestment from fossil fuels within a broader demand to address disproportionate criminalization and incarceration.

The report also called for cleaning pollution in black neighborhoods as part of a path toward economic justice, and bolstering the financial support for black farmers.

A major reason for such a bright spotlight on environmental justice issues this year was Sen. Bernie Sanders' presidential run, which included an entire platform on environmental justice—something rarely mentioned in presidential politics.

"These injustices are largely the product of political marginalization and institutional racism. The less political power a community of color possesses, the more likely they are to experience insidious environmental and human health threats," read Sanders' racial justice outline, which called for a clean energy transition, bolstered Superfund cleanups and more stringent permitting of polluting industries.

SACRED WATER, STANDING ROCK AND SOVEREIGNTY

The Standing Rock Sioux's opposition to the Dakota Access pipeline perfectly embodied the intersection of civil rights, human rights, and the environment, while also adding to the conversation important questions of indigenous sovereignty, Pellow said.

"People are really seeing and connecting what's happening with Native communities and the rest of planet," he said. "These are not just Native or oil pipeline issues. It affects us all."

Kyle Powys Whyte, Timnick Chair in the Humanities at Michigan State University and a member of the Citizen Potawatomi Nation in Shawnee, Oklahoma, said the way Standing Rock happened was crucial to the attention it grabbed and ultimate success.

"It's an important idea, not just the protest that we can succeed at, but how we design protest," he said. Standing Rock camps became functional communities, with people supporting each other with food, water, prayer. The Standing Rock and ally tribes insisted that they were not protestors but water protectors.

Standing Rock is the visible tip of a tribal justice movement focused on race, political representation and the management of natural resources.

I saw much of this firsthand. For our yearlong series, Sacred Water, I visited reservations where tribes are fighting for clean water. While touring the Crow Reservation with Three Irons, I saw multiple streams and rivers tainted with bacteria and heavy metals, exacerbating tribal health problems and economic woes.

Along the Puget Sound, which has dwindling salmon populations due to development, pollution and climate change, tribes are fighting to bring back the cultural icon for traditional ceremonies and spiritual well-being, but also for financial security. Commercial fishing is suffering badly.

In Michigan's Upper Peninsula, a proposed open-pit mine threatens the cultural headwaters of the Menominee Indians of Wisconsin. Ancient burial mounds sit nearby and the river is the center of their creation story.

Similar to Standing Rock, the call for environmental justice for the Menominee is based on a feeling of political marginalization and a system that doesn't take into account tribal values.

"Putting a mine on this location is just the same as if they were to put an open pit sulfide mine in the Garden of Eden for the Christians. Imagine what they would say when asking them to describe how it feels to see this mine polluting their sacred area," wrote Menominee Guy Reiter in an essay for our series.

This issue of sovereignty—which has long been a moving target—will continue to play out over the coming year. "We understand sovereignty as a way of life: autonomy, independence and community cohesion," Whyte said. "The U.S. government often understands sovereignty in a much more limited sense."

The highly visible fight over the Standing Rock pipeline has transformed the justice conversation in the U.S. and thrust Native Americans and grassroots organizing back into the mainstream consciousness. It worked in North Dakota: The Obama Administration rejected a crucial permit last month needed to complete the Dakota Access pipeline and gave, for now, a victory for the Standing Rock Sioux and allied tribes who have camped for months.

Rev. Fletcher Harper, executive director of GreenFaith, a faith-based organization focused on environmental stewardship, said it is "truly the best of times, worst of times" for environmental justice.

That Standing Rock victory? That's the "best" part, Harper said. The other side, of course, is president-elect Donald Trump.

"The Trump Administration has already sent signals that it may further privatize indigenous lands for resource extraction," Whyte said. "We might be in for four to eight years of fighting for the bare right just to be consulted."

OPPOSE—AND BUILD

Speak to those concerned about environmental justice [under] President-elect Donald Trump and there's bound to be silence, sighs, swearing or all of the above.

Trump's campaign was filled with racially charged rhetoric and calls to double down on polluting fossil fuels. He's mentioned wanting to exit the Paris Climate Agreement and has denied the existence of man-made climate change. His Cabinet is a who's who of climate change deniers and fossil fuel friends.

Perhaps most concerning is the unknown of a Trump Environmental Protection Agency. If his pick to run the agency, Oklahoma Attorney General Scott Pruitt, is any indication it will be a sharp departure from what has been an increasing recognition of and focus on environmental justice.

This year the EPA released a report outlining their environmental justice [goals] through 2020. "By 2020, we envision an EPA that integrates environmental justice into everything we do," said the report, which laid out three major goals—improving the health and environment of overburdened communities, expanding partnerships within those communities, and showing documented progress on disparities in lead exposure, drinking water, air quality and proximity to hazardous waste sites.

Pruitt is a climate change skeptic and has shown disdain for the very agency he will head, taking part in a multi-state lawsuit against the EPA over proposed regulations to curb the potent greenhouse gas methane from oil and gas operations. It remains to be seen what he makes of the environmental justice initiatives at the agency.

Optimism and opportunity remain and the refrain is consistent: the movement will have to thrive at the local, county and state level. "I think a lot of [environmental justice] organizations will get stronger as more people realize they can't sit on their hands," said J. Timmons Roberts, a professor of environmental studies and sociology at Brown University.

States have long been leaders on progressive environmental justice policies, Roberts said. In his home state of Rhode Island, for example, the 2014 Resilient Rhode Island Act seeks to mitigate climate change impacts while also looking for ways to boost the economy and lift up low-income residents.

California this year extended its cap and trade program, tilting the revenue spending toward urban, poor communities. Gov. Jerry Brown has made no secret that he's willing to spar with Trump when it comes to the environment.

"We have a lot of firepower! We've got the scientists. We've got the universities. We have the national labs. We have a lot of political clout and sophistication for the battle. And we will persevere!" Gov. Brown said in a fiery speech at the annual meeting of the American Geophysical Union last month.

Such progressiveness in spite of federal action or inaction could be vital during the Trump tenure, Pellow said.

"We need to stop imagining the EPA or federal government will be the source of solutions for environmental justice," Pellow said.

Part of the local approach means moving beyond simple opposition—protesting a polluting power plant, for example—and building local resiliency, such as energy cooperatives, land trusts, urban gardens, Pellow added.

"We need to be building something positive, not just opposing something bad."

FROM ENVIRONMENTAL JUSTICE TO JUSTICE AND THE ENVIRONMENT

The documents in this section illustrate some of the ways—new and old—that activists have blended social justice concerns with environmental ones in the twenty-first century. The first document, "Bali Principles of Climate Justice," frames climate change not only as a scientific reality, but also as an environmental justice issue with significant human rights implications. Drafted by a coalition of groups in 2002 using the "Principles of Environmental Justice" as a model, the coalition announced its adoption of the principles at the Rio+10 Earth Summit in Johannesburg, South Africa, setting the stage for the expansion of activism around climate justice. The second document is a blog post and poem by Kathy Jetñil-Kijiner, a poet, spoken word artist, and climate justice activist who was selected to speak on behalf of civil society during the opening ceremony of the 2014 United Nations Climate Leaders Summit in New York City. As a resident of the Marshall Islands, where significant environmental justice issues related to U.S. nuclear weapons testing in the 1940s and 1950s have now been compounded by the threat of flooding from climate change, Jetñil-Kijiner speaks to key themes, such as women's leadership, toxic exposure, and a destabilized climate. But she also insists on giving these issues a human face, showing how those who face the greatest risks of climate change nevertheless continue to live lives dominated by everyday concerns, activities, and aspirations.

The third document, which summarizes a scholarly study of how African Americans use public parks, discusses some of the ways that the legacies of segregation, racism, and limited access continue to shape patterns of use. The fourth document, an interview with the activist LaDonna Redmond, discusses the rise of "food justice" concerns as a distinct area of activism at the intersection of environmental and social justice issues. The fifth document, Van Jones's keynote address at the Power Shift summit in 2009, was delivered to some 12,000 participants, half of whom participated in the largest citizen lobby day in the nation's history. Speaking less than a month before President Obama appointed him as the Special Advisor for Green Jobs, Enterprise and Innovation to the White House's Council on Environmental Quality, Jones, the author of *The Green Collar Economy* (2008), argued that the United States needed to "build a green economy strong enough to lift people out of poverty."

In the final document, the prominent EJ leader Tom Goldtooth, the executive director of the Indigenous Environmental Network, reflects on the quarter century of activism since the first People of Color Environmental Leadership Summit in 1991. In a wide-ranging interview, he notes ongoing patterns of environmental racism, the successful formation of international EJ alliances, and the growing importance of climate justice as an EJ issue. He also reflects on the ways that EJ activism has transformed environmental activism more broadly. "Looking back," he says, "our Indigenous Peoples and people-of-color within the environmental and economic justice movement have put soul into the environmental movement."

"BALI PRINCIPLES OF CLIMATE JUSTICE," AUGUST 29, 2002

PREAMBLE

Whereas climate change is a scientific reality whose effects are already being felt around the world;

Whereas if consumption of fossil fuels, deforestation and other ecological devastation continues at current rates, it is certain that climate change will result in increased temperatures, sea level rise, changes in agricultural patterns, increased frequency and magnitude of "natural" disasters such as floods, droughts, loss of biodiversity, intense storms and epidemics;

Whereas deforestation contributes to climate change, while having a negative impact on a broad array of local communities;

Whereas communities and the environment feel the impacts of the fossil fuel economy at every stage of its life cycle, from exploration to production to refining to distribution to consumption to disposal of waste;

Whereas climate change and its associated impacts are a global manifestation of this local chain of impacts;

Whereas fossil fuel production and consumption helps drive corporate-led globalization;

Whereas climate change is being caused primarily by industrialized nations and transnational corporations;

"Bali Principles of Climate Justice," August 29, 2002, available from *Corps Watch*, www.corpwatch.org/article.php?id=3748.

Whereas the multilateral development banks, transnational corporations and Northern governments, particularly the United States, have compromised the democratic nature of the United Nations as it attempts to address the problem;

Whereas the perpetration of climate change violates the Universal Declaration on Human Rights, and the United Nations Convention on Genocide;

Whereas the impacts of climate change are disproportionately felt by small island states, women, youth, coastal peoples, local communities, indigenous peoples, fisherfolk, poor people and the elderly;

Whereas local communities, affected people and indigenous peoples have been kept out of the global processes to address climate change;

Whereas market-based mechanisms and technological "fixes" currently being promoted by transnational corporations are false solutions and are exacerbating the problem;

Whereas unsustainable production and consumption practices are at the root of this and other global environmental problems;

Whereas this unsustainable consumption exists primarily in the North, but also among elites within the South;

Whereas the impacts will be most devastating to the vast majority of the people in the South, as well as the "South" within the North;

Whereas the impacts of climate change threaten food sovereignty and the security of livelihoods of natural resource-based local economies;

Whereas the impacts of climate change threaten the health of communities around the world—especially those who are vulnerable and marginalized, in particular children and elderly people;

Whereas combating climate change must entail profound shifts from unsustainable production, consumption and lifestyles, with industrialized countries taking the lead;

WE, representatives of people's movements together with activist organizations working for social and environmental justice resolve to begin to build an international movement of all peoples for Climate Justice based on the following core principles:

1.   Affirming the sacredness of Mother Earth, ecological unity and the interdependence of all species, Climate Justice insists that

communities have the right to be free from climate change, its related impacts and other forms of ecological destruction.

2. Climate Justice affirms the need to reduce with an aim to eliminate the production of greenhouse gases and associated local pollutants.

3. Climate Justice affirms the rights of indigenous peoples and affected communities to represent and speak for themselves.

4. Climate Justice affirms that governments are responsible for addressing climate change in a manner that is both democratically accountable to their people and in accordance with the principle of common but differentiated responsibilities.

5. Climate Justice demands that communities, particularly affected communities play a leading role in national and international processes to address climate change.

6. Climate Justice opposes the role of transnational corporations in shaping unsustainable production and consumption patterns and lifestyles, as well as their role in unduly influencing national and international decision-making.

7. Climate Justice calls for the recognition of a principle of ecological debt that industrialized governments and transnational corporations owe the rest of the world as a result of their appropriation of the planet's capacity to absorb greenhouse gases.

8. Affirming the principle of ecological debt, Climate Justice demands that fossil fuel and extractive industries be held strictly liable for all past and current life-cycle impacts relating to the production of greenhouse gases and associated local pollutants.

9. Affirming the principle of Ecological debt, Climate Justice protects the rights of victims of climate change and associated injustices to receive full compensation, restoration, and reparation for loss of land, livelihood and other damages.

10. Climate Justice calls for a moratorium on all new fossil fuel exploration and exploitation; a moratorium on the construction of new nuclear power plants; the phase out of the use of nuclear power world wide; and a moratorium on the construction of large hydro schemes.

11. Climate Justice calls for clean, renewable, locally controlled and low-impact energy resources in the interest of a sustainable planet for all living things.

12. Climate Justice affirms the right of all people, including the poor, women, rural and indigenous peoples, to have access to affordable and sustainable energy.

13. Climate Justice affirms that any market-based or technological solution to climate change, such as carbon-trading and carbon sequestration, should be subject to principles of democratic accountability, ecological sustainability and social justice.

14. Climate Justice affirms the right of all workers employed in extractive, fossil fuel and other greenhouse-gas producing industries to a safe and healthy work environment without being forced to choose between an unsafe livelihood based on unsustainable production and unemployment.

15. Climate Justice affirms the need for solutions to climate change that do not externalize costs to the environment and communities, and are in line with the principles of a just transition.

16. Climate Justice is committed to preventing the extinction of cultures and biodiversity due to climate change and its associated impacts.

17. Climate Justice affirms the need for socio-economic models that safeguard the fundamental rights to clean air, land, water, food and healthy ecosystems.

18. Climate Justice affirms the rights of communities dependent on natural resources for their livelihood and cultures to own and manage the same in a sustainable manner, and is opposed to the commodification of nature and its resources.

19. Climate Justice demands that public policy be based on mutual respect and justice for all peoples, free from any form of discrimination or bias.

20. Climate Justice recognizes the right to self-determination of Indigenous Peoples, and their right to control their lands, including sub-surface land, territories and resources and the right to the protection against any action or conduct that may result in the destruction or degradation of their territories and cultural way of life.

21. Climate Justice affirms the right of indigenous peoples and local communities to participate effectively at every level of decision-making, including needs assessment, planning, implementation,

enforcement and evaluation, the strict enforcement of principles of prior informed consent, and the right to say "No."

22. Climate Justice affirms the need for solutions that address women's rights.

23. Climate Justice affirms the right of youth as equal partners in the movement to address climate change and its associated impacts.

24. Climate Justice opposes military action, occupation, repression and exploitation of lands, water, oceans, peoples and cultures, and other life forms, especially as it relates to the fossil fuel industry's role in this respect.

25. Climate Justice calls for the education of present and future generations, emphasizes climate, energy, social and environmental issues, while basing itself on real-life experiences and an appreciation of diverse cultural perspectives.

26. Climate Justice requires that we, as individuals and communities, make personal and consumer choices to consume as little of Mother Earth's resources, conserve our need for energy; and make the conscious decision to challenge and reprioritize our lifestyles, re-thinking our ethics with relation to the environment and the Mother Earth; while utilizing clean, renewable, low-impact energy; and ensuring the health of the natural world for present and future generations.

27. Climate Justice affirms the rights of unborn generations to natural resources, a stable climate and a healthy planet.

Adopted using the "Environmental Justice Principles" developed at the 1991 People of Color Environmental Justice Leadership Summit, Washington, DC, as a blueprint.

Endorsed by:
CorpWatch, US
Friends of the Earth International
Greenpeace International
groundwork, South Africa
Indigenous Environmental Network, North America
Indigenous Information Network, Kenya

National Alliance of People's Movements, India
National Fishworkers Forum, India
OilWatch Africa
OilWatch International
Southwest Network for Environmental and Economic Justice, US
Third World Network, Malaysia
World Rainforest Movement, Uruguay

KATHY JETÑIL-KIJINER

"RISING SEA LEVELS," 2016

Here in the Marshall Islands, International Women's Day immediately follows a national holiday. On March 1, Nuclear Victims Remembrance Day commemorates the legacy of US nuclear testing on our islands. As these two events collide, I find myself wrestling with connections between gender, international power, nuclear legacies, climate change, and lost land.

From 1946 to 1968, 67 nuclear weapons were detonated, which is the equivalent of 1.7 Hiroshima bombs being exploded daily for 12 years in terms of radiation exposure. Just the Bravo shot alone, a 15-megaton hydrogen bomb, was 1,000 times more powerful than the atomic bomb that was dropped on Hiroshima.

Women disproportionately bear the burden of the trauma their society has been exposed to—in this case, they bear the burden of a nuclear legacy. It was women who found themselves with birth defects after exposure to the radiation and fallout. "Jellyfish babies" is what they call them. Tiny beings with no bones.

Limeyo Abon is a Marshallese elder and nuclear survivor who spoke at the ceremony this past Tuesday. She was only 14 years old when the Bravo shot was detonated. The fallout from the Bravo shot rained on her home island of Rongelap. She thought it was snow. In her speech, she stated that the only thing she'll be able to pass on to her children is sickness and a rootless existence. Since the day radiated ash fell on her island, she has been exiled from her island.

Kathy Jetñil-Kijiner, "Rising Sea Levels: 'Our Islands Will One Day Be Wiped Off the Map: What Will Happen to Our Women?'" *The Elders* blog, March 7, 2016, theelders.org/article/rising-sea-levels-our-islands-will-one-day-be-wiped -map-what-will-happen-our-women. Used with permission.

I have been passionately advocating against climate change because of my deep sense of fear that our islands will one day be wiped off the map, due to the rising sea levels. But I never realized that we, some of us more than others, have already known the pain of lost homelands. Three islands have been literally vaporized because of the power of the bombs. Bikini and Rongelap atoll are forever lost to our people because of high levels of radiation. This is a loss we've had to bear "for a greater good"—a reasoning that is very similar to those who are convinced that our need for consumption outweighs the livelihoods of others.

This is all the more devastating when you consider the impacts that loss of land could have on women's already struggling statuses here in the Marshalls. Our culture is among the few around the world that is still matrilineal. Our mothers bestow land rights and chiefly titles. We believe that it is through our mothers that we receive power.

But what will happen to that power if there is no land to pass down?

In regards to the possible loss of our islands, I've asked myself many times—what will happen to our culture? It is only today that I ask—what will happen to our women?

As a November 2015 report from U.N. Women read, "No policy response to climate change is gender neutral." This makes me think of two women.

The first is a woman I met while running errands. She was fundraising with her sisters by the side of the road, selling plates of barbeque chicken for two dollars. The funds go towards their family's sea wall—a wall that most Marshallese people have along the lagoon and ocean side to prevent the tide from destroying their house. Their sea wall had been destroyed during the last flooding from high tides. It wasn't her husband who organized, cooked, packed, and stood by the side of the road for hours selling those plates—it was her and her sisters.

The second is my cousin. I've just received a text message from her inviting me over to a house warming ceremony tomorrow. The construction of her family's new house is finally done. Her old home, the one she'd lived in all her life with her family, was also destroyed during the last king tides. Her family has spent the past two years moving from place to place, taking out loans, and navigating new sources of family tension. This tension would, more often than not, explode onto my cousin. As the eldest daughter, she bears the burden of responsibility.

In both cases, it was the women rebuilding a new life. And so it would be with our work in climate change. The policies from the Paris agreement will not be successful without proper engagement of women—without structures set in place specifically to support women. But what does this look like? I'm not sure. I only know that it's a path we need to begin walking down—the sooner the better. Our women lived and survived through the nuclear testing, and we will weather the storms of climate change as well, if given the proper support.

I'd like to close with a poem I wrote about my cousin after she lost her home. It celebrates her resilience—a viewpoint rarely seen when discussing monumental issues such as these. As we've seen with the horrific experience of "jellyfish babies," sometimes, women give birth to the traumas they've experienced. And sometimes, if given support (and even sometimes without it) they give birth to a new life, to fresh possibilities. For this International Women's Day, I celebrate the resilience and strength of our Marshallese women.

THERE'S A JOURNALIST HERE

there's a journalist here
who wants to interview you
they want to hear
about your old old house
older than you
its cracked plywood walls
like dry, sunburnt skin
how it collapsed
like a lung
as the water rushed in
they want to hear
about your journal
how you awoke
to soggy pages—ink
staining the floor
staining your hands
they want to hear
about the glass shards

from your window
how they carved
jagged pathways
along your stepmother's leg

they want to hear
how you blame yourself
the way the neighbors
blamed you
women
shouldn't stare
at the ocean
too long
they said
it was your
boldness
that dared it to come

that's
what they want to hear

they don't want to hear
that maybe
you're imagining
a house
with new doors
new windows
on a grassy hillside
they don't want to hear
that, weeks later
you found your breath
filling and expanding your lungs
that all you want now
is to move
forward

BRENTIN MOCK

"FOR AFRICAN AMERICANS, PARK ACCESS IS ABOUT MORE THAN JUST PROXIMITY," 2016

A new study shows that the legacy of racial discrimination still looms heavily.

The Trust for Public Land has just released its annual scores and rankings on city parks across the U.S., as Laura Bliss reports. These scores claim to evaluate what the trust considers the "three important characteristics of an effective park system: acreage, facilities and investment, and access."

While this assessment is supposed to be the gold standard for determining park quality, its criteria is severely undermined by its failure to consider the legacy of racism in the U.S. park system. This holds especially true when looking at access, which the TPL defines as "the percentage of the population living within a 10-minute (half-mile) walk of a public park."

This is a limited definition, to say the least. We know from the many failed instances of desegregation in the U.S. that mere proximity or an open-door/floor plan doesn't necessarily mean equal access for all. It certainly hasn't meant that for African Americans and parks, as University of Missouri scholar KangJae Lee recently discovered. In Lee's study, published June 1 in the journal *Leisure Sciences*, he attempts to answer a long-unresolved question: How come black people don't go to the park? Or, put better: What keeps black people away from parks?

Excerpted from Brentin Mock, "For African Americans, Park Access Is about More Than Just Proximity," *CityLab*, June 2, 2016, www.citylab.com/design/2016/06/for-african-americans-park-access-is-about-more-than-just-proximity/485321.

. . . The people he interviewed were of varying ages and income levels. Each provided differing perspectives on why they didn't frequent Cedar Hill State Park, and even on why they felt that black people don't go to parks in general.

Risty*, a city government worker in his thirties spoke in the report of the racism black people encounter at the park:

It is very prevalent. I witnessed or experienced it throughout my whole professional life since I began working in the field of parks and recreation. . . . I can give you a perfect example. I've been on the June-teenth committee for two years here. . . . We have a really nice park over here that has an amphitheater that seats about 2,000 people, so we decided to have a free concert, for the community, kind of celebra-tion. . . . We planned for about 1,800 people, but we ended up having 6,800. Yeah, so that was the best Juneteenth celebration we ever had in the four cities [around CHSP]. It was [an] unbelievable success. Well, we were awarded a national award through the NRPA [National Recreation and Park Association] . . . when it was the time to go and receive the award . . . not one African American was on the trip. . . . Yeah, it was all White Americans. So, to the African American employees, that's like, you know, a slap in the face.

Jennifer*, also a city government worker, in her mid-fifties said:

They don't really say anything to encourage us to come. All we hear is that some groups went, if we hear that any people of color went there, nothing positive that they say about it, so we stay away from there. . . . My kids who go everywhere . . . haven't had a desire [to visit the park] . . . they just don't go. They make it sound like it's not for us. People talk about it, but they talk about it like it's their [whites'] place that they go.

Sam*, a former city government employee, in his late fifties and "very familiar with the history of the community" said:

Years ago, we couldn't stay at hotels. You couldn't go to the diners. You have to go around. Negros only, Whites only. So it has to, you are right [about the origin of recreation culture] . . . it has the root, right? So where you might have Caucasians, they can go anywhere they wanna go and enjoy whatever they wanna enjoy, Negros couldn't. . . . That culture was, well, it was embedded in us, all right? Maybe that's all we thought we can do. And we feel, well, say stay home, right? So we don't have to deal with it [racism].

And here's Susan, a graduate student in her late twenties, bringing it back to the issue of access and how racism distorts that concept:

We have to talk about access when we talk about the history of leisure, because there was no access to it [outdoor recreation], so how do you expect me [to] appreciate these things if my parents didn't appreciate it, my parents' parents couldn't appreciate it? . . . So I feel like it's, it's gotten passed down [from] generation to generation to where, "Oh, no we just don't do these things. We just don't. We don't go camping. That's just not what we do." It's something that settled in the Black community, but [a long time ago] it was like, "We can't do that."

What Lee learned from listening to black people share their lived experiences was that the threat of or the real presence of racism marred their ability to have an enjoyable park experience. Lee also found that the Cedar Hill park has failed to produce culturally relevant attractions for black people. . . .

The responsibility of creating a fair and just starting point falls largely on park authorities. But it's a non-starter to talk about "access" without respecting the concerns that Slaughter raises. Today's segregated spaces and activities are the direct result of a certain kind of place-based conditioning: Black people constantly being told—often through violence—that the price of admission to certain places is your dignity, and possibly your life. There can be no scoring or discussion of park access without park authorities compensating for that conditioning.

*NOTE: Lee used pseudonyms for his interviewees in the study.

NORMA SMITH OLSON

"FOOD JUSTICE," 2013

When LaDonna Redmond couldn't find an organic tomato within 10 minutes of her home in her Chicago neighborhood, she decided to become an urban farmer. Her urban garden led to a grass-roots movement of citywide—and then national—conversations about food justice. It is her quest to see that every citizen has a right to food. She now lives in Minneapolis and is the founder of a new organization (Campaign for Food Justice Now) to be a one-stop shop for individuals and organizations working on issues of food justice.

What sparked your concern about our food systems?

I became interested and concerned about food justice issues when my son developed food allergies to shellfish, dairy products and peanuts at an early age. I realized that the right kinds of food for him were not readily available to me in my neighborhood—non-GMO [genetically modified organism], foods that were fresh and free from his allergens.

At the time, I lived on the West Side of Chicago. My husband and I started urban farming in our backyard and it grew from getting vacant lots to developing urban farm sites and selling food at farmers markets. That was the beginning of my work of rebuilding local food systems, first around my neighborhood and now around the country.

Norma Smith Olson, "Food Justice: For LaDonna Redmond, This Is the Civil Rights Issue of the 21st Century," *Minnesota Women's Press*, June 2013, www.womens press.com/main.asp?Search=1&ArticleID=4318&SectionID=1&SubSectionID= 20&S=1. Brackets in the original.

What does "food awareness" mean to you?

It's about knowing where your food comes from, knowing who grew the food, under what conditions and to what degree those products are healthy for the land.

Is it healthy for your body and healthy for the planet? Is it healthy for the people who are enslaved by the food system, people who are forced to work for pennies so that we can have tomatoes, when they cannot afford to buy those same tomatoes? Knowing just a little more about food might slow some people down when they are eating highly processed foods.

How do you define "food justice"?

I define food justice as the activity to shift the injustice in the food and agriculture systems. Filling the gap, for example, in worker rights, making sure that the workers are treated fairly; making sure that all communities have access to healthy food; and if people want to grow food, making sure that they have access to land and materials or capital necessary to grow it. Also, to have seeds that are free from genetic engineering and land that is not contaminated by pesticides and other chemicals.

I think everyone has a right to eat. We should have a system that protects people from being hungry. But instead of just feeding hungry people, how do we get food to everyone? This would really mean pushing against corporate control of our food system.

Food justice means we talk about the things that help people get food, for example, raising the minimum wage would help people have food; making sure our immigration policies are fair to those harvesting our food; making sure that women with children have child care so that they can work. "Food justice" links all of these different issues.

Talk more about your work, what you're envisioning.

The issue of food is political at a corporate level but not at the consumer level. We need consumers to be educated to know when their legislators are not supporting the right to food. When legislators are not supporting SNAP benefits [also known as food stamps] or if they are supporting genetically modified foods, we need to call people's attention to that and help them make a decision to support candidates who support the right to food.

When you look at Wal-Mart being the largest purveyor of groceries in the United States . . . Why don't we have the diversity in our food corporations that we are asking for in our food? Particularly in agriculture, we know that mono crops are not good. So mono crops and mono corporations? There should not be one corporation that is dominating any field. We need to diversify and bust corporate control of our food system.

What is the role of women in the food justice movement?

Women who have had children have an intimate relationship. We are the first food through breast feeding—being food for someone else. Often moms are the ones who do the cooking and are the protectors of the nutritional value in the home. I think that is a really important voice, underrepresented in the movement.

I call myself the "urban food goddess" and I want to capture the voices of women, politicize them about the food that is available in our communities.

You've talked about dreaming bigger. What does that mean to you?

Dreaming bigger means that we can have a healthy, fair and just food system all at the same time. Instead of just trying to have more organic food or give more food to hungry people, why don't we dream of a world where we don't have hungry people, where we don't have poverty? We've compartmentalized the work on food systems—one group of people working on organic foods, other people working on closing factory farms. What we really want is a fair, just and healthy food system. For me, one of the absolutes is that we've got to get rid of hunger. We should not have hungry people.

VAN JONES

"POWER SHIFT KEYNOTE," 2009

Greening this economy is not just a technological challenge or a political challenge or a legislative challenge or a business challenge, it's a moral challenge. . . . [W]e have to create a green economy that Dr. King would be proud of. We have to create a green economy that includes everybody, that has a place in it for everybody. That's why we say "Green for All." And you have the ability and the power to do that. But the challenge is: will you settle for eco-apartheid? The challenge is: will you settle for green for some? I don't believe that your generation will do that. . . .

Now if we are going to have a movement that includes everybody, we've got to really include everybody. Let me tell you what that means. That means this movement has to also include the coal miners. The coal miners. They are people, too. They are people, too! And they have to be included. . . . [O]ur sisters and brothers who go into those coal mines every day, who risk their health, who risk their lungs, who are now being asked to blow up their grandmother's mountains and just scrape out the coal—they don't set the energy policy in this country. They suffer because of the energy policy in this country, and we stand with them, and we want them to have a better future, too. We want them to have a better future, too! . . .

We talk about green for all, green for everybody. Where was it written that only men could put up solar panels? Where was it written that only men could manufacture wind turbines? If the green economy has the same sorry track record of sexism—if women in the green economy

Excerpted from Van Jones, "Power Shift Keynote," Power Shift, Washington, DC, 2009, www.youtube.com/watch?v=IVNtoAiOh1k.

are making 70 cents to the dollar just like they're doing in the pollution-based economy—something's wrong with our movement! Something's wrong with our movement. We need to have gender equity in this movement. We mean green for everybody! . . .

What about our Native American brothers and sisters? . . . They told us a long time ago that this was sacred land. And the sacrifice zones of the pollution-based economy have to become the sacred zones in the new clean and green economy. Those communities that were locked out of the pollution-based economy and pushed down by the pollution-based economy need to be lifted up in the clean and green economy. That needs to be a moral principle. . . .

What about our immigrant sisters and brothers? What about people who've come here from all around the world who we're willing to have out in the fields with poison being sprayed on them—poison being sprayed on them because we have the wrong agricultural system, and we're willing to poison them and poison the earth to put food on our table, but we don't want to give them rights and we don't want to give them dignity and we don't want to give them respect? . . .

If the green economy can't open its arms and welcome everybody, something's wrong. Lastly, what about our sisters and brothers that are in prison right now? What about the formerly incarcerated? We need to have a green economy that doesn't have any throwaway species. We need to have a green economy that doesn't have any throwaway resources. We need a green economy that doesn't have any throwaway people, either. No throwaway people! We can't have a green economy that's passionate about reclaiming thrown away stuff but indifferent to reclaiming thrown away lives. We can't have a green movement that says we're going to do everything we can to give dead materials a second chance through recycling . . . but if you've been to prison we have no place for you in our economy. We won't give living people a second chance. That's not the green economy we need to build, sisters and brothers. We need to build a green economy that reclaims people, too. That reclaims community. . . .

If all we do is take out the dirty power system, the dirty power generation, in a system, and just replace it with some clean stuff, put a solar panel on top of this system, but we don't deal with how we are consuming water, we don't deal with how we're treating our other sister and brother species, we don't deal with toxins, we don't deal with the way we treat each other, if that's not a part of this movement, let me tell you what you'll have. This is all you'll have. You'll have solar-powered bulldozers, solar-powered buzz saws, and bio-fueled bombers, and we'll be fighting wars over lithium for the batteries instead of oil for the engines and we'll still have a dead planet. This movement is deeper than a solar panel! . . . We're not going to put a new battery in a broken system. We want a new system! . . .

Your generation will determine whether we as a species are locusts or honeybees. Are we locusts or are we honeybees? . . . We're a busy species, we're gonna work. We can't not work. The question is will our work be a curse on this planet? Or will it be a blessing for all creation? That is the significance. You will determine—you will determine—whether we are locusts, or whether we are honeybees. . . .

If you stand up as a generation and say that you refuse to compromise, you refuse to back down . . . you will build a coalition with every color, every class. You will achieve something that no generation of Americans has ever achieved: You will build a green economy strong enough to lift people out of poverty. You will connect the people who most need work to the work that most needs to be done. You will beat pollution and poverty at the same time. You will beat this recession and global warming at the same time. And you will be the generation that we look back on and say, "They didn't give us the coalition that we always wanted, they gave us the country we always wanted, and they saved the earth!"

Don't back down, young people. We need you! Thank you very much.

"'FOR A CHANGE OF PARADIGM': INTERVIEW WITH TOM GOLDTOOTH FROM THE INDIGENOUS ENVIRONMENTAL NETWORK," 2016

What does "environmental racism" mean to you?

In the late 1980's and early 1990's in the United States, there were studies conducted that discovered the environmental and public health laws of this country discriminated against Indigenous peoples and people-of-color. By people-of-color, I mean the African American, the Latin American and the Asian American people. Since the early 1970's there were strong national environmental laws enacted that also required the States to comply with. These were clean air, clean water and many other environmental and health laws and standards. However, in the 1980's it was found that many corporations and factories were building polluting industries in the backyards of people-of-color communities with no regard of these people's health. And, large-scale toxic waste dumping was being done near the communities of these ethnic people including our Indigenous Tribal nations (communities). In the early 1990's the United States and the nuclear industry [were] pushing plans to dump highly radioactive waste from the nuclear energy reactors in Indigenous lands and territories. The government promised millions of dollars as benefit-sharing agreements to each tribal member to obtain their

Excerpted from World Rainforest Movement, "'For a Change of Paradigm': Interview with Tom Goldtooth from the Indigenous Environmental Network," *World Rainforest Movement Bulletin 223*, May 9, 2016, wrm.org.uy/wp-content /uploads/2016/05/Bulletin223.pdf.

support of using our lands as a nuclear and toxic waste dump. However, with all these toxic, radioactive, and ecological destructive forms of industrial developments, the US government did not apply the federal environmental laws equally. We called this environmental racism.

This also applies to the extractive industries related to mining and fossil fuel development. The US government, through its Bureau of Indian Affairs programs brokered mining deals with our Tribal governments with false promises that these mining deals and fossil fuel developments would be beneficial. But, the provisions of applying effective environmental standards and regulations to protect water and air quality and the health of our people and the ecosystem and traditional food systems was never addressed. This is ecological and health injustice.

The fact that remotely located Tribal lands across North America contain much of the remaining energy resources, coupled with the desire by the US to achieve "energy independence" using fossil fuels, means that both government and industry are aggressively targeting Tribal lands to meet the US (and Canada) energy needs. This push to exploit fossil fuel resources in indigenous lands is of great concern to all who are working on energy and climate issues.

Because many Tribal communities are economically depressed and Tribal governments are under pressure to provide solutions, the energy industry is able to leverage the promise of short-term economic benefits to gain access to tribal lands and resources. Possession of energy resources coupled with depressed economies result with our many Indigenous Tribes of the North being vulnerable to the destructive and short term economic "solutions" of the dominant world.

Now, this "racism" is practiced worldwide. Elites of the countries in the global South that push their national agenda to exploit the natural environment have no regard for the Indigenous peoples of their countries. Globally, the exploitation and plunder of the world's ecosystems and biodiversity, as well as the violations of the inherent rights of Indigenous Peoples that depend on them, have intensified. Our rights to self-determination, to our own governance and own self-determined development, our inherent rights to our lands, territories and resources are increasingly and alarmingly under attack by the collaboration of governments, transnational corporations and conservationist NGOs.

Indigenous activists and leaders defending their territories continue to suffer repression, militarization, including assassination, imprisonment, harassment and vilification as "terrorists." The violation of our collective rights faces the same impunity. Forced relocation or assimilation assault our future generations, cultures, languages, spiritual ways and relationship to the earth, economically and politically. This is happening all over the planet—all over our Mother Earth. All this is an injustice.

And what does this mean for the struggle of Indigenous Peoples?

Looking back at the past 26 years, our Indigenous Peoples and people-of-color within the environmental and economic justice movement have put soul into the environmental movement, taking environmental protection out of its square box; making changes in policies, and building the base for strategic resistance of grassroots communities disproportionately affected by polluting industries, but more so, for social and economic change, as well.

The struggle for our Indigenous peoples is a rights-based struggle. We, Indigenous Peoples from all regions of the world are defending our Mother Earth—our forests, water, and all Life, from the aggression of unsustainable development and the overexploitation of our natural resources by mining, logging, mega-dams, exploration and extraction of petroleum. Our forests suffer from the production of agro-fuels, biomass, plantations and other impositions of false solutions to climate change and unsustainable, damaging development.

We are also fighting the commodification of all Life—of Nature—of Mother Earth and Father Sky. The capitalism of nature is a perverse attempt by corporations, extractive industries and governments to cash in on Creation by privatizing, commodifying, and selling off the Sacred and all forms of life and the sky, including the air we breathe, the water we drink and all the genes, plants, traditional seeds, trees, animals, fish, biological and cultural diversity, ecosystems and traditional knowledge that make life on Earth possible and enjoyable.

Mother Earth is the source of life which needs to be protected, not a resource to be exploited and commodified as a "natural capital." As Indigenous Peoples, we understand our own place and our responsibilities within Creation's sacred order. We feel the pain of disharmony of the world when we witness the dishonor of the natural order of Creation and the continued economic colonization and degradation of Mother Earth and all life upon her.

The modern world cannot achieve economic sustainability without environmental justice and without strong environmental ethics that recognizes our human relationship to the sacredness of Mother Earth. The future of mankind depends on a new economic and environmental paradigm that fully recognizes the life-cycles of nature and recognizes the Rights of our Mother Earth.

In addition to our fight for our Rights as Indigenous Peoples, the struggle is for the recognition of the rights of the water to be healthy; and the rights of the Forest and the Sacred Woman of the Forest to be healthy, this is our struggle. . . .

How do you think the solidarity movement on social and environmental justice can help the fight against environmental racism in all its forms?

In the North, in the early 1990's when the height of the environmental racism and cry for our demands for environment justice is recognized, we came together as Indigenous Peoples with the minorities, with people-of-color. We did this as a political strategy to build our power for change. As Indigenous Peoples, we are the "First Nations" and indigenous to the lands and territories of the US, and we said to the people-of-color and social justice movements that we will stand together with them, as long as they would also stand in solidarity with our rights as Indigenous Peoples. We saw a need to build a power base of solidarity with other social and environmental justice movements to strengthen our voices for change in the US. This strategy continues within the climate movement, as we have applied "justice" to climate. In this climate justice movement, we share many of the same problems with other communities that are poor, who face racism and poverty, and who are being marginalized and discriminated by the dominant society of the US. So, we have formed our own climate justice alliances and mobilizing communities in struggle and who are on the frontlines of the fossil fuel economy to stand with one voice demanding system change, not climate change.

Dialogue is needed amongst Indigenous Peoples and non-Indigenous people and frontline communities to put pressure on their governments to reevaluate a colonial legal system that doesn't work. This solidarity is needed to build a power base, to develop popular education to inform communities that have historically been oppressed of what is happening to our Mother Earth. Through popular education and principles of community based organizing, more people are recognizing the need for a body of law that recognizes the inherent rights of the environment, of animals, fish, birds, plants, water, and air itself.

Now, we are seeing social Movements starting to see a power structure that has no respect for anyone, except the small 1% of the wealthy elites. They are now starting to see the wisdom and importance of indigenous cosmologies, philosophies and world views. It is a worthy effort to mobilize for system change with other non-Indigenous movements. We need people power to seek and achieve long term solutions turning away from prevailing paradigms and ideologies centered on pursuing economic growth, corporate profits and personal wealth accumulation as primary engines of social well-being. The outside pressures of the world will continue to have negative effects on our Indigenous Peoples. So, how do we change this? We network and build alliances with the non-Indigenous allies and with social movements. The transitions will inevitably be toward dominant societies that can equitably adjust to reduced levels of production and consumption, and increasingly localized systems of economic organization that recognize, honor and are bounded by the limits of nature that recognize the Universal Declaration on the Rights of Mother Earth.

Thank you.

INDEX

A

Abon, Limeyo, 273

accountability: in "Principles of Working Together" (Second People of Color Environmental Leadership Summit), 223, 224–25; SWOP letter to Group of Ten and, 165, 167

Acoma people, 165

"Administration Joins Fight for 'Environmental Justice' Pollution" (Healy), 188–93

African Americans: Black Live Matter and Movement for Black Lives, 261; "Black Survival in Our Polluted Cities" (Thomas), 99–103; census data for landfill areas and, 136*table*; *Chicago Ghetto on the South Side* (White), 118*photo*; "For African Americans, Park Access Is about More Than Just Proximity" (Mock), 277–79; "Great Louisiana Toxics March" (LTP), 159, 162*photos*; "Toxic Wastes and Race at Twenty" (Bullard et al.), 213–14, 226–32; "Toxic Wastes and Race in the United States" (United Church of Christ), 122, 142–48, 149*table*, 155; uncontrolled toxic waste sites and, 149*map*. *See also* recreational segregation; residential space and segregation; Warren County, NC, toxics and protests; workplace segregation

agricultural losses from chemical contamination, 127

air pollution, 102, 154, 184

Albuquerque Petroglyph National Monument, 165–66

"Alcatraz Proclamation" (Indians of All Tribes), 91, 93–94

Alston, Dana, 14, 19, 23, 178–79

American Indians. *See* Native Americans

Anaya, Toney, 176–77

anencephaly, 209–10

arms race, Cold War, 57, 91. *See also* nuclear testing; uranium mines

Asarco copper smelter, 236

Asian/Pacific Islander Americans, 146, 227–30

Atrisco Land Rights Council, 165

Audubon Society, 166

Augustine, Rose Marie, 171–72

auto workers, 62–63

B

Backed Up Sewer in Negro Slum District, Norfolk, Virginia (Vachon), 30*photo*

Bailer, Lloyd H., 62–63

"Bali Principles of Climate Justice" (2002), 265, 267–72

Baltimore City v. Dawson, 83–84

banks and lending, 25–26, 30, 47, 52

Baton Rouge, LA, 188, 191, 236, 246–47

U

"uncontrolled toxic waste sites," 144,
146, 149*map*
"Understanding Fair Housing" (US
Commission on Civil Rights),
53–55
unemployment rates, 72
"Unequal Protection: The Racial
Divide In Environmental Law"
(Lavelle and Coyle), 150–57
"Unifying Principles" (Indigenous
Environmental Network), 160, 170
United Church of Christ: Charles
Lee on environmental justice, 153;
Commission for Racial Justice, 143–
44, 157, 173–74; Justice and Witness
Ministries, 226; "Toxic Wastes and
Race at Twenty" (Bullard et al.),
226–32; "Toxic Wastes and Race
in the United States," 122, 142–48,
149*table*, 155, 213–14
United Farm Workers of America
(UFWOC), 97–98
United Nations Climate Leaders Sum-
mit (New York City, 2014), 265
United Nations Conference on Envi-
ronment and Development ("Earth
Summit," Rio de Janeiro, 1992), 17,
202
United Nations Millennium Develop-
ment Goals, 202
United States Travel Bureau, 79
University of Michigan School of
Natural Resources, 15, 156, 184–85
"Unlicensed #DAPL Guards Attacked
Water Protectors with Dogs &
Pepper Spray" (Goodman), 255–58
Unruh Act (CA), 66
Upper Peninsula, Michigan, 262
uranium mines, 57, 64*photo*, 96, 179
US Commission on Civil Rights:

"Understanding Fair Housing,"
53–55
US-Mexico border, 209–10

V

Vachon, John: *Backed Up Sewer in
Negro Slum District, Norfolk, Virginia,*
30*photo*; *Negro Children Standing in
Front of Half Mile Concrete Wall,
Detroit, Michigan,* 34*photo,* 35*photo*;
*Steel Mill Workers, Bethlehem Com-
pany, Sparrows Point, Maryland,*
60*photo*
Vancouver shipyards, 65–66
Virginia Key Beach, Miami, 82*photo*
Vitchek, Norris: "Confessions of a
Block-Buster," 42–48

W

"wade-in," Fort Lauderdale beach, 77,
85*photo*
Wal-Mart, 282
Walter, Earl, 66
Walter, Mildred Pitts, 65–67
Ward, Robert "Buck," 5
Ward Transformer Company, 5. *See
also* Warren County, NC, toxics
and protests
Warren County, NC, toxics and protests: census data, 135, 136*table*;
chain of events, 5–7; decision-maker
motives, 9; "dry tomb" design, 6, 8;
environmental problem, definition
of, 7–8; experts, level of trust in, 8–
9; overview, 3–4; protests, 5–7, 121–
22, 130–31*photo*; Reilly on, 184; siting
process and local voices issue, 8;
United Church of Christ on, 143; "A
Warren County PCB Protest Song,"
132–33